SECONDS TO MIDNIGHT

CASPER ANDERSEN AND HENRY NIELSEN

SECONDS TO MIDNIGHT

A History of Nuclear Weapons

AARHUS UNIVERSITY PRESS

SECONDS TO MIDNIGHT

Cover: Camilla Jørgensen
Cover illustration: Fangataufa Lagoon 1968, detonation
of France's first hydrogen bomb. Bettmann / Getty Images
Layout and typesetting: Carl-H.K. Zakrisson and Tod Alan Spoerl
Translated from the Danish by Magnus Skovhus
Publishing editor: Maria Schaldemose Kristensen
This book is typeset in Documenta and Kievit and printed on 120 g Munken Lynx
Printed by Specialtrykkeriet Arco, Denmark

Printed in Denmark 2025
1st edition, 1st impression

ISBN 978 87 7597 438 2 (printed book)
ISBN 978 87 7597 485 6 (e-pdf)
ISBN 978 87 7597 486 3 (epub)

Aarhus University Press
Helsingforsgade 25, DK-8200 Aarhus N
unipress@unipress.au.dk
aarhusuniversitypress.dk

The publication is funded by
Aarhus University Research Foundation
VELUX FONDEN

The carbon emission of this book is calculated to be 0,7 kg CO_2 eq according to ClimateCalc. CC-000157/DK

PEER REVIEWED

FSC
www.fsc.org
MIX
Paper | Supporting responsible forestry
FSC® C010493

NORDIC SWAN ECOLABEL
Ecolabelled printed matter
5041 0826

Contents

Preface

The first quarter of the 21st century has been characterized by crises that threaten to change the world as we know it irrevocably. Population growth, environmental disasters, pandemics, lack of vital resources and not least the consequences of global warming for life on Earth increasingly occupy our minds in modern society. Complex global crises abound but for a time after the end of the Cold War the nuclear threat seemed reduced to a somewhat theoretical issue. This changed on February 24, 2022 when Russian forces crossed the Ukrainian border and President Putin that same day in a TV speech threatened any outsider who might consider getting involved in this "special military operation" with the "greatest consequences in history". This was a barely concealed hint that, in such a situation, Russia would not hesitate to use nuclear weapons. If that were to happen, it would be the first time since the USA in August 1945 dropped a nuclear bomb over each of the two Japanese cities Hiroshima and Nagasaki.

The nuclear threat is now back in the news after having played a secondary role after the end of the Cold War in comparison with the other crises mentioned above. However, this return is testament to the fact that the nuclear weapons issue was never resolved. Even though vast numbers of missiles and nuclear warheads were removed and dismantled in the 1990s, thousands are still left. Or, rather: elderly weapons have been replaced by fewer but more sophisticated ones. Furthermore, several countries are in possession of nuclear weapons. There are currently nine states with nuclear weapons at their disposal, and several others who consider – and in some cases work actively towards – joining the exclusive group of nuclear weapon states. How did the world end up in this precarious situation? What has been done thus far to remedy the nuclear threat hanging like a sword of Damocles above the heads of the entire world population? Is it possible to keep fending off the nuclear apocalypse? And how are the nuclear threat and the climate crisis connected in current and future risk scenarios? These questions have preoccupied us for many years, and they were our motivation for writing this book, which deals with the issue of nuclear weapons in a long historical perspective and addresses a broad audience.

The extent of the book is modest, but its topic is far-reaching. A significant part of the writing process consisted in selecting the most solid, thorough and seminal works within each topic of the book. We would like to warmly thank the authors of these splendid works as well as our many colleagues and friends who have offered greatly appreciated advice and comments during the writing process. Special thanks to the anonymous peer reviewer, who we have subsequently learned was Professor Casper Sylvest, University of Copenhagen, who gave many valuable comments and suggestions for improving a previous version of the manuscript. Profound appreciation, too, to our valued colleagues Professor Matthias Heymann and Senior Lecturer Kristian Hvidtfelt Nielsen, Center for Science Studies, Aarhus University, and Senior Researcher Henrik Knudsen, Danish National Archive, Viborg. We extend our sincere gratitude to Emeritus Professor Svein Sjøberg from the University of Oslo, whose invaluable contribution made our Danish book accessible to Norwegian readers. Professor Sjøberg not only translated the book from Danish into Norwegian but also wrote a thoughtful and engaging introduction tailored specifically for a Norwegian audience. Last but certainly not least, we are deeply grateful to Emeritus Professor Christopher Pethick from the University of Copenhagen and Nordic Institute for Theoretical Physics, for his generous and much-appreciated assistance in refining our English manuscript. His expertise not only helped to enhance the clarity and precision of the language but also provided valuable input on the content itself. Without the help and support of these colleagues, this book would probably never have been written.

A special thanks goes to the publishing editor of the book, Maria Schaldemose Kristensen, who has made an invaluable contribution to this book during several years of collaboration. At Aarhus University Press we are also indebted to Magnus Skovhus, Henrik Jensen and Alastair Ward for their work and professionalism. A great thanks to the Aarhus University Research Foundation (AUFF) and to Velux Fonden for their financial support for the publication.

Aarhus, June 2025
Casper Andersen and Henry Nielsen

Abbreviations

ABM	Anti-Ballistic Missile
AEC	Atomic Energy Commission (USA)
AEK	Danish Atomic Energy Commission
AERE	Atomic Energy Research Establishment
CEA	Commissariat à l'Energie Atomique (the French Atomic Energy Commission)
CIA	Central Intelligence Agency
CND	Campaign for Nuclear Disarmament
CTBT	Comprehensive Test Ban Treaty
EDF	Électricité de France (French energy provider, controlled by the French State)
ERL	Engineering Research Laboratory, Pakistan
FAS	Federation of Atomic Scientists (now Federation of American Scientists)
FBI	Federal Bureau of Investigation
FDO	Physical Dynamics Research Laboratory, the Netherlands
GAC	General Advisory Committee
HEU	Highly Enriched Uranium
IAEA	International Atomic Energy Agency
ICAN	International Campaign to Abolish Nuclear Weapons
ICBM	Intercontinental Ballistic Missile
InAEC	Indian Atomic Energy Commission
IsAEC	Israel's Atomic Energy Commission
INF	Intermediate-Range Nuclear Forces Treaty

IPCC	Intergovernmental Panel on Climate Change
IPPNW	International Physicians for the Prevention of Nuclear War
IRBM	Intermediate Range Ballistic Missile
JCPOA	Joint Comprehensive Plan of Action
KGB	Komitet gasudarstvennay bezopasnosti (Committee for Soviet State Security)
KRL	Khan Research Laboratories (previously Engineering Research Laboratories)
LEU	Low-Enriched Uranium
MAD	Mutual Assured Destruction
MIRV	Multiple Independently targeted Re-entry Vehicle
MRBM	Medium Range Ballistic Missile
NATO	North Atlantic Treaty Organization
NKVD	Naradnyy komissariat vnutrennikh del (People's Commissariat for Internal Affairs)
NPT	Nuclear Non-Proliferation Treaty
OSRD	Office of Scientific Research and Development
PAEC	Pakistan's Atomic Energy Commission
PNE	Peaceful Nuclear Explosion
PTBT	Partial Nuclear Test Ban Treaty
RERF	Radiation Effects Research Foundation
SALT	Strategic Arms Limitation Treaty
SDI	Strategic Defense Initiative (Reagan's "Star Wars" Project)
SLBM	Submarine-launched Ballistic Missile
START	Strategic Arms Reduction Treaty
TNT	Trinitrotoluene
TPNW	Treaty on the Prohibition of Nuclear Weapons
UNAEC	United Nations Atomic Energy Committee
UNESCO	United Nations Educational, Scientific, and Cultural Organization

Introduction

"Now I am become Death"

In the middle of July 1945, it had been more than two months since Germany was forced to surrender unconditionally to the allied forces: the USA, the United Kingdom and the Soviet Union. This had brought a conclusion to the Second World War in Europe, but war still raged in East Asia. Here, Japan refused to surrender, even though the country's army was pressed back on all fronts and a superior fleet of American war planes was bombing the Japanese mainland night and day. While the world's attention was turned to the fighting in the Far East and the victors' summit in Potsdam on the outskirts of Berlin, more than 10,000 km from each of these hotspots a dramatic event took place that would soon have a crucial impact on the war in the east.

On the night between July 15 and 16, physicist Robert Oppenheimer could not sleep. As the technical-scientific manager of the grand-scale, secret Manhattan Project, he had been extremely preoccupied in the preceding days with the last preparations for the world's first nuclear test, the Trinity Test.[1] According to plan, it was to take place on July 16 at 4 a.m., local time, in the chosen test site about 350 km south of Los Alamos and 100 km northwest of the city of Alamogordo in the New Mexico desert. The bomb, which the participants referred to as "The Gadget", was already mounted on the 30-meter-high steel tower that had been built for the purpose shortly before. On the afternoon of July 15, Oppenheimer had paid a last visit to the tower to check that everything was in order. Several hundred trusted technicians, scientists and military personnel were posted in shelters between 5 and 30 km from *ground zero*. Everything appeared to be under control.

But then the weather started to cause trouble. The meteorologists predicted thunderstorms and strong gusts of wind during the night. If the prediction held true, it might be necessary to postpone the test: partly because the technicians would be unable to carry out the planned measuring of the magnitude and effect of the explosion, and partly because those responsible for the experiment could not allow radioactive fallout from the explosion to be blown into the air above Alamogordo or some other city nearby. The mere

Professor Robert Oppenheimer (left) and General Leslie Groves, leaders of the Manhattan Project, stand in front of the remains of a steel tower in the desert in southern New Mexico. This tower was where the world's first nuclear bomb was detonated on July 16, 1945, at 5:29:21 a.m. Mountain Time.

thought of what that might entail in terms of deaths, radiation injuries and newspaper headlines must have made Oppenheimer shudder.

Between 2 and 3 a.m., a heavy thunderstorm with gusts of wind up to 15–20 meters per second reached the test area. The experiment was hanging by a thread, but then the weather slowly improved, and Oppenheimer and General Leslie Groves, the military manager, decided that the test would take place a few hours later – specifically at 5:30 a.m. Time crept by as the sky cleared and daylight slowly broke through. At 5:10 a.m., a speaker announced that the time was now "zero minus 20 minutes". The technicians checked the instruments one last time, and everyone got ready to observe the explosion from their shelters through dark sunglasses.

At exactly 5:29:21 a.m., the moment came that a host of scientists and technicians had been working towards for years.[2] A flash of light so powerful that for a moment it changed the gray morning to the brightest day shocked many of those present. But that was only the beginning of a scene that no one had ever experienced before. Everyone who was present at the Trinity test site that day had their own story to tell. One of them, physicist Isidor Rabi, described his experience as follows:

> Suddenly, there was an enormous flash of light, the brightest light I have ever seen or that I think anybody has ever seen. It blasted, it pounced; it bored its way right through you. It was a vision which was seen with more than the eye. It was seen to last forever. You would wish it would stop; altogether it lasted about two seconds. Finally it was over, diminishing, and we looked towards the place where the bomb had been; there was an enormous ball of fire which grew and grew and it rolled as it grew; it went up in the air, in yellow flashes and into scarlet and green. It looked menacing. It seemed to come toward one. A new thing had just been born; a new control; a new understanding of man, which man had acquired over nature.[3]

Everyone who witnessed the explosion was deeply shocked by what they saw and heard that day. The air pressure threw explosives expert George Kistiakowsky to the ground because he ventured outside the protective shelter. Physicist Robert Serber became temporarily blind because he looked directly at the explosion site without eye protection, and Nobel Prize laureate Enrico Fermi, who still had the composure to do a quick calculation of the impact of the explosion by observing how far small pieces of paper were blown by the shockwave, was unable to drive his car when heading back to Los Alamos. All the participants shared the immediate physical experience that the extreme power of the atomic bomb was something they would never forget.

Today's nuclear weapons developers have not experienced anything like this. According to anthropologist Joseph Masco, who has followed current weapons specialists closely for several years, this means that they adopt an abstract, almost techno-aesthetic attitude to their work, which consists in designing new, refined nuclear weapons on their computers. Due to the current all-encompassing nuclear test ban, these nuclear weapons cannot be tested in practice. Therefore their creators do not have a sensory experience like the one the participants in the Trinity Test had on July 16, 1945.[4]

How did the scientific manager of the Manhattan Project himself, Robert Oppenheimer, experience the explosion? Frank Oppenheimer, Robert's brother, was also present at Trinity, witnessing the test at his brother's side. Frank recalls that his brother immediately after the detonation said something like, "it worked!"[5] However, when Robert Oppenheimer was later asked to describe the thoughts that went through his head when the explosion happened, he claimed that they centered around a few lines from the ancient Hindu scripture *Bhagavad Gita*. Here, it is described how the god Vishnu, who appears in several different guises, reveals himself to the despairing hero Prince Arjuna in the shape of a fearsome creature that proclaims: "Now I am become Death, the Destroyer of Worlds."[6] And the well-read Oppenheimer, who had taken lessons in Sanskrit at university to be able to read *Bhagavad Gita* in the original language, used to add, "I suppose we all thought that one way or another." Even though everyone was relieved, pleased and proud that the ambitious project had come to a successful conclusion, they were also aware that the next nuclear explosion was likely to result in a large number of deaths and terrible suffering for survivors nearby.

Since the Trinity Test on July 16, 1945, the Earth's population has lived with the fact that humans are capable of releasing the immense energy stored in nuclei, and that it is consequently probable that we are also capable of wiping the entire species of *Homo sapiens* from the surface of the Earth. This book seeks to explain how various countries, organizations and individuals have attempted to tackle this challenge. It is a broad topic, but it is delimited in two ways because we have aimed to write a research-based history of nuclear weapons in one concise volume. Firstly, we cover the nine current nuclear weapon states, as well as some, but not all, countries that have had advanced nuclear weapons programs at some point. Secondly, we focus on nuclear technologies developed for military use, not on the use of nuclear technology in civil energy supply. However, it is important to note that this distinction is never absolute, as the boundary between military and civilian nuclear technologies – between bombs and energy – has never been clear-cut or stable. In fact, the divide between 'violent' and 'peaceful' nuclear technology has been shaped and maintained through various forms of technopolitics, many of which were not successful.[7] As this book will show, for example, some states have acquired nuclear weapons through the indirect route of civilian nuclear technology.

An important theme in the book is the impact of the development of nuclear weapons on the view of the sciences' ethical and political position in society, including the scientists' self-perception. Discussions about the ethical consequences of science have roots far back in history. However, they took a novel turn on that day in 1945 when Oppenheimer and his peers witnessed the immense flash of light from Trinity and concluded that the 'gadget' worked. In practice, science became more entangled with international politics, commercial interests and military projects. This raised new questions about the role and societal responsibility of scientists – also among scientists themselves.

Discussions on the topic have played out not least in the journal *Bulletin of the Atomic Scientists*, which scientists associated with the Manhattan Project founded a few months after the end of the Second World War. The *Bulletin* introduced the Doomsday Clock in June 1947 in an attempt to visualize how close, in their assessment, humanity was to the ultimate nuclear disaster at the time. The minute hand on the Doomsday Clock has been moved since the clock was created. Over the course of the following decades, it moved from time to time on the basis of decisions made in the circle around the *Bulletin*. Since 1947, the editorial and expert group have moved the minute hand 25 times in accordance with international political events, the development of new nuclear weapons technologies and the changing fortune of the peace movements.

Over the years, the editors of the *Bulletin* have given detailed arguments for changing the clock settings, which do not aim to predict the end of the world but to provide an assessment of the current threat level at which humanity finds itself as a consequence of the development and proliferation of nuclear weapons.[8] The clock settings can and should not be read as an objective declaration of how close humankind is to nuclear apocalypse. Rather, the Doomsday Clock is a political device that encourages political change in how the nuclear weapons issue is addressed. The clock is best understood as an initiative that aims to affect the receiver and, ultimately, encourage them to take action.[9] The changing settings of the Doomsday Clock have in many cases been intended and received as warnings that humankind is close to a nuclear disaster. However, the settings have also sometimes been intended and received as encouragement when one or more nuclear powers have set a course that the circle around the *Bulletin* approved of and hoped would be continued. In that sense, it is just as important to pay attention to the points in history when the clock has been set back as the points when it has been set forward. We intend to do so in this book, using the Doomsday Clock to structure our narrative of the history of nuclear weapons.

CHAPTER 1

Discovering the Secrets of the Uranium Nucleus

Nuclear Physics in the Year 1932

During the first three decades of the 20th century, physics underwent a development as dramatic as the scientific revolution in the 17th century. This development was represented by Albert Einstein whose Theory of Relativity, developed in the years 1905–15, wrapped up classical physics in the most satisfying way, as well as by Max Planck, Marie Curie, Ernest Rutherford, Niels Bohr, Werner Heisenberg and many others. Through their combined efforts, science achieved a deep understanding of the structure of atoms and the natural laws that govern atomic and nuclear processes.

In 1932, the physicists thus knew that all atoms consist of a very small, positively charged nucleus around which orbit a number of negatively charged electrons. In a neutral atom, the total negative charge of the electrons perfectly balances the positive charge on the protons in the nucleus. The lightest atom is the hydrogen atom, which only has one positive proton in its nucleus, and one negatively charged electron rotating around it. The physicists also knew that almost the entire mass of the atom is concentrated in the nucleus. Finally, they knew that all other nuclei than the hydrogen nucleus must contain something in addition to protons; otherwise, the masses would not add up. The second-lightest atomic nucleus is found in the element helium. Even though it only contains two protons, it has a mass that is approximately four times larger than the mass of the proton. The answer to this scientific riddle came in 1932, when English physicist James Chadwick demonstrated the existence of a hitherto unknown neutral particle whose mass was almost the same as that of the proton. He named this particle a neutron, and this new discovery made it possible to understand the composition of the different elements.

Each element is characterized by the number of protons in its nucleus, called its atomic number. A neutral atom of a given element contains exactly the same number of electrons as protons, because each proton carries one positive elementary charge and each electron carries one negative elementary charge. Further, any given element, in addition to the characteristic number of positively charged protons in its nucleus, may contain a number of neutrons, which carry no electrical charge. The total number of protons and neutrons is called the element's mass number.

In the Earth we find elements with atomic numbers between 1 and 92. The element with one proton in its nucleus is, as mentioned, hydrogen, which is designated by the symbol H. The element with two protons in its nucleus is helium (He). The element with eight protons in its nucleus is oxygen (O), and the element with 92 protons in its nucleus is uranium (U). Elements with more than 92 protons in their nucleus can only be produced artificially – they do not exist naturally on our planet, or at least only in extremely small quantities.

Elements appear in several varieties, called isotopes. Take, for instance, uranium. All uranium nuclei contain exactly 92 protons, but the number of neutrons can vary. The most important isotopes of uranium are U-235 and U-238, 235 and 238 being the mass number – i.e., the total number of protons and neutrons in the two isotopes. Of these isotopes, U-238 is by far the most common. 99.3 percent of the uranium found in the ground is U-238, while only 0.7 percent is U-235.

Some isotopes are stable, while others are unstable and decay spontaneously into a different element by releasing different types of radiation, usually alpha particles (identical to helium nuclei) or beta particles (identical to electrons). Unstable isotopes are also called radioactive isotopes. Element transformation thus takes place spontaneously in nature, but it is also possible to do it artificially, for example by bombarding an element with protons that are sped up through a specially designed machine called an accelerator. This was done successfully for the first time in 1932 in Rutherford's lab in Cambridge, when the physicists John Cockcroft and Ernest Walton bombarded the element lithium, which has three protons in its nucleus, with accelerated protons and found that this produced two helium nuclei, each of which contains two protons.

The Crafty Neutron

The discovery of the neutron made it clear that nature must harbor immense, hitherto unknown forces that held the atomic nucleus together. Think, for example, of a helium nucleus that consists of two protons and two neutrons. Based on ordinary understanding about electricity, it makes no sense that such a nucleus can exist. After all, the two positively charged protons are very close to each other and should repel each other with large electrical force. In order for the nucleus to remain as a unit, there must therefore also be some force of attraction between the protons and neutrons. And what is more, these forces must be much stronger than the electrical force of repulsion between the protons; otherwise, it would be easy to split atomic nuclei apart. And normally, it is not at all easy.

By accelerating positively charged protons through an accelerator and pointing them at, for example, helium, oxygen or uranium, physicists can calculate how much energy is required to split an atomic nucleus. Experiments like this were done in many places during the 1930s, finding that the energy with which a nucleus particle is bound in the nucleus is usually millions of times stronger than the energy with which an electron is bound in an atom.

The energy released by burning wood or in an internal combustion engine is called chemical energy and is only related to the rearrangement of atoms. Nothing happens to the atomic nucleus itself in chemical processes. Many scientists therefore asked themselves whether the much more potent energy stored in the atomic nucleus could be exploited in practice. Some prominent nuclear physicists believed so, having realized as early as in the 1930s that it must be such energy-releasing nuclear processes that take place in the center of the sun and other stars. But could similar processes be realized on our planet? This was a contested question. Most physicists, however, agreed with the famous experimental physicist Ernest Rutherford, Niels Bohr's mentor, when in 1933 he stated that all talk of exploiting the energy in the atomic nucleus was pure "moonshine".[10]

Even though scientists were not yet able to exploit nuclear power in practice, they could still study nuclear processes in their labs. Here, the neutron turned out to be the ideal projectile. While a positively charged proton has to be accelerated to a very high speed to overcome the electrical repulsion from another positively charged nucleus, a neutron – which is not electrically repelled – can sort of sneak its way into a nucleus and cause various nuclear reactions. These were relatively inexpensive experiments that did not require large accelerators, and they were carried out in many labs around Europe, but especially in Rome under the direction of physicist Enrico Fermi. He systematically bombarded one element after another with neutrons, in that way triggering unknown nuclear reactions and producing a number of new isotopes. At some point, he came to the element with the highest number of protons in its nucleus – i.e., uranium. Here, he observed some peculiar phenomena which he interpreted as the creation of transuranic nuclei, i.e. nuclei containing more than 92 protons. Observing electrons coming out, he imagined that a transuranic nucleus would be created when a uranium nucleus absorbed the incoming neutron, thereby becoming unstable and decaying by emitting a negatively charged electron.

The charge of the remaining nucleus had thus increased by one, meaning it would have 93 protons, instead of the 92 found in the original uranium nucleus. Or, if two electrons were emitted, the result would even be a transuranic nucleus with 94 protons. Fermi published his findings in 1934. Given his status as a prominent physicist, his conclusions were widely accepted by most of his colleagues. However, one German chemist, Ida Noddack, offered a different explanation. She suggested that instead of creating transuranic nuclei, Fermi's experiment might have actually broken the uranium nucleus into two or more fragments.[11] Unfortunately for Noddack, her hypothesis, being proposed by a relatively unknown female chemist, was largely dismissed at the time. While this was harmful to her career, the unjust dismissal may well have been fortunate for the world – for reasons that will become clear shortly!

In 1938, Fermi received the Nobel Prize in physics for his research into element transformation by means of neutrons. It was a great honor, and naturally he was invited to Stockholm for the prize ceremony on the day of Alfred Nobel's death, December 10. However, instead of returning home after the ceremony, he seized the opportunity to travel to the USA, where he had a standing invitation to become guest professor at Columbia University in New York. He was accompanied by his wife, Laura Fermi, who was Jewish. No doubt, Fermi anticipated the problems his family would soon face in fascist Italy, where the regime was introducing racial laws directed at Jews, just as had happened five years earlier in Hitler's Germany. Many, including Fermi, were aware that a new war was brewing, with Germany and Italy as allies. Germany had in the spring of 1938 annexed Austria without reprisals. In September of the same year, Hitler had obtained the approval of France and the United Kingdom – via the Munich Agreement – to seize control of the border region between Germany and Czechoslovakia. Without its border fortresses, Czechoslovakia could only wait for the inevitable German occupation. This took place in spring 1939. Shortly afterwards, Hitler started making demands for border revisions with Poland. However, this was when France and the United Kingdom put their foot down. Both countries pledged that they would declare war on Germany if the country went through with its threats against Poland.

The Christmas Holiday That Shook the World

The troubled years between 1932 and 1938 saw many attempts to exploit the 1932 discovery of the neutron to create element transformation. As mentioned above, Fermi had performed this kind of experiment for some years in Rome, but in the summer and fall of 1938, the well-known chemist Otto Hahn and his assistant Fritz Strassmann, both employed at the Kaiser Wilhelm Institute in Berlin, were also engrossed in studying the outcomes of bombarding uranium with neutrons. Like Fermi in Rome and the scientist couple Irène and Frédéric Joliot-Curie in Paris, they found that several new atomic nuclei were created. For many years, Hahn and Strassmann had collaborated closely with the talented Austrian physicist Lise Meitner. She had also contributed to the planning of the ongoing series of experiments, but in 1938 her Jewish ancestry forced her to flee from intensified Nazi persecution. Via the Netherlands and Denmark, Meitner arrived unharmed in Stockholm, where she was staying when, on December 21, she received a letter from Hahn in Berlin. In the letter, he wrote about the most recent attempts to identify the new particles created from neutron bombardment of uranium. And then came the great revelation: if Hahn had not been told over and over by his fellow physicists that an atomic nucleus under bombardment would only split off small parts such as protons, neutrons or helium nuclei, he as a chemist would have sworn that some of the new particles were nuclei of the well-known element barium, which has 56 protons in its nucleus – i.e., far fewer than the 92 protons in uranium. "Perhaps you can suggest some fantastic explanation," he added.[12]

On December 23, Meitner left Stockholm to spend the holiday visiting friends in Kungälv near Gothenburg. She arrived in the evening, and so did her nephew, physicist Otto Frisch, who worked at Niels Bohr's Institute in Copenhagen. After breakfast the next day, they ventured out into the beautiful winter landscape, eagerly discussing the contents of Hahn's letter. At first, Frisch flatly dismissed Hahn's claim, maintaining that the experiment must have been flawed.

© National Archives and Records Administration

Lise Meitner and Otto Hahn in their laboratory at the Kaiser Wilhelm Institute in Berlin, 1913.

Niels Bohr (second from the left) is pictured in Copenhagen in 1934, with four other nuclear physicists. Two of them, Edward Teller (fourth from the left) and Otto Frisch (fifth from the left), also made significant contributions to the development of nuclear weapons.

However, during their walk, the two came to think of the model of an atomic nucleus suggested by Niels Bohr a few years earlier. The model was called the liquid drop model because it compared an atomic nucleus to a drop of liquid, which is held together by chemical forces between its atoms, which give rise to surface tension. In an atomic nucleus, the electrical forces, which are repulsive, become stronger the more protons there are in the nucleus. The reason that uranium is the heaviest naturally occurring element must be that the long-range repulsive forces between the protons are only just kept in balance by the surface tension due to the strong short-range forces between the nuclear particles.

But what would happen if a uranium nucleus captured a neutron? Maybe the nucleus would start to oscillate, causing it at some point to become elongated like an American football – or perhaps even take on the shape of a dumbbell? In that case, it might be expected to break into two pieces of more or less the same size, if the long-range, repulsive forces between protons in the two pieces would overpower the short-range nuclear forces. Presumably, this would cause the two parts to separate at a tremendous speed, concluded Frisch and Meitner. Sitting on a fallen tree, they set themselves the task of calculating the amount of energy that is released when a neutron causes a U-235 nucleus (containing 92 protons and 143 neutrons) to split into a barium nucleus (Ba) and a krypton nucleus (Kr), say Ba-150 (56 protons and 94 neutrons) and Kr-85 (36 protons and 49 neutrons). Fortunately, Meitner remembered a semiempirical formula by which they were able to calculate the masses of the U-235, Ba-150 and Kr-85 nuclei. Using this formula they realized that a mass corresponding to roughly one fifth of a proton mass disappears during the splitting of a uranium nucleus by a neutron. But according to Einstein's famous formula $E = mc^2$, the mass lost is released as energy, which in this case is 200 MeV in round numbers, roughly 100 million times more than the energy released per atom in violent chemical reactions such as dynamite explosions. Furthermore, the result is almost identical if instead the U-235 nucleus splits into isotopes of cesium and rubidium (containing 55 and 37 protons, respectively) or tellurium and zirconium (containing 52 and 40 protons).[13]

Before the end of their Christmas holiday, Meitner and Frisch had written the draft of an article about neutron-induced splitting of uranium nuclei (soon to be called 'fission'), whose contents Frisch presented to Bohr in Copenhagen on January 3, 1939. Frisch recalls that he had barely started his account when Bohr put a hand on his forehead and exclaimed: "Oh what idiots we have been! Oh but this is wonderful! This is just as it must be!"[14] Frisch also recalls that Christian Møller, one of Bohr's colleagues, suggested to him that as the heavy uranium nucleus contains many more neutrons than protons, the fission products must have a surplus of neutrons and thus might be expected to emit one or more neutrons almost immediately.

On January 7, Bohr boarded a ship from Copenhagen to New York, taking with him the news from Berlin, and Meitner and Frisch's interpretation of the event as a neutron-induced splitting – soon to be called *fission* – of a uranium nucleus. This became a great sensation in scientific circles. Within a few days, physicists at several American and European labs confirmed Hahn and Strassmann's experimental discovery of the process of fission. The news spread like wildfire through the nuclear research community around the world.

Unprecedented Explosive Force

More than 100 articles on fission were published in 1939, including ones on experiments demonstrating that every fission process releases free neutrons. Exactly how many was still contested, but it was believed that it was more than two on average. This meant that science had made a huge leap toward the possibility of realizing a chain reaction. If one nucleus in a lump of uranium was split by a neutron from the outside, and if it thereby released, say, three neutrons, each of these neutrons could cause the fission of another uranium nucleus in the lump. This could release, say, nine neutrons, which in turn would cause new fissions, and so on at an extremely fast rate. The result would be a chain reaction which, in less than a millionth of a second, would release an immense amount of energy. However, if the uranium lump is too small, most of the released neutrons can be expected to leave the lump before hitting another uranium nucleus, in which case the chain reaction will not take place. In 1939 it was still unsettled how big the uranium lump had

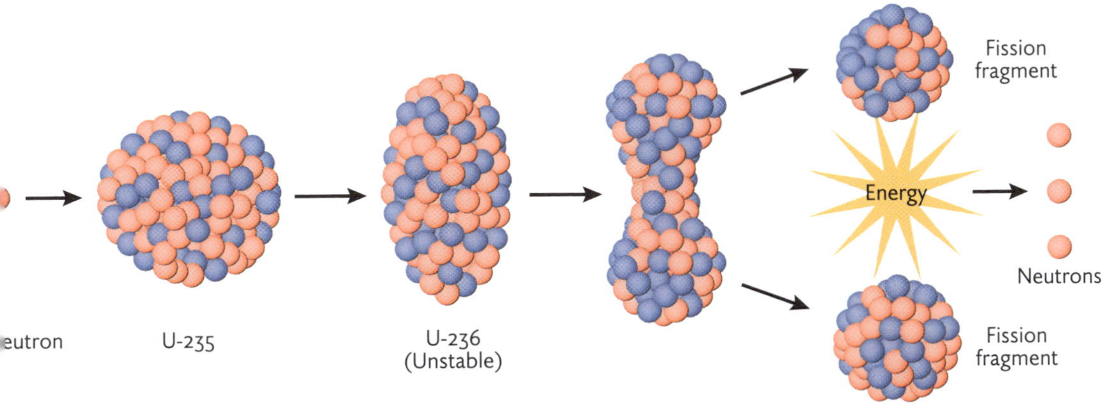

In the last days of December 1938, Otto Frisch and Lise Meitner proposed that the outcome of the uranium experiment conducted by Otto Hahn and Fritz Strassmann in the autumn of 1938 could be explained as the fission of uranium nuclei. A few weeks later, it became clear that the fission of uranium nuclei could trigger a chain reaction in a lump of uranium.
© Finn Petersen

to be, and how much energy could be released, but it was certain that the potential was huge. Leading nuclear physicists realized that they had stumbled upon a discovery that might lead to the development of a uranium bomb with unprecedented explosive force. Imagine what could have happened if Ida Noddack's hypothesis had been taken seriously in 1934. If fission in uranium and the possibility of a chain reaction in a lump of uranium had been realized in 1934–35 instead of 1938–39, all the major nations engaged in the Second World War could have been on the verge of developing nuclear weapons right at the outset of the war – a truly terrifying scenario.

However, there was one factor negatively affecting the prospects for a nuclear chain reaction: Niels Bohr and his American associate John Wheeler soon convinced their nuclear physics colleagues that it must be the rare uranium isotope U-235 that could be split when hit by a neutron, and not the far more common U-238.[15] As mentioned earlier, natural uranium consists of 99.3 percent U-238 and only 0.7 percent U-235, but how were scientists to distinguish between the two when they react identically in all chemical processes? They could only be separated by physical means due to their mass difference, which would be extremely difficult and costly. Thus Bohr and many other scientists doubted that chain reactions could be realized within a reasonable number of years.

Others were less pessimistic, including the Hungarian-born Jewish physicist Leo Szilard, who had also been forced to flee due to the extensive persecution in Germany, Austria and Hungary. In the fall of 1933, he was staying in London when he had the idea that the newly discovered neutron might be able to cause a chain reaction in one or more elements, meaning that Rutherford's talk of moonshine might not hold true. Szilard had no idea if there was any element that released more than one neutron each time its nuclei were hit by a neutron, but he toyed so much with the thought that in 1934 he applied for a patent based uponon his vague chain reaction idea for the exploitation of nuclear energy. The patent was granted in March 1936, but Szilard – fearing it might be misused – had assigned it to the British Admirality to ensure its secrecy. Consequently, Szilards patent was not published until 1949![16]

In 1935, Szilard emigrated to the USA. Over the next three years he seized any opportunity at different American laboratories to argue that either beryllium or indium, his favorite elements, would start a chain reaction when hit by neutrons. But in 1938, a few months before Enrico Fermi took up his posi-

Albert Einstein and Leo Szilard on the terrace at Einstein's summer house on Long Island, where on August 1, 1939 the two famous physicists wrote the letter to Roosevelt that – with some delay – launched the Manhattan Project. The photo was taken in connection with a reconstruction of the event after the war.

tion as professor of nuclear physics at Columbia University, Szilard had to admit that his work had been unsuccessful.[17] He did, however, stay in New York when he received Bohr's news from Copenhagen that uranium nuclei can be split by means of neutrons.

Suddenly, Szilard's hypothetical idea for a chain reaction became a realistic scenario. Naturally, this flattered him, but at the same time he was horrified at the thought of what would happen if Nazi Germany acquired a uranium bomb. He therefore tried to convince his fellow physicists not to publish the results of their research if it had anything to do with uranium nuclei, but in the beginning his attempts were in vain because the prospect of being the first to publish new, groundbreaking discoveries is one of the main drivers behind all science. One of the new discoveries that impressed nuclear physicists around the world was the report from the Joliot-Curies' lab in Paris in April 1939 that when it undergoes fission, a uranium nucleus normally releases two to four free neutrons, each of which can cause other uranium nuclei to undergo fission in turn. Szilard believed that the publication of this news was a terrible mistake because any able nuclear physicist could now readily conclude that science had come a big step closer to the possibility of building a uranium bomb.[18]

The many unsettling reports on uranium research in the spring of 1939 caused Szilard and his Hungarian physicist colleague Eugene Wigner, who had also fled from the Nazis, to contact Albert Einstein at his summer home on Long Island in August 1939. Although Einstein had not been involved in the new uranium research, he was without doubt the most famous scientist of his time. It was this fame that Szilard wanted to utilize by convincing Einstein to write a letter to Franklin D. Roosevelt, turning the president's attention to the frightening prospects associated with the current development in nuclear physics.

Einstein was sympathetic to the argument and, having pacifist leanings, let himself be talked into signing the letter that Szilard had more or less written in advance. The letter stated, among other things, that recent months' nuclear physics discoveries could most likely result in "a nuclear chain reaction in a large mass of uranium", and possibly "extremely powerful bombs" capable of destroying an entire harbor and its surroundings. Further, there were indications that the Germans were already looking into the possibilities, given that "Germany has actually stopped the sale of uranium from the Czechoslovakian mines she has taken over".[19] The letter was sent on August 2, 1939, only thirty days before the outbreak of the Second World War. Due to a series of unfortunate events, Roosevelt did not receive the letter until a few weeks later, but as soon as he read it, he sensed that this might be highly urgent. He immediately made sure that the letter was passed on to an American uranium committee that had been set up shortly before with Lyman J. Briggs as chairman. However, not much happened in the committee because the USA was not yet involved in the war, and Briggs therefore did not see any reason to deal with something as theoretical as making weapons out of uranium on this side of the Atlantic.

The Report in the Safe

After the outbreak of the Second World War, triggered by Hitler's attack on Poland on September 1, 1939, and the ensuing British and French declaration of war two days later, it was not long before the stream of articles on fission ceased. The warring parties had – upon request from the physicists – introduced a ban on the field. Instead, a number of secret uranium projects commenced in the United Kingdom, France, Germany, the USA, the Soviet Union and Japan. Everyone was aware that something was happening, but no one knew how far other countries' scientists had come.

We now know that the United Kingdom was ahead in 1939–40. The two German refugee physicists Otto Frisch and Rudolf Peierls, who had found a safe haven under the protection of Professor Mark Oliphant at Birmingham University, started on their own initiative to make calculations of whether creating a fission bomb based on the rare uranium isotope U-235 was possible. They were not privy to the exact nuclear physical data, but in the summer of 1940 they concluded, based on reasonable assumptions, that such a bomb was in fact most likely possible. They also estimated that the necessary amount of pure U-235 – called the critical mass – was no more than approximately one kilogram, and that if such a bomb were to explode, it would release energy equivalent to several tons of regular explosive (TNT). They wrote all this and more in the so-called Frisch-Peierls Memorandum that had the spectacular title: "On the Construction of a 'Super-Bomb', Based on a Nuclear Chain Reaction in Uranium."[20] The memorandum was immediately classified as top secret by the British military.

The estimate of the critical mass of U-235 made by the two physicists in 1940 was significantly lower than the 10–100 kg that prominent German physicists, including Otto Hahn, Werner Heisenberg and Friedrich von Weizsäcker, made in early spring of 1941 in Germany.[21] This difference may very well have contributed to the United Kingdom going forward with the uranium bomb idea, while the German physicists focused more on using uranium for an energy-producing reactor.

When Frisch and Peierls wrote their memorandum, the United Kingdom was under heavy pressure. All of Western Europe was occupied by Nazi Germany, and the United Kingdom could expect an invasion by Hitler's triumphant army anytime. Nevertheless, the British government had the wherewithal to set up a uranium committee, named the MAUD committee which, based on Frisch and Peierls' memorandum, was tasked with calculating more precisely how much U-235 was required to build a nuclear bomb, how long it would take and what it would cost.[22] The committee consisted of scientists from the British universities.

In June 1941, the final, top-secret MAUD report was ready. Assuming the average number of neutrons emitted per fission event is minimum 2.5 and using more precise data than was available to Frisch and Peierls in early 1940, the committee concluded that the critical mass of U-235 is approximately 43 kg for a U-235 sphere in free space, but only 13 kg if the sphere is fully tamped, i.e. surrounded by a thick sphere of steel or other massive material which reflects most of the escaping neutrons back into the uranium sphere. Although the new values for the critical mass of U-235 were more in line with the German estimate than with that of Frisch and Peierls, the committee nevertheless concluded that it would probably be possible to produce a uranium bomb before the end of the war. The development of the bomb was thus to be given top priority, and the committee estimated that the first bomb could be ready in December 1943. The committee also recommended that the development work should be done in collaboration with the USA, which had enormous financial and technical resources at its disposal. The production of the bomb itself was to take place in the USA, where the facilities would avoid German airstrikes.[23] The MAUD report was made available to the American government, given that the United Kingdom wanted the main technical facilities to be built on American soil. However, the American uranium committee did not respond to the report right away, which led Mark Oliphant, one of the leading physicists on the MAUD committee, to travel to the USA. Here, to his surprise, he found that Lyman Briggs, the chairman of the American uranium committee, had done nothing except put the MAUD report in his safe. Obviously, Oliphant could not accept this. He contacted some of the rank-and-file members in the committee who, although unfamiliar with the MAUD report, nonetheless took action. The entire American uranium committee gathered, Briggs was fired, and in December 1941 President Roosevelt appointed the legendary organizer Vannevar Bush, director of a newly founded organization, the Office for Scientific Research and Development (OSRD), as manager of the uranium project and other large-scale war-related projects.

This signaled the start of the top-secret Manhattan Engineer District that within less than four years would construct a number of nuclear bombs – two of which meant the definitive end of the Second World War.

CHAPTER 2

The World's First Nuclear Weapon State

The Manhattan Project

After Vannevar Bush was appointed manager of the OSRD, things moved quickly. Money for the nuclear project came rolling in, directly from "the president's deep pockets", as it was said about funding given by the American president without Congress having to approve it. The project was called the Manhattan Engineer District to confuse any German and Japanese spies on the lookout for snippets of information on new weapons projects. Manhattan Engineer District was purposely intended to sound dull. The work took place in close and, mostly, effective cooperation between military authorities, private companies and scientific institutions that made available a vast number of prominent nuclear physicists and other scientists to the project. However, the work was carried out in a secretive atmosphere the scientists were not used to, which sometimes caused tension. In an extensive study, historian Alex Wellerstein has established that attempts to keep confidential large parts of the nuclear weapons research and development in the USA has been the rule rather than the exception from the Manhattan Project up until the present day.[24] In special cases, scientists have been known to muzzle themselves, as was the case in the spring of 1939 when nuclear physicist Leo Szilard implored his colleagues in the USA and Western Europe to conceal all their research results regarding the element uranium because he feared they would help German physicists produce the first nuclear bomb.

Bush predicted the need for large, secret facilities for the Manhattan Project, a common abbreviation for "Manhattan Engineer District". On September 17, 1942 he appointed General Leslie Groves from the American military to manage the material construction and necessary security measures. Groves had previously demonstrated his talent for planning by managing the construction of the recently completed Pentagon. However, Groves soon realized that he would be unable to manage the large group of scientists, including several Nobel Prize laureates who had already been enrolled in the project. He did not understand them, and they did not understand him. Therefore, he needed to find a scientist with the ability and patience to explain to him the details of nuclear physics and who could manage the scientific and technical development of the nuclear bomb.

At the end of October 1942, after careful deliberation, Groves nominated American nuclear physicist J. Robert Oppenheimer, professor at the University of California, Berkeley. He was impressed with Oppenheimer's brilliant mind, even though the two had their political differences. Groves was an ardent conservative and hated communists, while Oppenheimer had many communist friends, including a mistress. During and after the Second World War, Groves always defended Oppenheimer against the security agents that suspected him of divulging classified information to his communist friends and thereby possibly to the Russians.

Groves and Oppenheimer collaborated on bringing the Manhattan Project to its conclusion: designing and producing a nuclear bomb. But before this could be done, the scientists needed more detailed knowledge about how many neutrons were released during the fission of a uranium nucleus after having absorbed a neutron. The number varied, but the scientists associated with the Manhattan Project soon confirmed that the average was 2.5, which was more than sufficient to facilitate a chain reaction. The scientists also needed a precise number for the critical mass of uranium, i.e., the weight of the smallest lump of uranium-235 in which a runaway chain reaction can be established. The critical mass turned out to be in agreement with the most pessimistic values in the Maud report, i.e. close to 43 kg if the uranium lump consists of 99 percent U-235 in free space.

Even before the necessary values had been conclusively established, a group of researchers led by chemist Glenn Seaborg had discovered that when the common uranium isotope U-238 is hit by a neutron, it occasionally transforms into a nucleus of an entirely new element named plutonium (Pu). Plutonium always has 94 protons in its core, but it can appear as different isotopes. One of these isotopes is Pu-239, which can also undergo fission when hit by a neutron. In other words: it suddenly seemed that a nuclear bomb could be developed via two very different paths.

The first path is called the uranium path. Here, the U-235 isotope needs to be separated from U-238 isotopes on a large scale, which – as was clear from the beginning – is an immensely difficult task. The two isotopes cannot be separated by chemical methods as they are essentially identical chemically.

Instead, they can only be separated by physical procedures relying on the fact that a U-238 atom is approximately 1 percent heavier than a U-235 atom.

The second path employs plutonium. Here, Pu-239 is produced in large quantities from U-238. This appears to be slightly less difficult, because when Pu-239 is created by bombarding uranium with neutrons, it is in principle easy to separate from uranium and other elements by using well-known chemical methods. The challenge, however, is how to bombard uranium with neutrons on a large scale. This can be done in a nuclear reactor via a *controlled* chain reaction.[25] The first and crucial step of the plutonium path was thus to demonstrate that it was possible to produce a functional experimental nuclear reactor. This option required study, but Groves did not have time to wait for the answer before launching the construction of four centers that he and Oppenheimer deemed necessary to realize the objectives of the Manhattan Project in the shortest time possible. All opportunities must be pursued, and time was the decisive factor as money was not an issue. We will return to the four centers below, but first let us take a look at an issue that Groves was strongly committed to: asserting control of the world's uranium resources.

The Most Coveted Element

The history of the element uranium is peculiar. Astrophysicists have long believed that the uranium atoms that in our time are embedded in uraninite and other minerals in the Earth's crust must originate from exploded stars, or supernovas.[26] The explosions of stars spread the heavy elemental atoms in interstellar space, where they mixed with the particles in dust clouds – mainly consisting of hydrogen atoms – which, over the course of some hundred million years, gathered in new galaxies as a result of the constant force of gravitation. One of these galaxies is the Milky Way. Approximately 4.5 billion years ago, the sun and a number of planets, including Earth, were created at the rim of this galaxy. And some of the uranium that happened to be here was embedded in the Earth's crust where it has remained relatively undisturbed ever since. Uranium was not described before 1789, when it was discovered by the German chemist Martin Heinrich Klaproth, and for more than 100 years it was used almost solely as a special yellow-green paint on bowls and jars.

© Union Miniere du Haut-Katanga 1906-1956

Most of the uranium used in the Manhattan Project came from the Shinkolobwe Mine in what was then the Belgian Congo. The mine continued to operate throughout the Cold War and until 2004.

Uranium's quiet existence changed abruptly when French physicist Henri Becquerel in 1896 discovered that uranium containing material emits radioactivity. Becquerel's discovery triggered an avalanche of new scientific discoveries that came to a temporary conclusion with Hahn and Strassmann's experimental neutron bombardment of uranium in Berlin in the spring of 1938 followed by Meitner and Frisch's interpretation of this experiment in December the same year. Uranium, which had long been viewed as an almost valueless material thereafter became the most coveted element on the planet.

General Groves was convinced that uranium was a very rare element only found in few places in the world in quantities large enough to be feasible to extract. Today, we know that this assumption was wrong, but neither Groves nor leading geologists knew this in 1942 when the Manhattan Project was launched. The uranium ore from which Marie and Pierre Curie in 1902 isolated the highly radioactive element radium came from the Joachimstal Mine in Bohemia. But since then, other richer uranium mines had been discovered, including the Shinkolobwe Mine in the former Belgian Congo and the Eldorado Mine in Canada. The Joachimstal Mine was located in an area occupied by the Germans and was thus not available to the Western allies, but Groves managed to gain control of the Shinkolobwe Mine and ordered the production of ore to be increased to the maximum possible. This was a lengthy process because the mine had been closed down for a few years due to the waning demand for uranium ore. The experts estimated that it would take about a year to get the mine up and running again. Lucky for Groves, however, it turned out that the Belgian mining company that owned the mine kept 1,250 tons of uranium ore in a storehouse in New York City! The director of the company, Edgar Sengier, had fled to the USA in 1939 and, on his own initiative, had the ore shipped from the Shinkolobwe Mine to New York at the end of 1940 when he started to worry that the Germans might invade the Belgian Congo. Most of the uranium used as raw material in the production of the nuclear bombs that exploded above Hiroshima and Nagasaki a few years later actually came from this stock – and thus originally from the Congo.[27]

However, Groves had bigger, longer-term plans. He hired experts in the American mining company Union Mines Development Corporation to pore over thousands of geological reports and journals with the objective of finding promising uranium deposits across the globe.[28] When such deposits had been identified, it was up to the newly founded Combined Development Trust – which was controlled by the governments of the USA, the United Kingdom and Canada – to offer the countries that owned the deposits lucrative export agreements on all the uranium they could produce. In the years 1943–46, agreements were made with, among others, Brazil, Belgium (concerning mines in the Congo), Portugal (concerning mines in the Portuguese colony of Mozambique) and the Netherlands (concerning mines in the Dutch colony of the Dutch East Indies – present-day Indonesia). The aim was to prevent Germany, Japan and not least the Soviet Union from gaining access to rich uranium deposits. This would obstruct these countries in any attempt to develop nuclear weapons. Groves was convinced that his initiative had been a roaring success. In November 1944, he thus estimated that the Trust already controlled over 90 percent of the world's uranium production.[29]

Four Secret Centers

The Met Lab, the abbreviation for the peaceful-sounding Metallurgical Laboratory, was the first of four centers involved in the Manhattan Project. It was situated in Chicago, at the University of Chicago. Over the course of 1942, a group of scientists gathered here, headed by American physicist and Nobel Prize laureate Arthur Compton. The group included Leo Szilard, the actual author of the letter from Einstein to Roosevelt in August 1939, and Enrico Fermi, who had arrived in the USA in December 1938. The group was tasked with constructing the world's first nuclear reactor, Chicago Pile Number 1 (CP-1), in which a controlled test was to be performed. The reactor fuel consisted of uranium metal and uranium oxide, and the reactor was equipped with a moderator of pure graphite, suited to slow down the fast neutrons. This could be done because graphite consists of carbon atoms, which are relatively light. When a carbon nucleus in the moderator is hit by a fast neutron, the neutron transmits a significant amount of its speed to the nucleus, just as a snooker ball loses most of its speed when hitting another snooker ball at rest. The moderator thus slows down fast neutrons, which is an advantage in a reactor given that lab experiments had shown that slow neutrons are more efficient than fast ones in causing fission of U-235 nuclei.

The reactor, which was constructed in a basement under the grandstands of a closed-down football stadium in Chicago, was therefore built on a layer of graphite blocks and columns of natural uranium.[30] Approximately 400 tons of graphite, 6 tons of uranium metal and 40 tons of uranium oxide formed the reactor core which was 8 meters wide and 6 meters tall. Further, the reactor was equipped with a number of wooden rods clad with cadmium that could be slid in and out through special ducts. Cadmium is a potent neutron absorber and therefore makes it possible to control a reactor.[31]

On December 2, 1942, the big day had finally arrived. Attended by the key researchers and engineers on the project, George Weil, one of Fermi's closest associates, pulled out one cadmium rod after the other. A battery of measuring instruments showed that the neutron activity in the center of the reactor kept increasing. When Weil slowly pulled out the last rod, the reactor went critical, meaning that every new generation of neutrons was now larger than the previous one. Fortunately, a small percentage (about one percent) of the neutrons that are released when a slow neutron causes fission in a U-235 nucleus are so-called 'delayed' neutrons that are only released up to several minutes after the fission has occurred. These delayed neutrons are crucial to preventing a reactor from getting out of hand as soon as it turns critical and make it controllable via rods of cadmium or other neutron absorbers.

This is exactly the effect that Fermi exploited in December 2, 1942. By having Weil pull out the cadmium rod and subsequently push it back in, Fermi could adjust the intensity of the reactor as he wished. Hereby, the

Atomic Age was a reality. The group celebrated with a bottle of Chianti that Eugene Wigner had brought for the occasion. However, the mood was probably dampened when Szilard shook Fermi's hand and said he thought the day would go down as a black day in the history of mankind.[32]

At the inconspicuous location of Oak Ridge in the state of Tennessee, a giant facility was built in the years 1943–44 under the codename Site X. The sole purpose of this facility was to separate U-235 from U-238. This was done by pumping uranium hexafluoride gas, which is the only gaseous compound of uranium, through a porous wall of nickel. If the holes are very small, U-235 passes through the wall slightly more easily than the heavier U-238, and the gas thereby contains a higher percentage of U-235 after passage than before. When the gas was pumped through a second membrane, the concentration of U-235 increased further and, after a large number of passages, reached approximately 90 percent, which nuclear physicists had estimated to be sufficient for use in a nuclear bomb. Researchers at Oak Ridge also tried to separate U-235 from U-238 by sending uranium atoms through powerful electromagnetic fields that deflect the lighter U-235 isotope slightly more than the heavier U-238 isotope. This process turned out to be even more challenging than the former, which is called a diffusion process. In the end, the technicians found a way to combine the two processes, but nevertheless it was not until the spring of 1945 that the Oak Ridge facility had produced quantities of U-235 that could be measured in kilograms. By then, Groves had managed to develop and build the world's largest building (K-25) at the time, bursting with labs and specially designed machines. K-25 was constructed as a U-shaped building on four floors. Each side of the U was almost 1,000 meters long and 120 meters wide. At its peak the Oak Ridge facility used as much electric power as the city of New York.

The small reactor CP-1 under the football grandstand produced plutonium as neutrons were absorbed by U-238 nuclei, but not nearly in the quantities needed. A much larger facility was required. However, if something went wrong, such a facility might cause dangerous radiation in the surrounding area. Therefore, Groves decided that the large reactors producing plutonium for nuclear bombs must be built far away from centers of population. The facility, called Site W, was built and operated by the large American chemical company Du Pont in a sparsely populated area near Hanford in the state of Washington in northwest USA.[33] In addition to being far removed from urban areas, there were plentiful quantities of river water to cool the reactors.

This was essential because the fission processes in large reactors give off enormous amounts of heat.

Site W also had its share of practical issues, but they were solved due to the ample funding and skilled staff. The reactors were soon running day and night. When the fuel rods had been inserted in the reactors for a few months, they were removed – now heavily radioactive – and cut up at a chemical factory called a hot cell facility. All processes here had to be operated remotely, including the processes by which the chemists separated Pu-239 from the other material. In June 1945, Hanford could finally send 5–10 kg of plutonium to the fourth and most important location in the Manhattan Project.

In 1943–44, in a remote part of the New Mexico desert, under the codename Site Y, the American military built a secret lab where all the threads of the Manhattan Project were gathered and some of the world's brightest minds were to design the bomb – or bombs. These people included Hans Bethe, Edward Teller, Richard Feynman, Ernest Lawrence and Niels Bohr – an impressive team of physicists. The team also included experts within other specializations that might come in handy, such as the explosives expert George Kistiakowsky. Oppenheimer and Groves had agreed to build the lab in this isolated location, because it would be relatively easy for the military to isolate the staff from the surrounding world. In addition, Oppenheimer was familiar with the area since he made a trip to it in 1922 when recovering from colitis and he and his brother rented a summer ranch in the neighborhood.

What the two main figures did not agree on, however, was how the work was to be conducted. Oppenheimer advocated that everyone inside the fence of Los Alamos should be allowed to discuss freely and openly because that was the custom in scientific communities and most scientists agreed that it generated the best results. General Groves, on the other hand, was a high-ranking military officer who was used to special knowledge being kept secret from everyone but the few who needed it. He was simply afraid of what might happen if everyone talked with each other. What if there were spies among them? Groves' suspicions were not just figments of his imagination: a few years after the war, it came to light that several of the researchers at Los Alamos had been spying for the Soviet Union.

One of the large nuclear reactors on the Columbia River in Washington State, which produced the plutonium that armed both the Trinity bomb and *Fat Man* bomb. The latter exploded over Nagasaki on August 9, 1945.

Two Types of Bomb

The staff at Los Alamos worked tirelessly on developing the two types of bomb. One was the uranium bomb, which the experts predicted to be plain sailing after Oak Ridge had started to deliver large amounts of uranium. The bomb itself was to be built as a pipe whose two ends were each equipped with a subcritical amount of U-235. A conventional explosive charge would ensure that the two lumps of uranium would at a predefined time be brought together in one supercritical lump, meaning that the majority of neutrons released in the process of fission could not escape the lump before causing new fissions in U-235. Or, described in more detail: the moment when the entire mass of uranium was gathered in one lump, a number of neutrons would be released in the middle of the lump by means of a so-called 'initiator'. Most of these neutrons would hit a U-235 nucleus, causing fission and generating an average of 2.5 neutrons, each of which would cause an even greater number of fissions, etc. Each generation would only last approximately 1/100,000,000 second, meaning that 60–70 generations could happen in a microsecond – the time the lump of uranium can remain whole before being dispersed so much that the chain reaction stops.

The Los Alamos experts estimated that over these 60–70 generations, approximately one percent of the U-235 nuclei in the supercritical lump would have undergone fission, and this would release energy equivalent to 10–20 thousand tons of conventional explosive (TNT).[34] The experts were certain the uranium bomb would work, and they deemed it unnecessary to waste precious U-235 on a test. As soon as the president wished, the first completed uranium bomb could be used in war.

The other type of bomb was based on the element plutonium. From the outset, the Los Alamos team reckoned that it would work according to the same principle as the uranium bomb, but this soon proved unfeasible. The problem was that the plutonium produced in the large Hanford reactors contained, in addition to Pu-239, smaller or larger quantities of the heaver isotopes Pu-240 and Pu-241 – especially the former. However, Pu-240 is radioactive and releases neutrons on its own. Calculations showed that if the lump contained even just a few percent of Pu-240, in the microseconds required to shoot one lump of plutonium into another, it would release so many neutrons from Pu-240 that it was likely to start a chain reaction in Pu-239 too early, reducing the potentially huge explosion to something best described as a dud. So, they had to come up with something else. The solution was to cover a small, 5–6 kilo subcritical lump of plutonium in several layers of explosive.[35] When this was brought to detonate in a carefully controlled manner, it would create an inward-directed blast wave that in a fraction of a microsecond would squeeze the plutonium lump into a much smaller ball. This process, called implosion, logically causes the plutonium nuclei to become much more compact than before the implosion. The chance that a neutron can escape the lump without causing fission in a Pu nucleus is thereby strongly reduced, and the lump goes from being subcritical to supercritical. At the exact moment that the lump is maximally compressed, an initiator releases a large number of free neutrons. They trigger a chain reaction that, over the course of approximately 70 neutron generations, builds up to an explosion equivalent to many tons of TNT.

It was extremely complicated to make the implosion processes work. Kistiakowsky and his staff carried out countless experiments with dummy bombs before they managed to achieve a perfectly symmetrical compression of the bomb core. The implosion challenge was without doubt the greatest technical issue the Los Alamos group solved over the two years the lab existed – that is, until the end of the war. In fact, Oppenheimer and his team were so uncertain the plutonium bomb would work that they found it necessary to carry out a test before introducing this type of bomb for war purposes.

Bohr, Churchill and Roosevelt

As the work progressed more or less according to plan on the different parts of the grand-scale nuclear project, some of the leading scientists began to discuss what would happen if they managed to fully develop the bomb before the war was over. In the series of initiatives regarding the future of the bomb, Danish nuclear physicist Niels Bohr played a central and somewhat tragic role. After fleeing from Denmark to Sweden with his family around October 1, 1943 when the Gestapo attempted to arrest all Danish Jews – Bohr's mother was Jewish according to the Nazi definition – he travelled to New York via England and from there on to Los Alamos. He arrived in Los Alamos at the end of December 1943 with his son, Aage.

In Los Alamos, Bohr soon learned that the nuclear bomb project was much further advanced than he had imagined. He followed the work but did not contribute much to the development of the bomb itself. Instead, he spent his time considering how the bomb would change the world, and what it would take to avoid a nuclear arms race between East and West after the war. He began writing a memorandum in which he advocated the importance of the Soviet government being informed about the nuclear bomb, and of the new, formidable weapon becoming subject to international control. However, before he had a chance to finish his memorandum, he suddenly had an opportunity to travel back to London and perhaps even be granted a private meeting with Prime Minister Winston Churchill. Thanks to Bohr's close friends, Finance Minister Sir John Anderson and Churchill's personal adviser Lord Cherwell, who were both educated in science, a meeting between the great physicist and the legendary statesman was indeed arranged on May 16, 1944.[36] Bohr reckoned that he would get the opportunity to present his thoughts in a relaxed atmosphere, and that he and Churchill would have a constructive dialog about the grave prospects looming on the horizon when the nuclear bomb became a reality.

However, the meeting turned out somewhat disastrously because Churchill was not a fan of Bohr's rather prolix manner. He interrupted Bohr long before the scientist had finished his account and stated that he cared very little for Bohr's thoughts on international control of the nuclear bomb. The meeting became a brief affair, and when Bohr asked permission to elaborate his thoughts in a letter, Churchill replied that he would be honored to receive a letter from Professor Bohr, but hoped it would not be about politics.[37]

Bohr was devastated over the failed conversation with Churchill, but that only made him even more eager to meet President Roosevelt. In the meantime, Bohr took time to finish the memorandum he had been working on for months, and when it was finished, he sent it to Roosevelt via a shared acquaintance, judge of the American Supreme Court Felix Frankfurter. The idea was that Bohr could go straight to the point if and when he was granted an audience with Roosevelt. Bohr did in fact manage to arrange a meeting on August 26, 1944 and this talk went much better than the one with Churchill – at least as far as Bohr was concerned.

Nevertheless, when Roosevelt and Churchill met on September 18, 1944, in the president's home in Hyde Park, New York, Bohr's hopes were dashed. The two statesmen agreed – or, rather, Churchill convinced Roosevelt – that there could be no talk of sharing the nuclear secret with the Russians before the war was over. Also, they agreed that the intelligence agencies should watch Bohr closely. In Churchill's eyes, Bohr presented a grave security risk

– partly because he had taken the liberty of discussing the nuclear bomb project with Felix Frankfurter, who had not been cleared to receive information on the secret project, and partly because he had corresponded with the well-known Soviet physicist Peter Kapitza, who had spent many years in the West. "Bohr ought to be confined or at any rate made to see that he is very near the edge of mortal crimes," wrote Churchill the following day in a note to Lord Cherwell.[38]

It is important to stress that nothing indicates that Bohr at any time disclosed nuclear secrets to Kapitza or other Soviet physicists. Nevertheless, all his attempts to set up new meetings with Churchill and Roosevelt were futile, and he further had to promise the FBI that he would refrain from working with nuclear energy at his institute in Copenhagen without clearance from the USA.[39]

What Should the Nuclear Bomb be Used for?

In May 1945, US Secretary of War, Henry L. Stimson, set up a so-called Interim Committee on the initiative of President Harry S. Truman, who had taken the presidential oath on April 12, a few hours after Roosevelt's death. The committee comprised eight members. Stimson was chairman of the group that included politicians, military personnel and three science politicians: Vannevar Bush, Karl Compton (brother of Arthur Compton, the manager of Met Lab) and James Conant. The most influential member would prove to be James F. Byrnes, who was the new president's personally appointed representative and about to become Truman's Secretary of State. The committee's job was to provide a recommendation for the president regarding what should happen with the nuclear bomb once it was ready to be employed in the war.[40]

The Interim Committee first met on May 9, 1945, the day after the German forces had capitulated across Europe. At that point, American nuclear experts, who had followed the invasion forces closely through occupied Europe, had established much earlier that the German nuclear bomb project was far behind the Manhattan Project.[41] The German effort in the field had been half-hearted, among other reasons because Hitler and his military advisers were only willing to provide massive funding for projects that were likely to result in weapons that could be used in the ongoing war – something that the leading German nuclear physicists did not dare to promise. After 1941, rivalling

German physicists therefore had to make do with modest funds, which they used on three or four uncoordinated attempts to make nuclear reactors with various designs work. By the end of the war in Europe, none of these groups had managed to build a critical nuclear reactor, which Fermi and his Met Lab group had already done in Chicago in December 1942.[42]

After May 9, 1945, the American bomb specialists could turn their full attention to Japan. This resulted in intensified interrogations of Japanese prisoners with physics backgrounds and studies of countless aerial photos of Japanese industrial facilities. This soon convinced the Americans that Japan had not prioritized nuclear bomb research and development during the Second World War. Hence, there was no reason for the Interim Committee to fear Japanese nuclear attacks on American territory when it began the work that would result in the clear recommendation to President Truman: to use the newly developed nuclear bombs against Japan. The committee set up a subcommittee, the Target Committee, and appointed four prominent scientific advisers – Robert Oppenheimer, Enrico Fermi, Ernest Lawrence and Arthur Compton – who were invited to take part in the next meeting of the Interim Committee.

The Target Committee consisted mainly of military personnel tasked with writing a prioritized list of suitable targets in Japan. No moral considerations were to be made – on the contrary, the case needed to be viewed cynically in answering the question: what is the optimal target in terms of likelihood that it will put an end to the war in the Far East? The resulting list contained the names of four cities, topped by the city of Kyoto – a metropolis with almost one million citizens and an important industrial center, in addition to being the cultural center of Japan. Next on the list was Hiroshima, a harbor city with approximately 380,000 citizens and home of a large weapons depot. The third city was the harbor and industrial city of Yokohama, followed by Kokura – a smaller city with large weapons factories.[43]

Tokyo and other big cities were not on the list because they had already been so destroyed by non-nuclear airstrikes that it would be difficult to document the effects of the nuclear bomb compared to an ordinary bombing. Also, the shock effect was expected to be greater if the citizens had not previously been exposed to airstrikes. It is worth noting that the city of Nagasaki – which became the target of the second nuclear attack a few months later – was not on the original list of prioritized targets either. The Target Committee simply assessed that it was less important than any of the four targets on the

A discussion at Los Alamos among some of the scientists and engineers involved in building the atomic bombs. Oppenheimer is in the second row wearing a jacket and tie.

list. Later in this chapter, we will return to why the city nevertheless suffered the ill fate of becoming the target of the second bomb.

The Chicago Rebellion

While Niels Bohr in the summer of 1944 had expressed his worries about the future of the world directly to Prime Minister Churchill and President Roosevelt, a new attempt was made in May/June 1945 to influence the American president – this time following normal protocol. However, this new initiative did not focus on the situation after the war, but rather on how the almost complete nuclear bombs were to be used in the current war. The initiative was launched by a group of scientists associated with the Met Lab in Chicago. They had not participated in the discussions at Los Alamos or in the Interim Committee in Washington, but they had nevertheless become aware that others were deciding how the bomb should be used. With Nobel laureate James Franck as chairman, and nuclear physicist Leo Szilard and biologist Eugene Rabinowitch as mouthpieces, the group hastily drew up a report called the Franck Report. Here, the group distanced themselves from the idea of using the bomb against a Japanese city in the current war. The report stated that exploiting nuclear energy would entail a monumental increase of USA's technological and military power, but also that it would cause serious problems, both nationally and internationally. It might be tempting for the USA – who undoubtedly had a significant head start compared to all other countries in utilizing nuclear energy – to try to keep the secrets of nuclear power in American hands, but it would not be feasible. As the report concluded:

> The scientific facts on which [the bomb's] construction is based are well known to scientists of other countries. Unless an effective international control of nuclear explosives is instituted, a race of nuclear armaments is certain to ensue following the first revelation of our possession of nuclear weapons to the world. Within ten years other countries may have nuclear bombs, each of which, weighing less than a ton, could destroy an area of more than five square miles.[44]

General Groves and other members of his staff had often claimed that the USA could prevent other countries from acquiring nuclear weapons by appropriating all the world's known uranium resources, but the authors of the report thought that this option was illusory. This was partly because the known deposits in Czechoslovakia were beyond American control, and partly because the authors found it unlikely that there were no rich resources of uranium in the Soviet Union, which covered more than a fifth of all land on Earth. The members of the Interim Committee and, ultimately, the American president, therefore needed to think long-term when deciding how to use the new, terrifying weapon that the USA possessed. It might very well turn out that the military advantages and American lives saved as a result of the decision to launch nuclear attacks without warning would be more than "outweighed by the ensuing loss of confidence and wave of horror and repulsion, sweeping over the rest of the world". In conclusion, the Franck Report gave an alternative recommendation:

> [The first] demonstration of the new weapon may best be made before the eyes of representatives of all United Nations, on the desert or a barren island. The best possible atmosphere for the achievement of an international agreement could be achieved if America would be able to say to the world. 'You see what weapon we had but did not use. We are ready to renounce its use in the future and join other nations in working out adequate supervision of the use of this nuclear weapon.'[45]

The report was dated June 11, 1945 and signed by eight people, the best-known being James Franck, Leo Szilard and Eugene Rabinowitch. Szilard, who in 1939 had convinced Einstein to write to Roosevelt, also wanted to send this report to the president, i.e., address "the Commander in Chief" directly, just as Niels Bohr had done in the summer of 1944 when Roosevelt was president. But James Franck, chairman of the Chicago group, preferred to follow the traditional line of command, which meant that on June 12 he went to Washington together with Arthur Compton, who was the manager of Met Lab and a member of the scientific board of the Interim Committee. Here, they tried to set up a meeting with US Secretary of War Stimson to hand over the report personally, but Stimson was out of the office, so they had to make do with one of his assistants. It is unclear whether Stimson ever read the report; in any case, the Chicago group never received any response. "Meanwhile we waited for some reaction and we waited and waited and we had the feeling we could as well have dropped this report into Lake Michigan," Rabinowitch said later.[46] In light of what was happening elsewhere, it is fair to conclude that the Franck Report had no influence on the crucial decisions of the Interim Committee and, subsequently, the White House.

The Fateful Decision

On May 31 and June 1, 1945, the Interim Committee met with the scientific advisors to discuss the different options of using the new nuclear weapons. Lawrence, who did not like the idea of an unannounced attack on a large Japanese city, initially suggested that President Truman should invite all relevant nations – including the Soviet Union and Japan – to dispatch military experts to witness a nuclear test on a remote island. It was Lawrence's hope that this would induce Japan to surrender and make Stalin pliable during the negotiations between East and West after the war. Oppenheimer, on the other hand, objected that this would ruin the element of surprise, and if the initiative was unsuccessful, it would only boost Japan's opposition. The American supreme command had already estimated that an invasion of the Japanese islands could cost the lives of approximately half a million American soldiers.[47] Based on this, Oppenheimer and the majority of the Interim Committee believed that once the war was over, the general American population would not forgive the American leaders in charge if they did not use the nuclear bomb against the enemy that attacked the USA on December 7, 1941, causing the US to enter a war that had claimed the lives of more than 100,000 American soldiers.[48]

A suggestion to bomb a Japanese city after warning the Japanese government about the attack, allowing for the citizens to be evacuated, was also turned down. The argument against this was that the Japanese air force would do anything to shoot down the attacking American aircraft, and if they succeeded it would be a terrible blow to the Americans. The majority of the committee ended up voting in favor of the suggestion made by newly appointed Secretary of State Byrne: the president should as soon as possible order an unannounced nuclear attack on a Japanese city of great military importance and with a significant population density in the vicinity of the target area, whether that be an ammunition factory, military barracks or harbor.[49] Only such an attack could be expected to generate sufficient shock in Japan that the proponents for peace could gain support for unconditional surrender.

The recommendation was handed over by Secretary of War Stimson to President Truman on June 6, 1945. However, Karl Compton received the Franck Report shortly after – on June 12 – and it is believed that Compton immediately passed it on to the other members of the Interim Committee. Consequently, another Interim Committee meeting was held on June 21 with the Franck Report on the agenda, but the outcome was that the committee stuck to its previous recommendation – an unannounced bombing of a Japanese city.

After the release of almost all relevant documents, it is now clear that in addition to the previously mentioned arguments for unannounced attacks on Japan, there was yet another argument, which might have been central:

keeping the Soviet Union from gaining influence in the Far East. Stalin had previously promised the American president that the Soviet Union would enter the war against Japan no more than three months after the German capitulation. However, if the Soviet Union managed to occupy parts of Japan, they could be expected to want the same agreement in Japan as in Europe, where the defeated Germany was divided into four occupation zones.

This was the last thing the USA wanted. Instead, Truman and Byrnes were eager to show Stalin that the USA possessed a formidable new weapon and that they could therefore be expected to play the key role in deciding the geopolitical development after the war. In July 1945, when waiting for news from General Groves about the Trinity Test, Truman let the remark drop that "if it [the Trinity bomb] explodes, I'll certainly have a hammer on those boys [i.e. Soviet leaders]".[50]

The Trinity Test

As mentioned in the introduction, the test of the plutonium bomb took place in the early morning of July 16, 1945 in the New Mexico desert. In the preceding weeks, a 30-meter steel tower had been built on the site. At distances of 5–30 kilometers from here, different posts had been built from which technicians and selected military staff could witness the detonation of the world's first nuclear bomb. Despite thunder and strong wind above the test area shortly before the planned time, Groves and Oppenheimer gave the green light for the test, which took place at 05:29:21 a.m. local time.

A key reason why Groves and Oppenheimer were hell-bent on performing the nuclear test on July 16 was that the newly appointed President Truman that day and the following was having meetings with Churchill and Stalin in occupied Germany at the Potsdam Conference for the victors in Europe. Truman was eagerly awaiting news of a successful test, hoping to seize the opportunity to impress Stalin and let him know that the USA had managed to develop a bomb of unprecedented power. A few days later, Truman brought up the topic of the successful test, but apparently to no effect. Stalin seemed rather uninterested; he did not ask any questions but merely made a remark along the lines of that being all well and good and hoping that the Americans "would make good use of it against the Japanese".[51]

The Trinity bomb being prepared at the top of the 100-foot steel tower at the testing ground in the New Mexico desert.

© U.S. Department of Energy / Wikimedia Commons

This made Truman and Churchill, who was standing a few meters from where Truman and Stalin were having their conversation, conclude that Stalin had probably not understood the issue at hand. However, they were woefully mistaken. Through his network of spies in the USA, Stalin already knew a lot about the Manhattan Project, and possibly even about the Trinity Test, when Truman told him the big news.

On July 5, President Truman wrote in his diary: "I have told the Sec. of War, Mr. Stimson, to use it so that military objectives and soldiers and sailors are the target and not women and children… He and I are in accord. The target will be a purely military one."[52] However, the official order to General Spaatz, issued two weeks' time later, mentions nothing of sparing women and children – merely that the selected Japanese cities are the targets.[53]

Kyoto – the first city on the Target Committee's list – did not become a target of the attacks because Secretary of War Stimson single-handedly decided to remove it on the grounds that he would not contribute to destroying the cultural capital of Japan.[54] Further investigations into the other targets on the initial list also led to Yokohama being deleted, replaced by two new cities. At the end of July 1945, the updated, prioritized list read: Hiroshima, Kokura, Niigata, Nagasaki.

Hiroshima and Nagasaki

At 2:45 a.m. on August 6, 1945, the B-29 bomber *Enola Gay* took off from the American military base on the island of Tinian, approximately 2,000 kilometers south-east of Japan. Aboard the aircraft was a crew of 11 and a uranium bomb called *Little Boy*. The course was set for the Japanese main island of Honshu. At 8 a.m. Japanese time, the aircraft approached the Japanese coast. In the meantime, it had been joined by two other planes; one was to photograph the event while the other was equipped with an array of measuring instruments. A few minutes later, at a height of approximately ten kilometers, the planes entered the airspace above Hiroshima – a city with a population of around 350,000. There was no panic among the citizens because the city had until then been spared of bombings. People were preparing breakfast, on their way to work, or already working at schools, factories, hospitals etc. There were hardly any air raid shelters. The weather was pleasant, the sky an almost perfect blue.

At 8:10 a.m., the aircrafts closed in on the site where the bomb was to be dropped. The bomb bay doors of *Enola Gay* were opened, *Little Boy* was released at 8:15 a.m., and the aircrafts made a sharp turn to get as far away from the explosion as possible. 45 seconds later, *Little Boy* exploded at a height of approximately 600 meters above ground. A sharp flash of light accompanied the explosion and a quickly expanding ball of fire with a core temperature of many thousands of degrees Celsius instantly killed tens of thousands of

OVERLEAF: Hiroshima a few days after the first nuclear attack in history. The city is almost demolished. A single concrete building remains standing although heavily damaged. This building later became a central part of the memorial park where thousands gather every year on August 6 to commemorate the attack in 1945.

© Handout/AFP/Ritzau Scanpix

people. This was followed by a shock wave that knocked down most buildings in a one- to two-kilometer radius and started fires everywhere.

From the aircraft, the crew witnessed how the city was demolished in an instant, followed by an enormous mass of smoke and dust that rose more than 10 kilometers into the atmosphere, spreading in a giant mushroom cloud. Based on the measurements made in the technical equipment aircraft, experts estimated the explosive force of the bomb to be equivalent to 12,000 tons of TNT. This is now believed to be conservative: the real power was probably as much as 16,000 tons.[55] Subsequent assessments have concluded that the Hiroshima bomb instantly killed 70–80,000 people and injured a similar number. Many of these died in the following days from radioactivity exposure or injuries caused by the collapsed buildings. By the end of 1945 the number of deaths had reached almost 140,000, and after five years, the total casualties were estimated at approximately 200,000.[56] Clearly, these numbers cannot be precise, and nobody would claim them to be so. In a recent article, historian Alex Wellerstein discusses why it is so difficult to "count the number of deaths in Hiroshima", but it is outside the scope of this book to go into further details here.[57]

President Truman received the news that *Little Boy* had been dropped over Hiroshima and worked according to plan while he was eating lunch aboard the American warship *Augusta*, which was transporting him and a large group of his entourage back to the USA after the Potsdam Conference. He was very pleased with the news: "This is the greatest thing in history. It's time for us to get home," he exclaimed spontaneously to his fellow diners.[58]

The next nuclear bomb, a plutonium bomb nicknamed *Fat Man*, was scheduled to be dropped on August 11, five days after *Little Boy*. The five-day interval was to ensure that the technicians had time to check all technical details of the much more complex plutonium bomb, which was being prepared at the Tinian Base. Also, the Japanese government was given time to surrender unconditionally before another bomb was dropped. But according to the commander-in-chief, American General George Marshall, the Americans had underestimated how long it would take for the government in Tokyo to gain a comprehensive overview of the destruction in Hiroshima because all the telegraph and phone lines between Hiroshima and Tokyo were down. Furthermore, the weather forecast for the southern part of the Japanese islands predicted poor weather for several days beginning from

August 10, which made General Spaatz advance the date of the second bombing from August 11 to August 9. The technicians protested but had to follow orders and check only the most vital parts of *Fat Man.*

In short, on August 9, 1945, the city of Nagasaki turned into a scene of chaos and suffering similar to Hiroshima three days earlier. Originally, it had been Kokura – which housed a large weapons factory – that had been the target of the second bomb, but as the clouds drew in above the city and the American supreme command had demanded clear photos from the explosion, the bomber *Bock's Car* continued on to the next target – Nagasaki. It was overcast here too, but just before the mission had to be cancelled, the pilot found a hole in the clouds and the plutonium bomb *Fat Man* was released at 11:01 a.m. 45 seconds later, the bomb exploded at a height of 500 meters above the city, approximately 3 kilometers from the preselected target. This significantly reduced the number of casualties compared to the original target, and similarly a smaller part of the city was destroyed. Nevertheless, because the explosive force was equivalent to approximately 21,000 tons of TNT, i.e., much stronger than the Hiroshima bomb, 40–70,000 people were killed instantly and another 30–40,000 were injured.[59] Five years later, the total fatalities in Nagasaki were estimated at around 140,000.[60]

On August 10, 1945, President Truman, who was back in the USA, addressed the American people in a radio speech:

> The world will note that the first atomic bomb was dropped on Hiroshima, a military base. That was because we wished in this first attack to avoid, insofar as possible, the killing of civilians. But that attack was only a warning of things to come. If Japan does not surrender, bombs will have to be dropped on her war industries and, unfortunately, thousands of civilian lives will be lost. I urge Japanese civilians to leave industrial cities immediately, and save themselves from destruction.[61]

It is striking – and uncanny – that Truman the day after the Nagasaki bombing still referred to Hiroshima as a "military base", having had the opportunity to look at the photos showing the enormous devastation caused by the bomb, and Hiroshima being a city with many different kinds of trade and a large civilian population. A majority of historians interpret the quote as proof that Truman knew better, while a few believe that he had never been properly informed about the composition of the population at the potential targets.[62]

Six days after the Nagasaki bomb, on August 15, 1945, Japan surrendered unconditionally, bringing the Second World War to an end. The same happened to the Manhattan Project, which had involved more than 200,000 people and cost the American taxpayers 2.2 billion dollars.[63] The American president had made these funds available to the project and now needed Congress to pass the expense as a supplementary grant. This proved unproblematic.

There is hardly any other decision made by an American president over the course of the last hundred years that has caused so much controversy among historians as President Truman's decision to authorize the bombings of Hiroshima and Nagasaki. The decision has divided historians into two camps – traditionalists and revisionists. A third group lies somewhere in between on this spectrum. Because Truman did not make it explicit in the instruction when Secretary of War, Henry Stimson on July 25, 1945 communicated it to General Spaatz, traditionalists as well as revisionists have made ardent efforts to discover documents and develop arguments to most convincingly explain what brought Truman to make the decision.

The traditionalists, who seem to make up the majority, emphasize that no American president would be able to justify to the American people the loss of possibly several hundred thousand American soldiers' lives to conquer the Japanese archipelago, which at least some of his generals believed would be required to make Japan surrender unconditionally. Experience from spring 1945 had shown that the Japanese almost always defended themselves to the last man standing when attacked. This had cost the lives of almost 20,000 American soldiers and navy personnel during the occupation of the remote, 1,200 km^2 Japanese island of Okinawa. The total number of American casualties, dead and wounded, was about 40,000, approximately 35 percent of the attacking forces. Based on this experience, the Americans potentially faced immense bloodshed when trying to take possession of the Japanese mainland, where they could expect every Japanese man and woman, young and old, to defend their country to the death. Using the figure of 35 percent to estimate the number of American casualties to be expected in the planned American invasion of the Japanese island of Kyushu with 750,000 soldiers in November 1945, a loss of more than a quarter of a million men could be expected.[64] In Herbert Hoover's "Memorandum on Ending the Japanese War", read by Truman on June 9, 1945, Hoover estimated that defeating Japan completely might cost between 500,000 and 1,000,000 American lives.[65]

In light of this, it is hardly surprising that Truman, who was heavily influenced by his Secretary of State, James Byrnes, seized the chance to – possibly – shorten the war by several months by using the new, revolutionary nuclear weapon as soon as it was ready. Not only would it probably save many American lives, it was also likely to make Japan surrender before the Soviet Union had a chance to occupy part of Japan – something that was also high on Truman and Byrnes' list of priorities.

While the traditionalists thus claim that Truman's decision to use nuclear weapons against Japan was mainly based on the wish to save the lives of hundreds of thousands of American soldiers, shorten the war and keep the Soviets out of Japan, the revisionists are trying to convince skeptics that Truman's paramount interest was to checkmate Stalin. The USA wanted to let the Soviet dictator know that they alone would occupy Japan and had a weapon at their disposal that far surpassed anything previously known. The main figure behind this interpretation is the historian Gar Alperovitz,[66] who builds his hypothesis on the view that Japan was close to surrender when the first nuclear bomb was dropped over Hiroshima on August 6, 1945. He and other revisionists find support for this claim in the fact that some of the members of the Japanese Supreme Council for the Directive of War ("the Big Six") had already put out feelers regarding peace to the Soviet Union, and that the USA could thus have ensured Japanese surrender without resorting to nuclear weapons or the full-scale invasion of Japanese coastal zones in November 1945 that had been planned by the American supreme command. The traditionalists blankly refuse this possibility, maintaining that only the shock caused by the two nuclear bombs could make the Japanese Supreme Council, which was dominated by high-ranking military personnel, capitulate.

The discussion between traditionalists and revisionists will probably never cease, considering that all relevant documents in the case have been thoroughly scrutinized; the discussion revolves more around convictions than cold facts.[67]

A few of the American soldiers who took part in the horrifying Pacific battles have made their contributions to the debate. One of them, Paul Fussell, who later became an author and debater, writes in the book *Thank God for the Atom Bomb* about the relief that he and his fellow soldiers in August 1945 felt when they received the news about the two bombs over Japan. The bombs put an end to the war they had not dared hope they would survive, having realized that they would most probably find themselves in the front line when the signal to invade the Japanese mainland came.[68]

The book prompted vehement protest from another author, Michael Walzer: "Paul Fussell's defense of the bombing of Hiroshima is written, as he tells repeatedly, from the standpoint of the ordinary GI. And that standpoint is human, all too human: let anybody die but me!" But it is easy for Walzer to write such a thing, counters Fussell, given that Walzer was only ten years old when the war ended and he was never at risk of dying on one of the beaches of Japan, even if the nuclear bombs had not been dropped. "My object was to offer a soldier's view, to indicate the complex moral situation of knowing that one's life has been saved because others' have been most cruelly snuffed out," Fussell concludes his piece.[69]

"I Feel I Have Blood on My Hands"

Obviously, Oppenheimer could not know exactly what was going on in the Soviet Union in the fall of 1945, but he was convinced that the American monopoly on nuclear weapons would be brief. This would present a major problem long-term, but even now, immediately after the end of the war, he was unable to savor the praise he received from all corners of American society as scientific manager of the Manhattan Project. As a scientific expert, he had at no point wavered in his recommendation to the Interim Committee that the USA should drop bombs without warning over two Japanese cities. As late as July 23, 1945, he had even, in a conversation with two high-ranking American military people who were involved in planning the bombing of Hiroshima, provided detailed instructions for the crew on the bomber:

> Got to see the target. No radar bombing; it must be dropped visually. [...] If they drop it at night there should be a moon; that would be the best. Of course, they must not drop it in rain or fog. [...] Don't let them detonate it too high. The figure fixed on is just right. Don't let it go up [higher] or the target won't get as much damage.[70]

But now, a few weeks later, Oppenheimer had become familiar with many details regarding the horrible consequences for the city's inhabitants, and he felt guilty. He was the one who had managed the development of the nuclear bombs, and perhaps his say had been instrumental when President Truman decided to follow the recommendations of the Interim Committee.

Therefore, Oppenheimer requested a meeting with Truman. The two met on October 25, 1945.

Truman had looked forward to meeting the man who had played such a decisive role in the development of the USA's new superweapon, but his enthusiasm soon dampened. During the entire visit, Oppenheimer kept wringing his hands, talking about his moral concerns, finally declaring: "Mr. President. I feel I have blood on my hands." Truman had no time for this. He replied coldly that the blood was on the president's hands, and that he slept soundly at night all the same. There was no reason for Oppenheimer to worry. Immediately after, Truman indicated that the meeting was over. According to Under Secretary of State, Dean Acheson, Truman later told him that he did not want to see that "son-of-a-bitch" in his office again.[71]

Evidently, Truman acted cool and determined when he defended his instruction to use nuclear weapons in the last phase of the war against Japan. However, in his diary he reveals a softer side than the persona he projected in his public speeches and memoirs after the war. On August 7 and 8, when he was aboard the warship *Augusta* on his way back from the Potsdam Conference, he thus expressed his regret to some of his trusted employees that "innocent women and children" had become victims of the Hiroshima bomb, and lamented the "terrible responsibility that such destruction" placed on the United States and upon himself.[72] And when the Nagasaki bomb had been dropped on August 9, he spoke with former Vice President, now Secretary of Commerce, Henry Wallace, who wrote down in his diary what Truman had told him: "Truman said he had given orders to stop atomic bombing. He said the thought of wiping out another 100,000 people was too horrible. He didn't like the idea of killing, as he said, 'all those kids'."[73]

It is relevant to dwell a bit longer on the exchange of words in October 1945 between the scientist Oppenheimer and President Truman. Truman's statement about blood being on his hands was his way of saying that the ultimate responsibility for the use of the nuclear bomb lay with him, not with the scientists – including Oppenheimer. This statement by Truman implied a specific understanding of the distribution of responsibility between science and politics, where it was the task of science to find out how nature *is* and make this knowledge available to the political decision-makers, who for their part were responsible for how to *use* this knowledge. There were scientists on the Manhattan Project who shared the president's view on the matter. For instance, Edward Teller, the Hungarian physicist who would later become known as the father of the hydrogen bomb and an uncompromising advocate for American nuclear armament, argued in 1950 for this distinction in respective responsibilities:

> The scientist is not responsible for the laws of nature. It is his job to find out how these laws operate. It is the scientist's job to find the ways these laws can serve the human will. However, it is not the scientist's job to determine whether a hydrogen bomb should be constructed, whether it should be used, or how it should be used. This responsibility rests with the American people and with their chosen representatives.[74]

For other participants in the Manhattan Project, this distinction was difficult – if not impossible – to maintain. Oppenheimer was one of them. As the scientific manager of the project, he was very much part of the political and military decisions, and the Interim Committee's recommendations had been instrumental in the decision to carry out unannounced nuclear attacks on Japanese cities – a decision Oppenheimer had backed. Truman's cool conviction that the responsibility lay with the president was to Oppenheimer insufficient balm to his sense of having blood on his hands. Like many other physicists, Oppenheimer's life and identity as a scientist were now linked to the nuclear bomb and the new world it had contributed to creating. It is sometimes said that Oppenheimer fathered the bomb, but equally the bomb created the persona of Oppenheimer and the Manhattan physicists. As early as August 17, 1945 – a week after the bombing of Nagasaki – Oppenheimer wrote to Secretary of War Stimson:

> The safety of this nation, as opposed to its ability to inflict damage on an enemy power – cannot lie wholly or entirely in its scientific and technical prowess. It can only be based on making future wars impossible.[75]

Oppenheimer was far from alone in pondering the role and responsibility of science in the new political and military situation to which science itself had contributed. Many scientists, within a range of disciplines and with varying motives, got involved in international politics as they came to realize the military potential of nuclear physics. This involvement continued after the end of the war and prompted the founding of the *Bulletin of the Atomic Scientists* and – consequently – the Doomsday Clock.

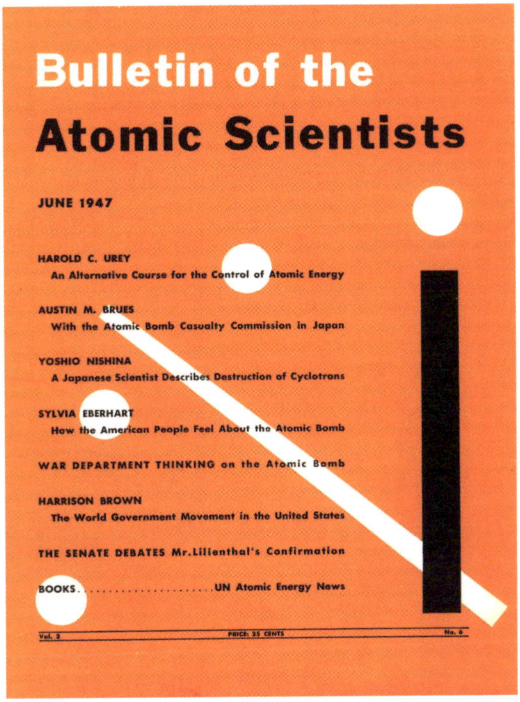

The cover of the *Bulletin of the Atomic Scientists'* June edition in 1947, when the Doomsday Clock was displayed for the first time.

Seven Minutes to Midnight (1947)

Shortly after Oppenheimer's disheartening meeting with President Truman, some of his and his scientific staff's qualms of conscience and worries for the future became publicly known. However, it was not Oppenheimer who initiated this but some of the scientists behind the Franck Report. Even though they had not succeeded in preventing the use of the nuclear bomb in the Second World War, their hard work during May and June 1945 still had an impact, in that the report became the primary inspiration for the newly founded Federation of Atomic Scientists. In 1946 the Federation published the famous book *One World or None*, following the launch of the newsletter the *Bulletin of the Atomic Scientists*.

From the first issue of the newsletter, which was published on December 10, 1945, edited by nuclear physicist Hyman H. Goldsmith and biophysicist Eugene Rabinowitch – the latter being one of the signatories of the Franck Report – the editors viewed it as their primary task to keep their colleagues and the American public informed about the scientific, technological and social problems associated with the use of atomic energy. The first three

© Used with permission of the Bulletin of the Atomic Scientists

Martyl Langsdorf, the artist who created the Doomsday Clock, soon to become an iconic image in the *Bulletin of the Atomic Scientists*.

issues were only six pages, but since the newsletter turned out to garner surprisingly wide interest, the issues gradually expanded until, beginning from June 1947, the format changed into a 32-page professionally designed color journal. As time went by, the extent and circulation of the journal increased even further. The cover of the June 1947 edition showed a list of contents, but apart from that, it featured a stylized clock that showed seven minutes to midnight.

The story behind the cover was that Hyman Goldsmith had asked the well-known artist Martyl Langsdorf, whose husband was a physicist and a participant on the Manhattan Project, to design a fitting cover for the new journal. At first, Langsdorf had planned to design the cover around a symbol for the element uranium, but the more she became familiar with the birth of the *Bulletin*, the more convinced she was that the cover needed to convey to the reader that this was an urgent matter – that humanity did not have much time to get the nuclear weapons under control. The end-product of her deliberations was the famous clock whose hands showed that the midnight hour – a well-known symbol for the apocalypse – was near.

This left the readers in no doubt that the editors were trying to illustrate how close in their view the world was to the ultimate disaster. The clock was soon named the Doomsday Clock and has been depicted in every issue since. However, the hands have not remained still over the decades. The minute hand has moved in response to significant changes in the technological and global nuclear situation which the editors-in-chief have found positive or negative in terms of world peace. The clock quickly achieved the iconic status it has had ever since. Only the mushroom cloud can compete with the Doomsday Clock in cultural distribution and impact as a symbol of the nuclear threat and nuclear arms race. Naturally, the clock became still more known as the *Bulletin* went from newsletter to journal with an increasing national and international readership. And even more importantly, newspapers, other journals, TV channels, various internet platforms and other mass media have used the Doomsday Clock throughout the years, contributing further to popular knowledge of its background and portrayal of time.

The minute hand on the Doomsday Clock has moved 25 times in the period 1947–2023, every time based on careful consideration. The only exception was June 1947, when the editors did not argue why they chose to have the first Doomsday Clock show precisely seven minutes to midnight. However, the clock being so close to striking midnight was a clear signal to readers that getting the nuclear bomb under control was an urgent matter. This impression was forcefully underlined on the cover's page two, where a group of the USA's most eminent scientists, spearheaded by Albert Einstein, in effective bullet points summarized the precarious situation in which the world found itself:

1. Atomic bombs can now be made cheaply and in large number. They will become more destructive.
2. There is no military defense against atomic bombs and none is to be expected.
3. Other nations can rediscover our secret processes by themselves.
4. Preparedness against atomic war is futile, and if attempted, will ruin the structure of our social order.
5. If war breaks out, atomic bombs will be used and they will surely destroy our civilization.
6. There is no solution to this problem except international control of atomic energy, and ultimately, the elimination of war.[76]

High-ranking politicians and military personnel challenged the concerned scientists' view of the nuclear bomb as a decisive gamechanger in international politics after the Second World War. This was probably to be expected, whereas it may have caused consternation that several other brilliant scientists considered even more powerful nuclear weapons as a viable guarantee for peace rather than attempting to exercise international control of the ones that already existed. We will return to this in the following chapters.

CHAPTER 3

All the Great Powers Become Nuclear Weapon States

Wasted Opportunities

It was not only those responsible for the Manhattan Project, but also – and in particular – politicians around the world who were facing a daunting challenge after the dramatic end of the Second World War: How could they prevent the new, terrifying weapon being used again in attempts to solve conflicts in the new world, divided East from West, that was becoming a reality?

During the Second World War, politicians from the allied nations had agreed to establish a new world organization, the United Nations, as a replacement for the League of Nations that had proven a failure in 1930s Europe. One of the first pressing issues for the organization was the nuclear situation. However, the UN never succeeded in finding a satisfactory solution as it soon turned out that the American and Soviet approaches to handling nuclear bombs were irreconcilable.

In December 1945, US Assistant Secretary of State Dean Acheson set up a committee chaired by himself and David Lilienthal, former director of the giant state-owned energy company, the Tennessee Valley Authority. Robert Oppenheimer was also a member of the committee, tasked with providing recommendations regarding American nuclear policy in the UN. The committee worked intensively during the first months of 1946 and in mid-March presented its report, which became known as the Acheson-Lilienthal Report. The most notable recommendation in the report was the foundation of an international organ with a monopoly on the production of raw materials for nuclear energy – i.e., enriched uranium and plutonium. According to the authors of the report, this was necessary because "A system of inspection superimposed on an otherwise uncontrolled exploitation of atomic energy by national governments will not be an adequate safeguard."[77] All less dangerous activities could be left to the participating countries, who at any given time could seek advice from the international organ. Further, the Acheson-Lilienthal Report suggested that the USA and the UN should encourage all member countries to come up with constructive contributions to the development of nuclear energy for peaceful purposes, rather than threatening dire consequences if a country were to misstep.[78]

However, the lenient attitude soon changed. Almost simultaneously with the publication of the Acheson-Lilienthal Report, President Truman, who in the meantime had been warned that there were hordes of Soviet nuclear spies and communist sympathizers ('fellow travelers') in the USA and Canada, appointed the man who in June 1946 would present the American suggestion to the UN. This was the 76-year-old financier and speculator Bernard Baruch, who was not willing to just follow the Acheson-Lilienthal proposal in every detail. At a meeting in Washington in the middle of May, probably in agreement with President Truman and Secretary of State Byrnes, Baruch added two notable conditions to the report: (1) that all nations must be ready to allow full territorial inspection before the USA would surrender sensitive nuclear technology to the UN's nuclear organ; and (2) that any nation breaching the nuclear agreements would immediately be subject to punitive measures from the UN. To avoid any misunderstandings, Baruch stressed that if the lawbreaker was a superpower (i.e., the Soviet Union), this nation's right to veto in the UN Security Council would be void.[79]

Now, it was clear to Acheson, Lilienthal and Oppenheimer that their carefully conceived suggestions, intended as the first proper American proposal for a round of negotiations in the newly founded United Nations Atomic Energy Commission (UNAEC) had been sabotaged by Baruch's additions. The reworked suggestion that was presented in the UN in 1946 was thus referred to as the Baruch Plan rather than the Acheson-Lilienthal Plan.

As could be expected – and probably as Baruch had wanted – the Soviet negotiators turned down the Baruch Plan because it would in their opinion put them in a position that benefitted the USA. In the summer of 1945, Stalin had already launched a large-scale secret project intended to ensure that the Soviet Union would become the world's second nuclear weapon state within a few years. Therefore, as we will see shortly, it did not want any restrictions on its nuclear activities. Rather than agree to the Baruch Plan, the Soviet delegate to the UN, Andrei Gromyko, suggested that all existing nuclear arsenals should be destroyed before the UN atomic commission was established. This suggestion was likewise completely unacceptable to the USA, which Gromyko (and Stalin) had obviously expected. No one took the suggestion seriously – not even the Russians themselves.[80] The widespread hope that there could be some form of international control of the development of nuclear energy for military as well as civilian purposes was thus dashed in 1946.[81] In December 1946, Baruch won a ballot on the Baruch Plan in the UNAEC, where only the Soviet Union and Poland refrained from voting, but this was inconsequential as the Soviet Union, on the last day of the year, vetoed the Security Council's implementation of the plan.

The opportunity of ongoing, high-profile negotiations in the UN regarding the future of nuclear energy had come and gone. Instead, the vast majority of nuclear energy efforts in the following years took place at a national rather than an international level. This suited Baruch and many large American corporations brilliantly, given that the USA – with its head start in military nuclear technology – had a realistic hope of dominating the anticipated large market for civilian nuclear technology within the foreseeable future. Truman, on the other hand, was not pleased. He later confided to Acheson that choosing Baruch for the UN job "was the worst mistake I ever made".[82]

General Leslie Groves, who had been the military manager of the Manhattan Project, assessed in 1945 that it would be at least 15–20 years before the Soviets would be able to produce a nuclear bomb. Even though leading nuclear physicists objected that this was wishful thinking, American nuclear policy focused for many years on keeping the 'nuclear secret' as long as possible. In practice, this meant that a newly established American Atomic Energy Commission (AEC), established by Congress in 1946 through the so-called MacMahon Act, assumed control of all nuclear research and development in the USA. The commission was extremely restrictive in terms of providing nuclear information to interested corporations or persons. According to the act, "It shall be unlawful for any person to operate any equipment or device utilizing fissionable materials without a license issued by the Commission authorizing such operation." A few lines below, the act establishes that no license could be issued to any foreign government or person that was not under American jurisdiction.[83] Even the USA's closest ally, the United Kingdom, was thereby cut off from utilizing the advances of nuclear technology that British scientists had contributed in connection with the Manhattan Project.

This restrictive policy meant that a number of other countries including the United Kingdom, Canada, France, the Netherlands, Norway and Sweden shortly after the Second World War started their own nuclear projects without direct use of American nuclear technology, resulting in several national nuclear reactors being constructed between 1947 and 1954. Even though most of these were small compared to the large American Hanford reactors, each one represented a vital step toward larger reactors designed to produce electricity and/or plutonium for nuclear weapons. The future looked anything but bright, anticipating a chaotic world in which many countries would desperately attempt to acquire nuclear weapons to keep hostile countries from attacking out of fear they might become victims of devastating nuclear retaliation.

In the short term, it was almost inevitable that at least the four countries (apart from the USA) that were referred to as great powers, and which had the right of veto in the UN Security Council, would do their utmost to develop nuclear weapons: initially nuclear bombs, and subsequently the much more powerful hydrogen bombs that had already been on the drawing board in Los Alamos, and which will be described further in chapter four. The four great powers were the Soviet Union, the United Kingdom, France and China – assuming that the Chinese seat in the Security Council, which was currently occupied by the nationalist government of Formosa (Taiwan), was to be replaced by China. Everyone expected that the Chinese People's Republic, with its almost one billion citizens, could and would take that seat. However, it did not happen until 1971 – the year that US President Richard Nixon and communist China's Chairman Mao initiated serious détente efforts between the two countries.

The Soviet Union: "Powerful things"

The nuclear bombs over Hiroshima and Nagasaki in August 1945 put a dramatic full stop to the Second World War. When the news of the sweeping and terrifying effect of the bombs reached the Kremlin, Stalin had an overwhelming fit of rage. Not even when Hitler's armies threatened to overpower Soviet defenses in 1941–42 had his staff seen him out of his wits like this. Stalin's efficient intelligence agency, by way of spies planted in Los Alamos, had long been reporting that the USA was producing a nuclear bomb, and during the Potsdam Conference in July 1945, President Truman had tried to tell Stalin that the Americans had successfully tested a very powerful new bomb a few days before. Nevertheless, Stalin now had to face the fact that despite the Soviet Union's enormous sacrifices during the war, and the superior conventional strength of the Red Army, these new "powerful things" prevented him from reaping the benefits of his endeavor: becoming a superpower on a par with the USA – a superpower with Europe as its sphere of influence.[84]

When Stalin had regained his composure, he ordered that the development of a nuclear bomb was to be the country's top priority. He immediately contacted the leader of the Soviet nuclear program, physicist Igor Kurchatov, reproaching him for not requesting sufficient resources to do the same as the Americans had apparently achieved. Kurchatov objected that his country had been destroyed and people were starving. The story goes that Stalin replied with the notoriously famous sentence: "If the baby doesn't cry, the mother doesn't know what he needs. Ask for anything you need. There will be no refusals."[85]

From this point on, the Soviet nuclear program was restructured and granted all the necessary resources. To manage the top-secret project, Stalin appointed the effective Lavrentij Beria – head of the secret intelligence service NKVD responsible for the death of millions of Soviet citizens. Beria made sure that the most indispensable scientists and technicians enjoyed extensive privileges, including the best imaginable work environments, but at the same time they were probably well aware that they could not expect to live unless their efforts were crowned with success within a few years.[86]

As mentioned, the Soviet nuclear program did not have to start from scratch after the war, given that Soviet spies who had contributed to designing *Fat Man* in Los Alamos had gathered reliable information. Two of the specialists, Klaus Fuchs and David Greenglass, were working on making the vital implosion mechanism function perfectly under the supervision of explosives expert George Kistiakowsky. They were both ardent communists and eager to help the Soviet Union in its desperate struggle against the Nazis. They were dismayed that the USA refused to share its nuclear knowledge with their ally in the east who had carried a disproportionate amount of the burden of the war. Even though most of the staff that worked at Los Alamos were cut off from the world and surveilled by a large security police force, Fuchs, Greenglass and several others still managed to smuggle out thousands of confidential documents, which were sent to Moscow. Here, the new information on nuclear research was immediately passed on to the lab that was set up in the fall of 1942 to investigate the possibility of constructing a nuclear bomb. The leader of this lab was the above-mentioned Igor Kurchatov. At that time, he had only limited financial and technical means at his disposal, but he did manage a small staff of highly skilled scientists and technicians, who were able to quickly separate the wheat from the chaff in the documents and develop plans for the future.

There was no shortage of ingenious Russian scientists. Apart from Kurchatov himself, his core team at the so-called Laboratory No. 2 in Moscow included famous people like Peter Kapitza, Yulii Khariton, Igor Panasyuk, Georgij Fljorov, Jakov Zeldovitj, Isaak Kikoin and Abram Alikhanov, several of whom came to manage important subprojects in the giant project that was to develop the Soviet Union's first nuclear bomb. However, the staff at Laboratory No. 2 were challenged by a lack of many things – most importantly, uranium.

The Soviet experts could provide an educated guess as to how much uranium was needed based on the official American report on the Manhattan Project, the Smyth Report, which at the request of General Groves had been published in the USA on August 12, 1945 – only three days after the second nuclear bomb was dropped over Nagasaki.[87] The Smyth Report was immediately translated into Russian and scrutinized by Kurchatov's team. What they learned was that approximately six tons of uranium metal had been used, in addition to a larger but unspecified amount of uranium oxide to build the test reactor that Fermi's team had made critical in Chicago on December 2, 1942. Obviously, much larger amounts were needed for reactors built to produce considerable amounts of plutonium. This meant that Soviet geologists would have to begin searching for uranium across the entire Soviet Union and Eastern Europe, which was under Soviet control by the end of the war.

The lack of infrastructure made it very difficult to find and extract uranium occurrences in the Asian part of the Soviet Union. These relatively inaccessible occurrences only became important later on; for the time being, some previously known and some recently discovered resources of uranium in Czechoslovakia, Poland and Eastern Germany were utilized. Tens of thousands of prisoners from the many prisoner camps known collectively as the Gulag Archipelago did most of the hard work in the mines.[88] As far as we know, there are no official Soviet numbers, but the CIA – who obviously might be biased – estimated at the beginning of the 1950s that somewhere between 175,000 and 240,000 people were working in the Eastern European mines. Human lives counted for nothing. The project – ensuring that the Soviet Union could have nuclear weapons as soon as possible – meant everything.[89]

The leading Soviet nuclear physicists Andrei Sakharov (left) and Igor Kurchatov in deep conversation, 1959.
Unknown photographer

Uranium mines were – and to some extent still are – dangerous working environments, regardless of which part of the world they are situated in and which country's military or civilian nuclear programs they provide with uranium. It is thus amply documented that uranium mining in the USA, Canada and France, and not least in the former African colonies of Congo, Madagascar, Niger, Namibia and Gabon, which for many decades have delivered large quantities of uranium to American and French nuclear weapons and nuclear plants, has had terrible human and environmental consequences.[90] That said, there is no doubt that the conditions in the Soviet-controlled mines that provided uranium for the first Soviet nuclear weapons were beyond comparison in terms of deaths and accidents. After the collapse of the Soviet Union in 1991, documents from the Soviet archives, which had until then been kept secret, told the story of the miserable security culture and non-existent environmental considerations in the Soviet nuclear industry.[91] For instance, we know today that the Soviet Union dumped large amounts of radioactive waste in shallow water in the Arctic Sea. We also know that the area that housed the plutonium production plants north of the city of Chelyabinsk in western

Siberia is today probably the most radioactively polluted place on Earth. Here, the Soviet nuclear industry during the Cold War deposited more than 26 tons of plutonium nitrate – 50 times as much as at the (also heavily polluted) American Hanford plutonium facility.[92]

As the uranium ore was unearthed, the uranium was extracted and transported to the almost abandoned industrial city of Elektrostal, approximately 70 kilometers east of Moscow. A former steel works and an ammunition factory existed in the area, and they were now turned into a uranium factory under the management of the German technician Nikolaus Riehl. During the war, he had worked on purifying uranium and manufacturing metallic uranium under the unsuccessful German uranium project. It took time to get the process up and running, but in September/October 1946, Elektrostal delivered approximately 3 tons of uranium metal a week to Kurchatov's Laboratory No. 2 in Moscow.[93]

In the meantime at the lab, efforts focused on the preparations for a nuclear reactor that was to become a landmark achievement in the Soviet nuclear bomb project. In the months leading up to June 1946, Kurchatov's team constructed a building specially designed to house the reactor. Furthermore, some of the team's experts had performed experiments with small amounts of uranium, which allowed them to calculate how large the reactor needed to be in order to become critical. They found that a reactor with a radius of 3 meters would be optimal, and that they would need 50 tons of pure uranium and 500 tons of pure graphite. The reactor with the code name F-1 came into being in Elektrostal in December 1946. Blocks of pure graphite mixed with graphite blocks with holes for uranium rods were built up layer by layer in a roughly spherical geometry until instruments measuring the neutron intensity at the core showed that layer number 62 would cause the reactor to cross the all-important limit of criticality.[94]

At 6 p.m. on December 25, 1945, the reactor was made critical for the first time. It was Kurchatov himself who was able to move the reactor control rods from a subterranean control room. He pulled out the final, decisive cadmium rod bit by bit until the increasingly frequent clicks from the measuring instruments turned into a constant noise. He even risked pulling out the rod a bit more until the ticking of the instruments in the control room itself became a constant buzz, meaning that the level of radioactivity in the reactor surpassed the natural background radiation by a significant factor. Then he let the vertical control rods drop down into the reactor, causing it to stop. Everything worked according to plan, which reportedly made him exclaim: "Atomic energy has now been subordinated to the will of Soviet man."[95] The patriotic statement was no doubt aimed at Stalin and Beria. Also, it most likely contributed to securing even more funding for the Soviet nuclear bomb project.

The question of funding was vital because Kurchatov and his team were now getting ready to build much bigger reactors with an eye to producing large quantities of plutonium for the many nuclear weapons that Stalin deemed necessary to keep the USA from attacking at some point. The Russians needed to find a location in the Soviet Union similar to Hanford in Washington State – i.e., a place that was far removed from urban areas, had a good power supply and rivers or large streams whose water could cool the reactors. They chose a location in the Ural Mountains, 80 kilometers north-west of the industrial city of Chelyabinsk. The area was named Chelyabinsk-40, 40 being the postal code for the area. Ordinary Russians – not to mention foreigners – were forbidden access to the area. Chelyabinsk-40 quickly grew. At one point, there were approximately 70,000 people working there – many of them prisoners – building reactors, factories, labs and accommodation in one of the many 'secret' cities in the Soviet Union.[96]

The first production reactor, Installation A, was ready around the end of 1948 and in early spring 1949 the two key figures, physicist Kurchatov and Commissar Vannikov, moved to Chelyabinsk-40 to supervise the inauguration of the reactor. The reactor was first made critical on June 7, and on June 22, it reached its planned maximum power of 100 MW. However, before it could start producing plutonium on a large scale, it was necessary to make some changes as the fuel rods deformed in the powerful neutron flux. The eternal skeptic Beria was convinced that it was due to sabotage, but Kurchatov managed to convince him that it was due to a design fault that could easily be fixed, and that this type of issue was unavoidable once in a while when lab tests were transferred to big industrial facilities.[97]

After the fuel rods had been inside the reactor for a few months, they were removed and transferred to Installation B in Chelyabinsk-40, where a team led by a chemist named Vitaly was tasked with separating the plutonium produced from the rest of the material. The B-facility started supplying plutonium at the beginning of 1949. There are no official records of the level of radiation the chemists and technicians involved were exposed to in those years, but it must have been quite intense considering the circumstances.

The increasing amounts of plutonium nitrate produced by the technicians at Installation B were transported to another facility called Installation V,[98] also in the Chelyabinsk-40 area. Here, the plutonium nitrate was transformed into metallic plutonium, which was the form of plutonium used in American as well as Soviet nuclear bombs. By the beginning of 1949, there was enough metallic plutonium to build the first Soviet nuclear bomb.

The bomb was built in another secret city named Arzamas-16, or sometimes "Los Arzamas" to stress the analogy to Los Alamos in the USA. The city was located at the Volga River, approximately 400 kilometers east of Moscow. Under the management of physicist Yulii Khariton, the team performed numerous explosives tests to squeeze the subcritical plutonium ball, which was the size of a softball, into a supercritical ball much smaller than a tennis ball. The subcritical ball was shaped like two symmetrical hemispheres with a hole in the middle for the detonator, which was to release neutrons and trigger a chain reaction in the imploding plutonium as the surrounding layers of conventional explosive blew up. Everything was designed more or less like the first American nuclear test, given that Stalin's ambition to possess a nuclear bomb as quickly as possible meant that there was no time for needless experiments. If the Soviet experts trusted the Smyth Report and the material that Klaus Fuchs and other Soviet spies had provided, they would simply have to do what the Americans had done.

The first Soviet nuclear test took place on August 29, 1949 in a deserted area northwest of the city of Semipalatinsk in Kazakhstan. At the site, which had been selected a few years before, a 30-meter tower had been built, and close to it a workshop where the bomb was to be assembled before being hoisted up in the tower. Around the tower, at distances up to ten kilometers, were huts, houses and various vehicles – including old tanks – all with the purpose of allowing the Soviet experts to evaluate the effect of the explosion on such objects at different distances. Just as at the Trinity test site four years earlier, there were hundreds of project workers as well as executives (including Beria) in bunkers about 15 kilometers from the explosion site, waiting to witness the great event. Also, a number of tank staff were positioned in tanks approximately 10 kilometers from the tower, ordered to start up the tanks and drive to the place where the tower had stood as soon as the bomb exploded.[99] There are no records regarding the level of radiation they were exposed to. Our indignation at this blatant lack of respect for the staff's health should, however, take into consideration that this was not much different from the experiments the American military conducted in connection with Operation Upshot-Knothole, Teapot and Plumbbob in the 1950s in the Nevada Desert. Here, platoons of soldiers were ordered to witness the nuclear tests from trenches or shelters located only a few kilometers from the explosion site.[100]

At 6 a.m. local time, Kurchatov, who was staying at a special command post 10 kilometers from ground zero with Khariton and Beria, pushed the button that triggered the detonation. A powerful flash lit up the morning sky, and when the blast wave reached the command post 30 seconds later, there was no question that the test was a success. Beria was over the moon, embracing Kurchatov and Khariton, who were no less excited. Khariton later stated that "When we succeeded in solving this problem, we felt relieved, even happiness – for in possessing such a weapon we had removed the possibility of its being used against the USSR with impunity."[101] Notably, all Soviet scientists involved in the development of the Soviet nuclear bomb have expressed similar thoughts – if they have spoken about it at all.

Three Minutes to Midnight (1949)

President Truman announced the first Soviet nuclear test to the world public a month later, on September 23, and shortly afterwards it was confirmed in an official statement from the Kremlin. The news sent shock waves through the Western world and soon generated vast political and military responses. It also caused Eugene Rabinowitch, on the cover of the *Bulletin of the Atomic Scientists'* October 1949 issue, to warn readers about the aggravated state of the world by moving the minute hand on the Doomsday Clock from seven to three minutes to midnight. This was the first time it had changed since the clock had been introduced in 1947, and came with an explanation. From October 1949, Rabinowitch had taken over all editorial responsibility, and he remained in the seat until his death on May 15, 1973. During his long editorship, he decided to change the time on the Doomsday Clock seven times in total. Naturally, he did not do so before discussing the matter with the board and sponsors of the journal, in addition to some of his personal friends. But ultimately, the decision was his.

After the first Soviet nuclear test, the nuclear race between the USA and the Soviet Union was a reality and was only expected to intensify over the following years. The October 1949 issue of the *Bulletin* reported what a number of the scientific participants in the Manhattan Project 1945–46 had said and written about other countries' prospects of developing nuclear weapons. Citations included the Franck Report from June 1945 and a number of individuals such as Leo Szilard, Hans Bethe, Frederick Seitz, Harold Urey, Harrison Brown and Irving Langmuir, who that year warned American politicians and high-ranking military officers that any industrial country willing to pull out all the stops would be able to develop and test a nuclear bomb within 3–4 years. In stark contrast to this, the *Bulletin* also printed citations by Leslie Groves and Vannevar Bush, also from the fall of 1945, suggesting that they operated with a very different timeframe. For instance, Groves was cited from November 29, 1945, when he gave evidence to the Senate Special Committee on Atomic Energy:

> ...one nation could catch up and produce a bomb, if they did it in complete secrecy, probably within from fifteen to twenty years, more likely the latter. If they did it without secrecy and with a great deal of help from the United States and from England and Switzerland – and I say Switzerland because she is a manufacturer of precision machinery – it could be done in five to seven years, probably seven.[102]

Vannevar Bush, who gave evidence to the same committee a few days later, was in agreement with Groves:

> I think if she [the Soviet Union] threw her full weight into it and if she imported freely those things which she does not herself manufacture adequately at the present time, then I think in four or five years she could have a plant in operation. On the other hand, if she did it relying entirely on her own resources and building those up as she proceeded [...] I think it would take somewhat longer, it might take as long as twenty years ...

Physicist James Franck, after whom the Franck Report was named, commented ironically on these testimonies following President Truman's report of the first Soviet nuclear test: "There has probably been no other occasion when we have been so unhappy that our prediction turned out to be right." To Franck and Rabinowitch, the nuclear race had gone from something they feared to an undeniable reality. Importantly, it was a race that they had argued all the way back from the first issue of the *Bulletin* could never be won by military means of any kind, no matter how powerful, but only through "international control of atomic energy and, ultimately, the elimination of war".[103] Other scientists and decision-makers from both sides of the Iron Curtain, however, saw the end of the American nuclear monopoly as a sign that they had to do anything they could to create an even more powerful nuclear weapon, which so far had only been on the drawing board: a thermonuclear weapon also known as the hydrogen bomb or just the H-bomb. A few years later, such bombs, which were 50–100 times more powerful than the one that destroyed Hiroshima, became a reality. In fact, the hydrogen bomb, which will be described in the next chapter, contributed to a complete change of the entire geopolitical situation regarding the nuclear issue.

The United Kingdom: "We've got to have this thing!"

The United Kingdom, one of the victors of the Second World War, was left in a rather miserable state, both economically and socially. Considerable parts of London and other large cities were in ruins after the German bombings, and the poorest segment of the population were living at subsistence level. In addition, large sectors of British industry and trade, including the workforce, had switched to war production, and the United Kingdom had amassed a huge debt to the USA during the war because the government had been forced to buy large quantities of supplies from the new superpower on the other side of the Atlantic. On top of all this, the crown jewel of the British empire, India, was in the process of claiming sovereignty, which would be a severe blow to the British economy, its military status and its self-image.

This called for a large-scale, advanced technological project that could rebuild confidence among the country's elite, as well as the common people, that the country, with its proud scientific and technological tradition, had a future as a great power on a par with – or at least not far behind – the two great superpowers, the USA and the Soviet Union. And what was more suited for this purpose than investing in independent British development of the nuclear technology that had more than proven its potential with the nuclear bombs that marked the end of the Second World War?

In this area, the United Kingdom might even prove to have a head start on all other countries except the USA. Firstly, because the foundation of the Manhattan Project had been laid in the United Kingdom via the MAUD project in 1941, and secondly because Churchill and Roosevelt in August 1943 had signed the so-called Quebec Agreement, which established that the USA and the United Kingdom from that time would merge their national nuclear projects up until that point. As a consequence, nuclear experts in Britain – including Niels Bohr, who had fled to England via Sweden in 1943 – were sent to the USA and Canada in the following months to participate in the Manhattan Project. After the war, the British government therefore took it as given that the Americans would help their closest ally enter the Atomic Age by making available the latest nuclear technical knowhow to the British nuclear experts as they returned home from the USA and Canada.

Their hopes were sorely disappointed, even though Clement Attlee, the newly elected prime minister for the Labour Party, on August 8, two days after Hiroshima, sent a congratulatory message to Truman, stating that he and Truman as "[the] heads of the Governments which have control of this great force, should without delay make a joint declaration of our intentions to utilize the existence of this great power [...] in the interests of all peoples in order to promote peace and justice in the world".[104] Attlee's message did not make much of an impression in Washington because Roosevelt's death in April 1945 had changed everything. The new government, under Truman's command and with Secretary of State Byrnes as a central figure, did not express any sense of obligation to honor the Quebec Agreement, and also were not keen to see the Labour Party taking the helm in the United Kingdom.

The Americans stalled the British until a new, restrictive American nuclear policy, the MacMahon Act, was passed by the American Congress in June 1946 and signed by Truman in August that year. The Act was a shock to Prime Minister Attlee, who had tried to contact Truman several times by sending him personal letters and sending British Foreign Secretary, Ernest Bevin, to Washington to remind the American Secretary of State, Byrnes, about the unmistakable wording of the Quebec Agreement. Minutes from a meeting in October 1946, when the British government was considering an application for increased funding for a nuclear power plant with military perspectives, testify to the unbearable humiliation Attlee and Bevin felt by the Americans' conduct:

> We've got to have this. I don't mind for myself but I don't want any other Foreign Secretary of this country to be talked at, or to, by the Secretary of State of the United States, Mr. Byrnes. We've got to have this thing over here, whatever it costs... We've got to have a bloody Union Jack flying on top of it.[105]

The British disappointment at the American rejection was considerable, but it only made the British government intensify its effort in nuclear energy development. As early as January 1947, a research and development center was established at the former RAF airfield Harwell, which was at a comfortable distance from both London and Oxford. Here, many British nuclear experts gathered at what was referred to as the Atomic Energy Research Establishment (AERE), managed by Nobel laureate Sir John Cockcroft. The collected team of returned experts from the USA and experts brought in from large British industrial corporations worked intently on constructing the United Kingdom's first test reactor, called GLEEP (Graphite Low Energy Experimental Pile). The reactor was made critical in August 1947, and only a year later the success was repeated with the larger BEPO reactor (British Experimental Pile O).[106] With these test reactors, which both used pure carbon as a moderator to slow down fast fission neutrons – the same technique Fermi and his colleagues had used in the CP-1 reactor in Chicago 1942 – the British could learn most of what they needed to complete the actual task: developing a British nuclear bomb.

As a consequence of the MacMahon Act, the top management of the British army, the Chiefs of Staff, had already in July 1946 recommended that the United Kingdom develop nuclear weapons. The argument was that the United Kingdom could not rely on help from the Americans if the Soviet Union were to attack, and the only hope to resist the conventional forces of the Soviet Union was to strike back with nuclear weapons. Obviously, the problem would only become worse when the Soviet Union at some point became an nuclear power, but the generals reckoned that this would not happen until the mid-1950s. They definitely believed that the United Kingdom would succeed in developing nuclear weapons several years before the Soviet Union.[107]

The formal decision that the United Kingdom was to develop nuclear weapons of its own was made by an ad hoc committee set up by Prime Minister Attlee in January 1947. The committee consisted of only six Labour Ministers, including Attlee himself, Ernest Bevin and Minister of Defence A.V. Alexander. Few others were consulted before the committee, about a year later, announced the decision in the English House of Commons on May 12, 1948.[108]

But how many nuclear bombs should the United Kingdom aim to build once they had developed the weapon? This was also part of the considerations. The Attlee government set up a committee chaired by the famous chemist and radar specialist Henry Tizard to monitor developments in the nuclear weapons area. Tizard's committee provided ongoing reports for the government, and in July 1947 published a new report that addressed the question of the desired number of British nuclear bombs. The answer was simple and clear enough that the politicians could easily understand it. The committee built its recommendation on an investigation into how many nuclear bombs equivalent to the one over Hiroshima could be expected to wipe out the United Kingdom completely. The committee estimated that this number was 25, and as the Soviet territory was approximately 40 times bigger, the committee recommended that the ambition should be to build 1,000 nuclear bombs as soon as possible.[109]

The nuclear bomb project was to be concealed under the alias "High Explosive Research" and managed by Professor of Mathematical Physics William Penney, who was the head of British military research. Engineer Christopher Hinton, who during the Second World War had showed great organizational skill as director of the British weapons factories, was hired to manage the construction of the necessary production facilities, including a uranium factory at Springfields, a uranium enrichment facility in Capenhurst and two plutonium-producing reactors at Windscale.[110] In 1951, Penney and his staff of bomb designers moved into a new complex in Aldermaston, 70 kilometers west of London. As the British counterpart to Los Alamos in the USA, the United Kingdom's nuclear and hydrogen bombs were developed in this place.[111] It was also here the British nuclear protesters gathered some years later to demonstrate against the country's nuclear policy.

The two plutonium-producing reactors in Windscale were made critical in 1950 and 1951, respectively. After a few months, the fuel rods were removed from the reactors and transported to the processing facility in Windscale, where the produced plutonium was extracted. In the spring of 1952, bomb technicians built some of this plutonium into the first British nuclear bomb, which the military received in August that year. According to an agreement with the Australian government, the bomb was tested in Australia on October 3, 1952 under the code description Operation Hurricane. The bomb was brought to explode on an old British frigate that was moored in a lagoon in the Monte Bello Islands northwest of Australia. This introduced the United Kingdom as the third country to demonstrate its status as a nuclear weapon state.[112]

After the costly nuclear bomb project had proved successful, and the initial national pride had settled, the British government and military was forced to face the fact that they were not the nuclear frontrunners they had hoped. The Soviet Union had tested its first nuclear bomb back in 1949, and both superpowers, the USA and the Soviet Union, had in the years 1952–53 developed hydrogen bombs that were 50–100 times more powerful than the British nuclear bomb. This meant that the United Kingdom had the choice between playing second fiddle or launching an expensive, new weapons project aiming at developing British hydrogen bombs. The new Conservative British government, with Winston Churchill back at the helm, opted in July 1954 for the latter option, which was recommended by a Chiefs of Staff committee. The committee's main argument was that "it would be dangerous if the US were to retain their present monopoly," since Britain in that case would "be denied any right to influence her policy in the use of this weapon" and thus "could not expect to maintain our influence as a world power unless we possessed the most up-to-date nuclear weapons."[113] Prime Minister Churchill, who was famous for being succinct, said when presented with an estimate of how much a hydrogen bomb project would cost, and how long it would take to realize: "We must do it. It's the price we pay to sit at the top table."[114]

In 1954, William Penney launched no fewer than three projects, each of which was to follow a different path toward the goal: a British hydrogen bomb. The two simplest paths did not work according to plan, but 3–4 years later the British bomb engineers succeeded in building a real hydrogen bomb, which detonated successfully in April 1958 at the so-called Grapple Y-test off Christmas Island in the Indian Ocean. The explosive force of the bomb was measured at approximately 3 megatons.[115] Now there was no ignoring that the United Kingdom was in possession of a weapon of mass destruction. But the country still lacked modern means of delivering the weapons – i.e., intercontinental planes and missiles. Should the country develop these too or humble itself and ask the Americans for help and thus drop the ambition of being an independent nuclear power? In the beginning of the 1960s, the United Kingdom chose the latter option, purchasing American Polaris submarines with accompanying medium-range missiles, equipped with British warheads.

France: "This achievement will add to the radiance of France"

Like the United Kingdom, France was a relatively poor and devastated country in the post-war years. But in at least one respect, France's situation was even worse than the United Kingdom's. In contrast to the United Kingdom, who had held its own in its fight against the Nazis for almost six years, France had been defeated surprisingly quickly by its arch-enemy Germany in 1940. Many French people collaborated with the occupying power during the war, and this was a blow to the nation's pride and cohesion. Those French leaders who had been uncompromising saw it as their foremost duty to regain as fast as possible some of the French *gloire* and *grandeur*, in political, military and technological respects. The military man Charles de Gaulle, who during the war had led the Free French forces from his exile in England, felt deeply humiliated that he had not been invited to the Potsdam Conference in July 1945 – even though his forces had contributed to defeating the Germans.

Still, de Gaulle had big plans. Convinced that nuclear technology was the technology of the future, he – as the Chairman of the Provisional Government of the French Republic in the first year following the war – used his power to establish a French atomic energy commission, Commissariat à l'Énergie Atomique (CEA), which he did by way of a decree in October 1945.[116] Now, prominent French scientists, including physicist and Nobel laureate Frédéric Joliot-Curie and chemist Bertrand Goldschmidt, could prove their talents to the honor and benefit of the French people. An ardent communist, Joliot-Curie had been very active in the French resistance, whereas Goldschmidt as a French-Jewish refugee took part in the Manhattan Project: first at the Met Lab in Chicago, where he contributed to making CP-1 critical, and later as a member of the British-Canadian team in Montreal, where he made a crucial contribution to developing a method to extract uranium and plutonium from irradiated fuel elements – one that would become standard.

The purpose of CEA was, broadly defined, to be in charge of scientific and technical research with the aim of furthering France's use of nuclear energy in science, industry and defense. One of the first initiatives was the construction of a small test reactor, named ZOE, that was made critical in December 1948. This reactor utilized natural uranium as fuel and heavy water as moderator, in contrast to CP-1 in the USA and GLEEP in the United Kingdom, which both used graphite as moderator. Heavy water, which consists of water molecules in which the usual hydrogen isotope has been replaced by deuterium, a heavy hydrogen isotope consisting of one proton and one neutron, is a better moderator than graphite but also much more expensive. Like CP-1 and GLEEP, ZOE also produced a small amount of plutonium, and Goldschmidt and his staff were able to extract a few milligrams in November 1949 at a small plutonium lab nearby. The French president at the time, Vincent Auriol, paid a visit to ZOE on the occasion, where he exclaimed the grandiose words: "This achievement will add to the radiance of France,"[117] striking the familiar nationalist note that French politicians and intellectuals often employed when they emphasized France's role as the standard-bearer of civilization in the country's golden era before the Second World War.

ZOE demonstrated that France had experts and technology that could make the country an independent nuclear state if the politicians wished. However, this was not currently the case, given that de Gaulle had stepped down in 1946, unable to muster support for his proposal for a new French constitution with strong presidential rule. And the rapidly changing French governments during the 4th Republic were less interested in acquiring nuclear weapons than de Gaulle had been.

The increasingly intense Cold War around the end of the 1940s resulted in CEA, which had until then been dominated by left-wing scientists, getting rid of several communist employees including scientific manager Frédéric Joliot-Curie in 1950. The direct cause was that Joliot-Curie had publicly stated that he would under no circumstances contribute to producing a French nuclear bomb; if it were ever to be used, it would be against the Soviet Union, his great inspiration. And when the USA protested violently against France having a notable communist in such an important position, the nationalist French government decided to sack Joliot-Curie, who earlier had been highly regarded. Instead, CEA's board was supplemented with a number of engineers and bureaucrats.[118] Now, it was not sufficient to simply do experiments that the scientific staff found interesting. France was to build additional, larger reactors that could contribute to the power supply and rebuild the country to its former glory. This was in accordance with recommendations from CEA's powerful ally in the parliament, Félix Gaillard. In 1951, he had been appointed minister of nuclear energy – an area he was very enthusiastic about. He promised to present CEA's wishes for funding of larger reactors to the National Assembly, letting the CEA management know that it might be easier to secure 20 billion francs than 3 billion. It was time to think big.[119]

After careful consideration, CEA's steering committee came up with a five-year plan for the period 1952–57. The plan entailed that two large reactors – for the standard at the time – were to be built, fueled by natural uranium, moderated by graphite and using carbon dioxide for cooling. CEA opted for this technological solution partly to avoid having to enrich uranium, for which France did not have the facilities at the time, and partly because this type of reactor would produce large quantities of plutonium. Using Goldschmidt's extraction method, the element could relatively simply be separated from spent fuel elements and utilized as fuel in future, more advanced nuclear reactors or in nuclear bombs. However, it was not decided at the time that France was to become a state with nuclear weapons; on the contrary, the French government keenly promoted nuclear energy only for peaceful purposes. Nevertheless, the choice of reactor in the five-year plan left all future possibilities open, and it was clear to all involved that the decision might bring France close to being a nuclear weapon state.

When funding was granted, CEA launched the construction of what was to become a large nuclear facility, Marcoule, in south-east France. The commission ordered the construction of three reactors – G1, G2 and G3 – in 1952, 1955 and 1955, respectively. They were all to supply power to the electrical grid, so CEA called in assistance from engineers in the large, French-owned power company Électricité de France (EDF), but it was still CEA's people, with engineer and administrator Pierre Guillaumat in charge, who managed the project. Guillaumat did not much care whether the reactors were designed optimally with regard to power production; he was much more focused on optimizing the production of plutonium. In fact, G2 and G3 were designed so that the fuel elements could be changed while the reactors were running.[120] This allowed the removal of the irradiated but far from burnt-out fuel elements while they still contained considerable amounts of the fissile plutonium isotope Pu-239. This procedure also enabled the chemists to extract the Pu-239 before the plutonium was 'polluted' too much by the non-fissile isotopes Pu-240 and Pu-241, the relative content of which increases the longer a fuel element has been in the reactor. When the chemists subsequently cut open the removed fuel elements at the nearby plutonium factory, they could extract the plutonium, but as they could not separate the plutonium isotopes from each other by chemical methods, the end product contained a mixture of Pu-239, Pu-240 and Pu-241. This was problematic if the government wanted to use the plutonium in a nuclear bomb, because even a small amount of the two heavier isotopes was likely to make the bomb a dud. That is because these two isotopes are very short-lived and release unwanted neutrons, which could and probably would trigger a chain reaction in the imploding plutonium mass before it was sufficiently compressed. Hence, the fuel elements needed to be removed from the reactors long before they burned out.

EDF did not like this procedure because – as seen from a power supply perspective – it is a very irrational use of the uranium embedded in the reactor's fuel elements. In the 1950s, EDF insisted on building its own reactors, which led to a longstanding struggle between the two giants, CEA and EDF, who both wanted to play the lead in the build-up of the French nuclear industry.

With their choice of reactors and the plutonium factory in Marcoule, Guillaumat and his staff had made sure that France over the course of the 1950s was ready to enter the club of nuclear weapon states as soon as the government gave its say-so. The first steps were taken in 1954, when Prime Minister Pierre Mendès-France, in secrecy, gave his permission for a new military organization, Bureau d'Études Générales, to develop components for a nuclear bomb in an attempt to boost French morale, which had bottomed out after the loss of French Indochina. The bomb project gained further impetus with the United Kingdom and France's humiliating withdrawal from Suez in 1956 following the USA as well as the Soviet Union taking strong exception to the two countries' military occupation of the Canal Zone. It is hardly a coincidence that CEA and the French Ministry of Defense, on November 30, 1956, signed a secret memorandum obliging the parties to collaborate on developing and testing a nuclear bomb.[121] The definitive official order to make a French nuclear bomb was given by the last prime minister of the 4th French Republic, Félix Gaillard, on April 11, 1958.[122]

A month later, Guillaumat's old friend, Charles de Gaulle, returned to power to save the 4th Republic in the acute Algerian crisis 12 years after his former reign ended. He managed to do so, but following a referendum he terminated the 4th Republic and inaugurated a 5th Republic in which the president – de Gaulle himself between 1959 and 1968 – was bestowed with new, extensive, executive powers. He used these with the aim of restoring France, which during the 1950s had suffered military defeat in the French colony of Vietnam and was now losing the war against the rebels in Algeria. However, de Gaulle's focus was not on war but on rebuilding the

© Topfoto/Ritzau Scanpix

The G2 reactor at Marcoule. Notice the platform in the foreground from which fuel elements in the reactor could be replaced while it was running.

country by means of modern technology. A cornerstone in the technological development was enormous investments in civil as well as military nuclear infrastructure. The French version of nuclear technology – including the development of nuclear weapons – was designed to help the republic regain its former power.

Moreover, de Gaulle did not trust the USA to step in if the Soviet Union were to carry out a surprise attack on a European NATO ally. He therefore insisted that France was to build its own independent nuclear striking force, *Force de frappe*, which at any given time would be able to deal such massive blows on an attacker that the threat alone worked as a deterrent. Or, as the French General Pierre Marie Gallois expressed it: "Making the most pessimistic assumptions, the French nuclear bombers could destroy ten Russian cities, and France is not a prize worthy of ten Russian cities."[123]

In terms of developing nuclear weapons, Guillaumat, CEA and the Bureau d'Études Générales had already done much of the preliminary work. In 1959, de Gaulle ordered a test of the finished nuclear bomb and introduced a missile development project. The first French nuclear test, called *Gerboise bleue* (Blue Jerboa), took place in the Algerian desert on February 13, 1960.[124] It was an atmospheric test that resulted in considerable radioactive fallout in a nearby French military desert camp and the surrounding desert, where Tuareg nomads lived. Experts measured the strength of the bomb as equivalent to 70 kilotons of TNT. France performed two other atmospheric tests in the following months, but intense protest from several African countries meant that future tests were carried out underground and in another region of Algeria. This continued until February 1967, i.e., five years after Algeria had achieved independence from France and two years after France had launched its first satellite – also from a base in Algeria.[125]

However, the French government knew this situation could not continue – especially when the republic was going to test the country's first hydrogen bomb. Following careful investigations, de Gaulle decided in 1963 that when the tests stopped in Algeria, they would continue in French Polynesia, more specifically on the uninhabited atolls of Mururoa and Fangataufa. He backed up the decision with the claim that the inhabitants of the neighboring islands would be pleased when they realized that the tests would entail a sizeable improvement of the poor Polynesian economy. The island council accepted this argument, but immediately after the French nuclear tests began in 1966, the island population started powerful protests.[126] Nevertheless, France performed no less than 181, including 46 atmospheric nuclear and hydrogen bomb tests in the years 1966–96. The tests sparked worldwide protests as time went by – e.g., in the form of boycotts against French wine – criticizing what most non-French (and many French) viewed as the ruthless abuse of the indigenous population by a former colonial power.

The first French hydrogen bomb test went under the codename "Canopus" and had a strength of 2.6 megatons. It took place on August 24, 1968. The last test in Polynesia took place on January 27, 1996.[127] Subsequently, excess mortality has affected the islanders as well as the French test participants who were exposed to high doses of radiation. In 2009, the French government agreed to pay 10 million euros to the surviving victims and 80 million dollars as compensation for environmental damages on the island of Hao, which had served as a base in the 30 years the nuclear weapons tests took place.[128]

China: "The atomic bomb is a paper tiger"

Just under two years after the communists, led by Mao Zedong, had seized power over the entire mainland China in 1949, distinguished Chinese radiochemist Yang Chengzong visited French Nobel laureates Frédéric and Irène Joliot-Curie in their laboratory in Paris. Before Yang went back to China, Frédéric asked him to send his regards to Mao and say that China must obviously distance themselves from nuclear weapons – while making sure to get their hands on them. Irène gave Yang ten grams of radium salt because she wanted "to support the Chinese people in their nuclear research".[129] The Joliot-Curie couple with their strong communist leanings had thus done their part in breaking American dominance and helping the world's most populous nation become the world's fifth state with nuclear weapons.

The formal decision to make China a nuclear power was taken by the communist party's Politburo under Chairman Mao's management on January 15, 1955. In the preceding years, as hundreds of thousands of Chinese soldiers had fought and died on North Korea's side in the Korean War, Mao had appeared unfazed by the press rumors that the USA was considering using nuclear weapons against Chinese targets. Nuclear bombs were merely "paper tigers" as he liked to say. In reality, however, he was well aware of the danger associated with President Eisenhower's New Look Strategy. This implied that the USA might choose to defend itself against even minor provocations from a hostile power with a massive nuclear counterattack, a harsh reality that Mao could not afford to ignore.[130] In fact, it threatened to render impossible his plan of taking back the large island of Formosa, present-day Taiwan, from his arch-rival Chiang Kai-shek, who had fled there in 1949 with the remains of his nationalist army.

Apart from Mao and the Politburo, participants in the meeting on January 15, 1955 included Foreign Minister Zhou Enlai and a group of physicists led by Qian Sanquiang, director of the physics institute of the Chinese Academy of Science. Qian had studied nuclear physics under Frédéric and Irène Joliot-Curie in Paris, who as committed communists had been more than willing to tell him everything they knew about the Manhattan Project in the USA. They had also helped him acquire scientific equipment so that he, together with Chinese colleagues, could pursue advanced nuclear research after his return to China. He had done so, but probably not on the scale he had hoped when he said goodbye to the couple in Paris. However, now, in January 1955, Zhou Enlai had invited him to give a popular talk to Mao and members of the Politburo on nuclear physics – especially on the element uranium and the properties that allow it to be transformed into an explosive with massive destructive power.

Mao followed the talk eagerly and was excited to learn that China had rich deposits of uranium and that Qian and his colleagues were ready to commence a Chinese nuclear bomb project if the Chairman wished. Mao certainly did. Before securing the backing of the Politburo for large investments in nuclear research for military purposes, he stated:

> During the past years we have been busy doing other things, and there was not enough time for us to pay attention to this matter [nuclear weapons]. Sooner or later, we would have had to pay attention to it. Now it is time for us to pay attention to it. We can achieve success provided we put it on the order of the day. Now, [because] the Soviet Union is giving us assistance, we must achieve success! We can also achieve success even if we do this by ourselves.[131]

The following years saw a major rise in Chinese nuclear research due to a large increase in Chinese investments and Soviet assistance. Many young Chinese were sent to universities in Moscow and other cities in the Soviet Union to study nuclear science and nuclear technology, at the same time as numerous Soviet experts came to China to help build the facilities needed to ensure that the "Middle Kingdom" could become a nuclear state inspired by the Soviet

Union. They worked on the construction of a test reactor, a small facility to extract uranium from uranium ore and parts of a gas diffusion facility to produce enriched uranium. Things progressed according to plan for a few years, but soon the relationship between the leaders of the two communist brother countries, Soviet First Secretary Nikita Khrushchev and Chinese Chairman Mao Zedong, began to turn sour.

Even though Khrushchev and Mao might agree that communism would eventually triumph across the world, they disagreed on which strategy was best suited to reach this goal. Khrushchev was convinced that it was paramount to avoid a disastrous nuclear war between the capitalist and the communist worlds; instead, the communist countries should rely on conquering capitalism in a struggle based on peaceful co-existence, which would make ever more countries realize gradually that communism was the superior of the two societal ideologies.

Mao strongly disagreed, claiming that the USA was merely a capitalist "paper tiger" that needed to be confronted consistently wherever it appeared. The paper tiger had reared its ugly head in Korea, and China had stood up firmly against it, while the Soviet Union had only provided some weapons. But now the tiger was on the prowl again, this time on Formosa, threatening to use nuclear weapons if China went through with an attempt to conquer Formosa or other small islands controlled by Chiang Kai-shek. Mao believed that this posed no real threat. "We have no experience in atomic war. So, how many will be killed cannot be known. The best outcome may be [that] only half of the [Chinese] population is left, and the second best may be only one-third." Regardless, it would be worth the sacrifice because a nuclear war would mean "total elimination of capitalism" and herald an era of "permanent peace", said Mao in a speech at the eight-party congress of the Communist Party in Beijing in the spring of 1958.[132]

Terrified by the thought of being dragged in on the Chinese side of a nuclear war with the USA, Khrushchev ordered the technical assistance to China to be reduced to a minimum. By the end of 1956, Chinese administrators and experts started complaining over delays in the Soviet deliveries to the promised nuclear facilities, as well as imprecise blueprints. As 1958 went by, the assistance all but stopped. This included the Soviet Union having promised to hand over a prototype of a Soviet nuclear bomb to China, but shortly before reaching the Russian-Chinese border, it was withheld in Soviet territory.[133] After that, the mutual trust between China and the Soviet

Union was almost gone, and it was only a matter of time before there would be a parting of the ways. This happened in August 1960, when the last remaining Soviet nuclear and missile experts left their posts in China's strategic weapons program.[134]

While Mao had previously counted on the Soviet nuclear umbrella to keep the USA in check if China were to attack Formosa, that illusion was taken from him in 1958 – if not before. Mao concluded that China had to rely on its own resources in all forms of technological development, including the development of Chinese nuclear weapons. This conclusion contributed to his launching the sweeping societal experiment referred to as the Great Leap Forward, which resulted in the loss of millions of Chinese lives because it entailed the degrading of experts and expertise at the expense of investments in the creative abilities of farmers and workers in almost all aspects of society. For example, Mao's attempt to multiply China's iron and steel production by having millions of villagers build small, primitive blast furnaces was a huge failure because the iron produced proved to be of inferior quality. Meanwhile, traditional farming was neglected, which resulted in a disastrous shortage of food and an ensuing famine.[135]

The reason that China nevertheless managed to develop nuclear weapons in the period between 1958 and 1964, when the first Chinese nuclear bomb was tested, was more than anything else that most of the nuclear project work was managed by the Chinese military. The Chinese armed forces had a clear command structure and were not subject to unprofessional interference from the outside – such as from political actors – to the same extent as other sectors of Chinese society. This meant that scientists and technicians could work relatively undisturbed on the projects under the nuclear program that had been planned by the Central Military Commission in the summer of 1958. The project included the search for uranium deposits all over China, running uranium mines like the Chenxian Mine in Hunan Province and production of uranium hexafluoride at the large Jinquan nuclear complex in Gansu Province, where the Chinese also built reactors for plutonium production. Finally, the project included a giant facility for production of enriched uranium from uranium hexafluoride, using the gaseous diffusion method which the Americans had employed at Oak Ridge during the Second World War. When the economic situation deteriorated at the beginning of the 1960s following the failed Great Leap Forward, the latter facility was exempt from the cuts that hit the plutonium facility. This resulted in the first Chinese nuclear bombs being based on uranium in which the fissile isotope U-235 had been concentrated to approximately 90 percent.[136]

The first Chinese nuclear bomb exploded on October 16, 1964, at 3 a.m. in a remote area at Lop Nor in the Province of Xinjiang in north-western China – a region with approximately 20 million inhabitants of many different ethnicities. The explosion was measured to have a strength of approximately 20 kilotons of TNT, but the experts wanted to be completely sure they had really witnessed a nuclear explosion before they dared inform Chairman Mao and Premier Zhou Enlai in Beijing. Shortly afterwards, when Radio Beijing announced the news, celebrations began all over China.

China had now proved that the country's scientists and technicians were capable of developing nuclear weapons. But China did not stop at this. Mao immediately gave orders to speed up work on the production of ordinary nuclear weapons – i.e., uranium and plutonium bombs – for the country's defense, at the same time as bomb experts were instructed to develop a Chinese hydrogen bomb. It might be unthinkable for Mao that China would ever be the first country to use nuclear and hydrogen bombs in a conflict, but if an enemy were to use that type of weapon against China, he would not hesitate to strike back with such weapons so that the enemy would be utterly destroyed. Hence, China needed hydrogen bombs as soon as possible. This turned out to take only three years. On June 17, 1967, amidst the worst excesses of the so-called Cultural Revolution, China tested the country's first hydrogen bomb. It was dropped from a Hong-6 bomber and measured at approximately three megatons of TNT. China was now one of the front-runners in the rampant nuclear arms race.[137]

Since the first Chinese nuclear tests in 1964, China has performed an additional 44 nuclear and hydrogen bomb tests at Lop Nor – half of them atmospheric and half underground. The Chinese authorities claim that only very few people have been exposed to radiation exceeding the internationally accepted norms in connection with the tests. However, given that China does not allow foreign experts access to the Chinese data, there is widespread skepticism regarding this information. This skepticism is not least represented by experts in the organs set up to monitor nuclear weapons tests and their environmental consequences around the world – most notably the Preparatory Commission for the Comprehensive Nuclear-Test-Ban Treaty Organization (CTBTO)[138] and International Physicians for the Prevention of Nuclear War (IPPNW).[139] The latter organization published in 1991 the book

© Pictures From History / Akg-Images / Ritzau Scanpix

The detonation of the first Chinese nuclear bomb took place in the Lop Nor test area in western China on October 16, 1964.

Radioactive Heaven and Earth, which provides an estimate of the amounts of radioactive isotopes that have been released in the soil and atmosphere due to the superpowers' nuclear weapons testing. The estimate is staggering, but probably the effects are underestimated– especially in relation to the Chinese tests.

As described, by the middle of the 1960s all five so-called great powers had become nuclear powers. This meant that they all had the capacity to commit instant massacres of hundreds of thousands of people in addition to massive destruction in any country that were to confront them in conflict. But over the course of the nearly twenty years that passed from when the USA became the first nuclear power to when China joined the club, many countries, organizations and individuals fought to put a stop to, or at least slow down, the nuclear race that in reality started when the Second World War ended in 1945. The following decades saw a struggle between nuclear weapons armament and protests against them, which gave rise to the institutions and treaties that remain seminal in attempts to minimize the nuclear threat. The following chapter is devoted to the question of atoms for peace and war.

CHAPTER 4

"Atoms for Peace" and "Atoms for War"

Science as a Concerted Human Effort

As the world's great powers developed into nuclear weapon states, nuclear physics and geopolitics became inextricably entangled. This is still the case today. In fact, even by the end of the Second World War, it was generally acknowledged that war and peace in the world were now closely linked to nuclear technology and how it was handled politically. The first nuclear detonations and the establishment of the UN system were thus also two closely connected world historical events. The family of UN organizations included the then recently founded United Nations Educational, Scientific, and Cultural Organization (UNESCO), whose aim was to promote peace between people and nations through education, science and culture. The original plan had been an organization for education and culture only (UNECO), and the S was a last-minute addition.[140] UNESCO was founded three months after the bombings of Hiroshima and Nagasaki, and the inclusion of science in the organization was decided in the shadow of the mushroom clouds. As British Minister of Education, Ellen C. Wilkinson, said during the concluding UNESCO negotiations in London 1945:

> In these days, when we are all wondering, perhaps apprehensively, what the scientists will do to us next, it is important that they should be linked closely with the humanities and should feel that they have a responsibility to mankind for the result of their labors. I do not believe that any scientist will have survived the world catastrophe, who will still say that they are utterly uninterested in the social implications of their discoveries.[141]

The mood in 1945 was clearly marked by concern. But just as importantly, there was also hope in the post-war years that humanity during the war had hit rock bottom, and that the new situation was a *Stunde Null* with new opportunities for peaceful human coexistence despite – or, according to some, due to – the novel understanding of the potential of nuclear power. This view was promoted by physicist Arthur Compton, who became the US representative in UNESCO after the end of the war. Compton, who had received the Nobel Prize in Physics in 1927 for his discovery that electromagnetic radiation can in some instances act as a stream of particles, had played a central role in the Manhattan Project. He was also a member of the scientific committee that advised President Truman about how to use nuclear bombs over the Japanese cities.[142]

After the war, Compton left his career as an active scientist and became an internationally known figure. In this capacity, he debated the philosophical and societal implications of the latest advances in nuclear physics, not least as a representative for the USA in the UNESCO headquarters in Paris.[143] In the first years after the war, he argued that nuclear weapons could and would contribute to maintaining a peaceful world. His argument was that nuclear weapons are so destructive that they have a preventative effect in relation to new acts of war – an argument that was particularly appealing to him at a time when there was still an expectation that the USA would maintain its monopoly on nuclear weapons for some years to come.[144] Even more importantly, however, he argued that the development of the nuclear bomb had demonstrated the fundamental, inherently international character of science. The development of nuclear technology, as he argued in UNESCO in 1947, was a product of unprecedented international collaboration. The scientific foundation had been laid by contributions by scientists from numerous large and small countries, including France, Germany, Japan, Denmark, the United Kingdom, the Soviet Union and the USA. During the Manhattan Project, he had further experienced firsthand the most comprehensive collaboration ever between highly diverse people on a science-based project:

> Scientific specialists of a thousand types, engineers, managers, labor, skilled mechanics, construction crews, secretaries, Army and Navy, whites and negroes, Americans and Europeans, all worked with co-ordinated efforts. Many differences arose, but all were intent on completing the job. Differences were set aside in order to reach the common goal.[145]

Through collaboration, the participants had transcended the autocratic power structures. The development of nuclear technology had, according to Compton, demonstrated that modern science and technology by nature constituted an incentive for human collaboration and generated mutual international interconnectedness. This was the reason why science was perfectly suited to promote internationalist values and, ultimately, ensure peace after the end of the war.

Scientists were truly citizens of the world, claimed Compton. Unlike business people, who were dependent on the market, and military people, who were dependent on their nation, scientists were first and foremost preoccupied with ideas and knowledge, which knew no national boundaries. However, the new developments also came at a price. The nuclear bomb had tied humanity together in a communality of fate. Humankind had taken another step on the long journey from small social groups to what Compton referred to as "planetarian society".[146] The situation after the Second World War thus entailed a choice between one world or none – a phrase that was often used and first coined in the best-selling book *One World or None: A Report to the Public on the Full Meaning of the Atomic Bomb*, which was published in 1946 with a preface by Compton.[147] Science had created these new, terrifying conditions, but science was also the solution because, by its nature, it relied on collaboration and supported internationalist values. Therefore, scientists, according to Compton, were obliged and able to contribute to peaceful coexistence.

Compton may have expressed worry, but also the hope that existed in the first years after the war. And he was not alone in doing so. Historian Glenda Sluga mentions these years as "the curiously utopian moment bracketed by the end of the Second World War and the onset of the Cold War".[148] The curiously utopian moment soon evaporated. A few years after the end of the war, the world became the stage of a nuclear race between the former allies, seeing the nuclear weapon states becoming able and willing to develop ever more powerful nuclear weapons. This was the new reality that the public, politicians and, not least, scientists had to get used to in the following years. Among the latter was Niels Bohr.

Niels Bohr's Open Letter to the UN

At the end of September 1949, when the American government announced the news of the first Soviet nuclear test, it made Niels Bohr react. During the four years since the war ended, he had – due to his promise to the FBI – been prevented from pursuing the use of nuclear power in Denmark. However, this had not kept him from continuing his efforts to convince the American government to be more open with the Soviet Union about nuclear energy. During a stay in 1948 at Princeton University, Bohr had the opportunity to dine with American Secretary of State George Marshall. The two had a good rapport – at least in Bohr's mind – and before they parted, Bohr promised Marshall to send a letter in which he elaborated his views. On June 10, he sent the letter, which was an abbreviated and updated version of the memorandum that Judge of the Supreme Court Felix Frankfurter had delivered to President Roosevelt on Bohr's behalf in summer 1944. Bohr followed up on the letter with an addendum on June 19, 1948.[149] However, despite kind words of thanks from Marshall, the American government did not take any concrete steps in the direction suggested by Bohr. In fact, quite the opposite. Although Marshall established a board to evaluate the pros and cons of Bohr's ideas, the board rejected them as unrealistic. Bohr did not receive word of this until much later, but as time went by, he could deduce that his appeal had been shelved at some level in the American State Department.[150]

The Soviet nuclear test in 1949 caused Bohr to make another attempt to stop the nuclear arms race, which was no longer just a bleak prospect. But having learned from past experience, he now knew that further appeals to the American and Soviet governments would be to no avail. Instead, he wanted to appeal directly to all UN member countries. Therefore, he wrote a 12-page open letter over the winter of 1949–50, which he handed to the UN on June 9, 1950. Three days later, on June 12, Bohr held a press conference in his honorary residence at Carlsberg in Copenhagen, where he summarized the main points of his initiative and handed out copies to the press. Apart from the introduction, the conclusion and some transitions, the text mostly consisted of extracts of the memoranda he had sent to Roosevelt in 1944 and Marshall in 1948.

In the letter, Bohr drew attention to the fact that the mutual relationship between the countries of the world relied on the unique development of science and technology, which "holds out such great promises for the improvement of human welfare" but at the same time has placed "formidable means of destruction in the hands of man".[151] This paradox was reiterated and expanded throughout the text. The open letter contained no concrete suggestions for how the world could escape the grave crisis, although Bohr stressed that an open world based on exchange and collaboration was an unconditional necessity if individuals and governments were to succeed: "An open world where each nation can assert itself solely by the extent to which it can contribute to the common culture and is able to help others with experience and resources must be the goal to be put above everything else."

Hence, openness was the takeaway message in Bohr's letter, as was emphasized in the conclusion in which he stated that "the effort of all supporters of international co-operation, individuals as well as nations, will be needed to create in all countries an opinion to voice, with ever increasing clarity and strength, the demand for an open world".[152] Bohr's open letter received much attention in Denmark and the other Nordic countries, while the reactions in the UN were less enthusiastic. Nevertheless, the Danish ambassador in Washington, Henrik Kauffmann, managed to make American security adviser George Kennan promise that the American State Department would study Bohr's letter carefully. But before this had been done, something happened that removed any possibility that Bohr's initiative could become the topic of serious discussions – whether in the UN Security Council, the American State Department, or other contexts.

On June 25, 1950 at 4 a.m., local time, only 15 days after the UN had received Bohr's letter, North Korean troops crossed the 38th latitude, which was the border between North and South Korea, in an attempt to reunite Korea under communist rule. The American government was convinced that Stalin was the mastermind behind this attack, and that the aim was to test whether the USA really intended to live up to the Truman Doctrine from March 1947. This doctrine, which came into being when Greek communists, backed by the Soviet Union, were about to seize power in Greece, entailed that the USA would intervene anywhere in the world where the Soviet Union tried to seize power by a coup in a non-communist country. This was to happen with no regard of whether it took place with Soviet forces or by means of proxies – as was the case in Korea.[153]

It took Stalin only a few days to realize that the Truman Doctrine was meant in earnest, because by then, the UN Security Board – which the Soviet Union was boycotting at the time – passed a resolution proposed by the USA that large UN forces, the majority of them American, would be deployed on the South Korean side of the Korean War. The war lasted from June 25, 1950 to July 27, 1953 and probably cost the lives of between two and three million people, civilian as well as military, on both sides of the front, but estimates of casualties are wide-ranging. The USA alone lost approximately 36,000 soldiers, and China, which entered the war on North Korea's side, is estimated to have lost as many as 600,000 soldiers on the battlefield. As always in modern warfare, however, it was the civilian population that suffered the biggest losses. North and South Korea together probably lost around two million human lives, civilian and military, during the Korean War.[154]

The Super

In the years after the Second World War, the American defense budget suffered severe cuts as military personnel were reduced from more than 10 million to 1 ½ million. Most American politicians agreed that this was the right policy because it was time to kick-start civilian production again. But the outbreak of the Korean War gave rise to a new, sizable increase of the American defense budget, almost a quadrupling from 1949 to 1952, when it was at its highest.[155] The majority of the increased funding went into training a large number of army units, and to provide them with weapons, albeit only conventional weapons. The American military leaders – and the government in Washington – discussed several times whether to use nuclear weapons in Korea or in the border region between China and North Korea. However, the proposal was turned down every time by the Truman and (from January 1953) Eisenhower governments. No obvious military targets for nuclear weapons existed, and the potential dangers of using nuclear weapons – especially in the case that the Soviet Union would get involved and the fighting in Korea would develop into a world war – seemed greater than the immediate advantages for the UN troops. But the threat of the USA using nuclear weapons was hanging in the air, which made Eisenhower and leading members of his government draw the conclusion that it was this very threat that made North Korea and China hesitant and weak: in fact, so weak that a ceasefire was established in 1953, when the frontline was close to the 38th latitude.

The ceasefire gave further impetus to faith in the efficiency of 'nuclear diplomacy' – i.e., that the USA with its nuclear weapons at the ready could force through conflict solutions that would otherwise have been unacceptable to the opponent. Historian George Herken has argued that the notion of the nuclear bomb as a *winning weapon*, diplomatically as well as militarily, was established in the first years after the Second World War, when the USA's nuclear monopoly seemed to warrant that kind of possibility. After the monopoly was broken, focus changed to maintaining the American head start in the nuclear race, which was seen as a precondition for effective nuclear diplomacy. Based on this logic, peace still depended on nuclear striking power.[156] This conception – which was apparently confirmed by the conclusion of the Korean War – had wide-ranging consequences for the American nuclear strategy throughout the 1950s.[157]

The heavily increased defense budgets contributed to speeding up the development of thermonuclear weapons that exploit fusion of lighter atomic nuclei such as hydrogen and deuterium. The hydrogen bomb was also known as *the Super*. Work on developing a hydrogen bomb began slowly in the Los Alamos years 1943–45. Hungarian physicist Edward Teller, who was part of the Los Alamos team, concluded early on that all crucial scientific and technical problems concerning the atomic bomb had been solved. He therefore pressed Oppenheimer for clearance to use his talents to investigate whether a hydrogen bomb was an option in practice. Oppenheimer accepted, but because he needed all available resources to develop the atomic bomb as quickly as possible, he was not willing to set up a special team devoted to developing a hydrogen bomb.

After the war, Teller campaigned for the USA to embark on a new, large-scale arms development project inspired by the Manhattan Project. The aim would be to develop a hydrogen bomb with far greater explosive force than the atomic bombs that destroyed Hiroshima and Nagasaki. His campaign was futile for a long time, partly because Oppenheimer was opposed to the idea and, as a member of the influential General Advisory Committee, which gave advice to the American government on security questions, had influence at the highest level. This founded an almost lifelong animosity between the two highly intelligent and politically influential nuclear physicists – an animosity that would have dire consequences for Oppenheimer in the early 1950s.

The power dynamic between Oppenheimer and Teller changed dramatically in 1949 when the Soviet Union had become a nuclear weapon state. The Soviet bomb became known as Joe-1 in the USA, and it sent shivers down the spines of both civilian and military leaders in the USA, not to mention ordinary Americans, who had felt safe in their conviction that the USA had a monopoly on atomic weapons. Suddenly, the monopoly had been broken, and the general population expected President Truman to respond forcefully to the Soviet challenge. He did so after a few months' deliberations, during which he was put under heavy pressure by Teller and his supporters – a group that was rapidly growing. Their arguments for a fast launch of the hydrogen bomb project rested mainly on the notion that the Soviets might already be working on something similar and that it would be a disaster if they beat the Americans to the superbomb. If that were to happen, Stalin would see his ultimate dream come true: having the means to force the West to surrender.[158]

Truman could not oppose this logic, even though Oppenheimer and his staff explained that when the USA at this point had almost 300 atomic weapons at their disposal – and the number was rising – the American military had more than enough to obliterate the Soviet Union. Further, they argued, the hydrogen bomb could not be regarded as a military weapon because military targets that required such weapons for destruction did not exist anywhere.[159]

On January 31, 1950, Truman gave his order to launch a project aiming to quickly establish whether a hydrogen bomb was a realistic option.[160] Just a few months later, the project changed into a *crash program* – i.e., a program that must be implemented ASAP at any cost – for the development of hydrogen bombs that could be transported by plane to the target area. This was no simple task, and it was a great challenge for Teller and his closest associate Stanislaw Ulam to conceive of a construction that could ensure the desired result. The first test detonation took place at the Eniwetok Atoll in the Pacific on November 1, 1952. This test did not involve a proper bomb but rather a large stationary facility with a nuclear bomb, a cooling unit, and an amount of deuterium that had been cooled to -250°C. The entire facility weighed 82 tons and could thus not have been transported on any existing plane. However, the aim was simply to test Teller's idea, which passed with flying colors considering that the new 'gadget', codenamed Mike, was measured to have an explosive force of 10 megatons – i.e., almost a thousand times the Hiroshima bomb.[161]

In the Soviet Union, scientists were also ready to test a fusion weapon as early as August 12, 1953, and although it was less powerful than Mike, it had the advantage of being transportable. The American nuclear arms experts could hardly believe their eyes when analyses of the radioactive fallout from the detonation showed signs of fusion processes. Joe-4, which was their name for the test, was a real shock to many of them because it proved that the Soviet bomb constructors were right behind them – maybe even about to overtake them. The Americans now had to acknowledge that the Soviet nuclear experts were just as skilled as the Americans.[162]

The Soviet nuclear weapon that was tested on August 12, 1953 was not as powerful as the American one that exploded at Eniwetok nine months earlier. However, an official message signed by Lewis Strauss, head of the

© Wikimedia Commons / U.S. Department of Defense

US Atomic Energy Commission (AEC) on August 20, admitted that the Soviet explosion had "involved both fission and thermonuclear reactions".[163] Most probably, this was therefore an early version of a hydrogen bomb.

It took many years before the Americans learned the name of the physicist who had played the same role in the development of the hydrogen bomb as Teller in the USA. His name was Andrei Sakharov; he was a theoretical physicist but had in 1950, together with other young, promising physicists, been summoned to the secret city Arzamas-16 to aid the older, distinguished physicist Igor Tamm in developing a superbomb. Sakharov received the Stalin Award in 1953 for his efforts and was named Hero of Socialist Labor.

The Castle Bravo hydrogen bomb detonation on March 1, 1954. It was the first in a series of American nuclear tests at the Bikini Atoll in the western Pacific.

The first 'proper' American hydrogen bomb, in a test codenamed Castle Bravo, was detonated on March 1, 1954 at 6:45 a.m. at the Bikini Atoll in the Marshall Islands in the Pacific. The liquid heavy hydrogen had been replaced with heavy hydrogen in a chemical compound that was solid at ordinary temperatures. The explosive force of the bomb surpassed all expectations, measuring close to 15 megatons TNT, which was more than double the experts' calculations.[164] But the American joy at this record was soon overshadowed by the news of a drama that was playing out approximately 130 kilometers from the detonation site. Here, a Japanese fishing boat, *Lucky Dragon No. 5*, was sailing with 23 fishermen on board, when they suddenly and unexpectedly saw a huge ball of fire to the west. It was as if the sun was rising both in the east and the west that day, said one of the fishermen. Soon after, radioactive ashes started to rain down over the boat, but the crew did not know what it was as they had not been warned of the test. The fishermen continued their work and only returned to harbor on March 14, long after they had started to get sick. They were immediately transferred to intensive care, and for some time they were the center of the attention of the world press. One of the fishermen died from the effects of the radiation, which contributed to the event becoming an eye-opener for people around the world.[165]

With the hydrogen bomb, both superpowers now were in a position to develop weapons with almost unlimited destructive force. At a press conference after the Castle Bravo test in March 1954, Lewis Strauss explained the new situation to the invited reporters:

> A: Well, the nature of an H-bomb ... is that, in effect, it can be made as large as you wish, as large as the military requirement demands, that is to say, an H-bomb can be made as large as – large enough to take out a city.
> (*A chorus of 'What?'*)
> To take out a city. To destroy a city.
> Q: How big a city?
> A: Any city.
> Q: Any city, New York?
> A: The metropolitan area, yes.[166]

Strauss's sober, almost impatient statement at the conference hardly contributed to alleviating the concern of a public that was only just beginning to understand the power of thermonuclear arms technology. With the hydrogen bomb, the destructive potential of nuclear weapons had reached an entirely new level. The superpowers, USA and the Soviet Union, were spearheading the development of the new technology, but the other great powers – the United Kingdom, and, subsequently, France and China – were also launching programs to ensure they had hydrogen bombs at their disposal. The hydrogen bomb was the topic of Churchill's last great speech to the British parliament in March 1954, shortly before a series of strokes put a stop to his active political career:

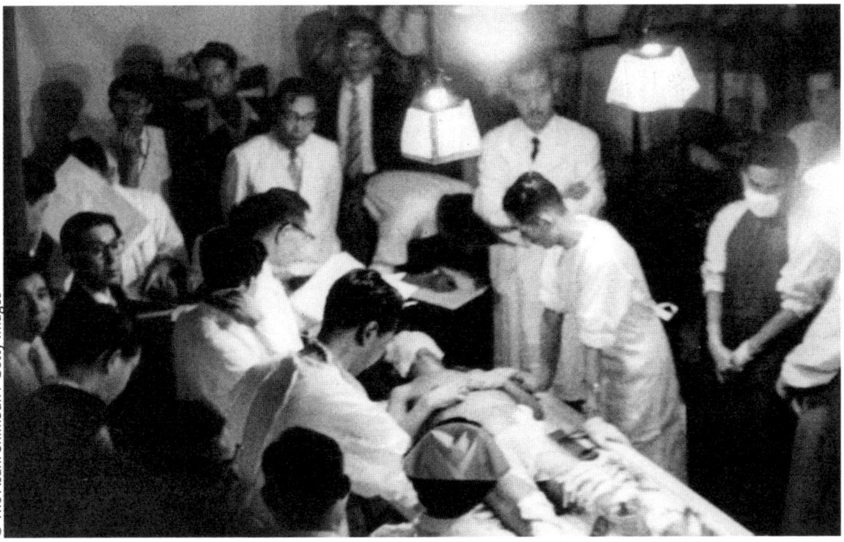

© The Asahi Shimbun / Getty Images

Aikichi Kuboyama, the radio operator on the fishing boat *Lucky Dragon*, died in a Japanese hospital on September 23, 1954 as a result of exposure to nuclear radiation from the American Castle Bravo hydrogen bomb test.

> Which way shall we turn to save our lives and the future of the world? It does not matter so much to old people; they are going soon away; but I find it poignant to look at youth in all its activity and ardour and, most of all, to little children playing their merry games, and wonder what would lie before them if God wearied of mankind.

Nevertheless, he maintained that the hydrogen bomb was a precondition for the survival of the United Kingdom because

> a curious paradox has emerged. Let me put it simply. After a certain point has been passed it may be said 'The worse things get, the better'. The broad effect of the latest developments is to spread almost indefinitely and at least to a vast extent the area of mortal danger. This should certainly increase the deterrent upon Soviet Russia by putting her enormous spaces and scattered population on an equality or near-equality of vulnerability with our small densely populated island and with Western Europe.[167]

At this point, the nuclear powers seemed to be deadlocked in a logic according to which ever-stronger weapons were viewed as the only viable guarantee to avoid destruction.

Two Minutes to Midnight (1953)

The recent American and Soviet hydrogen bomb tests in 1952 and 1953 caused such a stir that the *Bulletin of the Atomic Scientists* made last-minute changes to their September 1953 issue. The most dramatic and eye-catching change was that the Doomsday Clock on the cover had been set forward one minute, so that it now showed two minutes to midnight – the closest the clock had been to midnight until January 2020. The editors also used the back cover of the journal to direct an urgent appeal to the world's leaders, especially the leaders of the two superpowers. With a blurry mushroom cloud as backdrop, the central passages read:

> We live in an age of peril ...
> These words, directly from the lips of our national leaders, are addressed not only to Americans but to all nations. That we live in imminent danger, a tense world to erupt in flames of nuclear or thermonuclear warfare, that there will be 'no place to hide' for the great masses of civilized mankind – these are the torturous facts which compel our leaders to spell out for us the tragic nature of the times in which we live.

The editors stressed the deeply serious security situation, but also expressed a very tentative hope that the possibilities of peaceful use of nuclear energy might become a reality if the nuclear threats were addressed and managed properly:

> The hands of the clock on the *Bulletin's* cover now stand at two minutes to midnight. Not to terrify, certainly, but to warn and to awaken, the clock is intended to be symbolic. Wishing will not stop the clock. The *Bulletin* may be wrong. It may actually be one minute – perhaps seconds – to midnight. The specter of atomic perils hovers constantly near. Yet one thing is sure. The *Bulletin* will never experience a happier moment than the day it can settle back with the hands of the clock set at the beginning of a major new world era, already heralded by the marvelous prospects afforded by developments in the peaceful utilization of atomic energy.[168]

According to the *Bulletin*, the world was in an extremely precarious situation in September 1953. If the leaders of the two superpowers continued the nuclear armament by developing and deploying hydrogen bombs in their arsenals, the world would almost inevitably end in a global, nuclear apocalypse because the destructive potential of the hydrogen bomb was almost unlimited. While one nuclear bomb had proven powerful enough to destroy a city the size of Hiroshima, one hydrogen bomb could destroy huge cities such as New York and Moscow, as well as extensive surrounding areas. In that sense, the hydrogen bomb was a true gamechanger.

However, if the world leaders would think twice and focus on exploring nuclear energy for peaceful purposes instead, the world could become a better, more prosperous, and happier place, wrote the editor of the *Bulletin*. This sounded almost too good to be true, but nevertheless it was this message that the new American president, Dwight D. Eisenhower, tried to sell to the world only three months after the *Bulletin* had published its strongest ever appeal and warning to world leaders. There is no question that the president and his advisers were inspired by, among other, the *Bulletin* in formulating their message. Many nuclear physicists subscribed to the journal, which could also be found at more or less all American and Western European physics institutes, and it was precisely among nuclear physicists that Eisenhower recruited many of his advisers on nuclear issues.

Peaceful Atoms

On December 8, 1953, President Eisenhower gave a groundbreaking speech to the UN's General Assembly. Together with his advisers, he had spent the preceding months analyzing the dramatic development in nuclear arms technology after the Second World War. This development was ominous – not least from an American perspective. From having been in a comfortable situation in the first four years after the war, when the USA had a monopoly on nuclear weapons and counted on holding on to it for many years to come, they now had to face the fact that in 1953 there were no fewer than three states in possession of nuclear weapons: the USA, the Soviet Union and the United Kingdom. The latter had tested its first atomic bomb in 1952, while shortly afterwards both superpowers had tested hydrogen bombs with unfathomable destructive capacity. A lethal arms race had begun. Eisenhower did not believe that this fact should be kept from the public because it would only cause all the more fear when it finally came to light. Rather, he and his advisers held the view that the widespread nuclear fear constituted a threat to public morale in all Western states and to international support for US agendas. In order to secure the sympathy and trust of the population, it was important that fear should not be allowed to stand alone. Eisenhower therefore insisted that the well-prepared speech in the UN should also convey real hope for humanity.[169] The speech was named *Atoms for Peace*.

Eisenhower began by saying that if the USA were to be attacked with nuclear weapons, it would be capable of retaliating so effectively that the aggressor's country would be totally destroyed, and it would not hesitate to do so. However, obviously this was not an objective in itself. "To pause there would be to confirm the hopeless finality of a belief that two atomic colossi are doomed malevolently to eye each other indefinitely across a trembling world. To stop there would be to accept helplessly the probability of civilization destroyed." This was not how things ought to be. "My country's purpose is to help us to move out of the dark chamber of horrors into the light," Eisenhower continued. And the road to the promised land was "Atoms for Peace", i.e. developing nuclear energy for peaceful purposes. In that way the atom would become a symbol of hope for mankind instead of signaling fear and destruction.[170]

More specifically, Eisenhower proposed the establishment of a new UN organization called the International Atomic Energy Agency (IAEA) to manage the peaceful development of nuclear energy. Countries already in possession of a stock of enriched uranium or plutonium were to hand over part of it to the IAEA, and to prove that the USA was willing to take the lead, Eisenhower promised that they would donate an unspecified amount of enriched uranium to the new agency. Further, the proposal entailed that the IAEA should offer uranium fuel and information about peaceful use of it to member states that were willing to subject themselves to international control. In this way, the USA could prevent a number of countries from commencing nuclear energy development on their own, while exploiting its own head start to conquer a significant part of the expected large and lucrative world market for civilian nuclear reactors.

Eisenhower's speech prompted enthusiastic response across the Western world and some level of understanding east of the Iron Curtain. The ongoing nuclear race had increased the fear of nuclear weapons, and the peoples of East and West needed a message like *Atoms for Peace* to build hope for the future. At the same time, there were signs of tentative thawing in the relationship between East and West following the death of Soviet dictator Josef

Stalin in March 1953, which gave impetus to the American suggestion, and ensured the USA a clear propaganda victory in relation to the Soviet Union.[171] Many countries – industrialized as well as developing – announced their interest in receiving scientific and technological aid to start developing peaceful nuclear energy. But because the establishment of the IAEA dragged on, most of the countries that requested assistance for nuclear energy research ended up getting it by entering into bilateral agreements with one or several of the three nuclear powers: the USA, the Soviet Union and the United Kingdom, or with France, which was soon expected to become one.

"Our Friend the Atom"

The *Atoms for Peace* speech launched an ambitious campaign to win over people's hearts and minds in the global Cold War, which also had a strong cultural dimension in which the mass media played a central role. Propaganda was 'the fourth weapon' after the military, political and financial instruments of the Cold War. Eisenhower was strongly influenced by this mentality, and during his eight-year presidency he put great efforts into information and propaganda regarding the nuclear question. Historian Kenneth Osgood notes that "Atoms for Peace was quite possibly the largest single propaganda campaign ever conducted by the American government".[172]

In his speech to the UN's General Assembly, Eisenhower also suggested that a large nuclear energy conference be arranged for participants from across the world. The aim should be to share experiences with peaceful use of nuclear energy and discuss the future potential in the field. The conference took place in Geneva August 8-20, 1955, but in 1954, the head of the US Atomic Energy Commission, Lewis Strauss, had anticipated the event with his optimistic prediction that "Our children will enjoy in their homes electrical energy too cheap to meter".[173]

The conference in Geneva was attended by approximately 1,400 delegates and 3,400 associated experts from 70 countries. An army of reporters covered the event, which they were surprisingly unanimous in describing as a roaring success. The leading American newspaper *The New York Times* featured the Geneva Conference on its cover on 10 of the 12 days it lasted, and many other news media followed suit. The day after the opening of the conference, the world's newspapers already announced in headlines that the Nuclear Age was now a reality.

The many reports from Geneva portrayed nuclear energy as humanity's relief from global energy shortage. Readers were told that nuclear energy could unproblematically be used to produce electricity and soon also to power ships, planes and cars. Radioactive isotopes produced in nuclear reactors, the reports predicted, would have a vast impact in the future of biological research and would also find broad application in medicine and agriculture. It was as if any critical sense had been put aside for a time. It was as if all the gloomy thoughts prompted by the current military race between East and West were suppressed for some weeks or months by uncritical enthusiasm and expectations that soon proved impossible for the nuclear experts heralded as society's true heroes to meet. However, these issues were still in the future; for the time being, people who were still worried could find renewed faith in the future in chemist Heinz Haber's book *Our Friend the Atom*, published in the USA in 1957, with a preface by Walt Disney and featuring lavish illustrations by more than 20 artists from Walt Disney Productions. The book was published in many countries over the following years.[174]

In the book, Haber describes how the development of science from ancient times to the present is in fact a tale of increasing insight into the world of atoms: how the atom was discovered, how humans learned about its many strange secrets, how the power of the atom was unleashed, and finally how the atom will become our friend and servant. The artful narrative employs the figure of the serving genie in the *One Thousand and One Nights* tale, who has been captured in a lamp for ages but is released by an old, poor fisherman. As a token of gratitude, the fisherman is allowed three wishes that the genie promises to fulfil. However, the question is whether the fisherman is able to make wishes that will benefit himself and his family without harming others. This question remains unanswered in Haber's book as this is where he leaves behind the old tale at the expense of the new.

Just as the fisherman released the powerful genie from the lamp, writes Haber, humanity has released the atomic spirit from the lamp with the invention of the nuclear bomb. It has the power to destroy everything for us, but we can also make it fulfil three wishes ensuring that humankind will live happily ever after. But which wishes are wise? The author answers this question on our behalf: The first wish is "Power", which the atomic spirit can provide in the form of inexhaustible, peaceful atoms; the second is "Food and health", which it can provide in the form of radiation to preserve food and treat diseases; the third is "Peace", which we can also achieve if we choose the atomic spirit as our friend forever.[175]

At present, we can conclude that the atomic spirit has only delivered on a fraction of the first two wishes. And as far as the third wish goes, the best we can say is that we have at least so far avoided wars in which the atomic spirit has had a chance to prove that it is in fact capable of obliterating the world.

The Opponents' Manifesto

Not everyone was convinced that Eisenhower's optimistic *Atoms for Peace* initiative would result in a peaceful, happy world. Among the skeptics was the famous author and philosopher Bertrand Russell, by then 82 years old.[176] On February 11, 1955, he wrote an open letter to Albert Einstein in the USA in which he expressed his nightmarish concerns about the ongoing arms race between East and West and his regret that nothing had been done so far to put an end to it. "I think that eminent men of science ought to do something to bring home to the public and Governments that disaster may occur," he wrote, continuing that it was no good to try to reach an agreement that banned hydrogen bombs because "such an agreement would not be considered binding after the war has broken out". Instead, Russell wanted to emphasize that "thermonuclear war may very well mean the extinction of life on this planet", which should be enough to make the individual citizen understand that the arms race is very much his or her concern.[177]

Einstein agreed with Russell's views and promised to support an initiative that would hopefully have an impact on the general public and the political leaders around the world. However, he had little opportunity to contribute to the writing of what would become known as the Einstein-Russell Manifesto, as he became sick and died on April 13, 1955. Still, Einstein's moral support meant so much to Russell that he only accepted slight changes to the original version of the manifesto, which Einstein had approved, although some of the other signatories – not least the communist physicist Frédéric Joliot-Curie – tried to convince him to make changes.

The finished manifesto, in addition to Russell and Einstein, was signed by eight prominent physicists from six different countries: Percy Bridgman from the USA, Cecil Powell and Joseph Rotblat from the United Kingdom, Hideki Yukawa from Japan, Frédéric Joliot-Curie from France, Max Born from Germany and Leopold Infeld from Poland. It was also signed by American geneticist Hermann Muller, but no Soviet or Chinese scientists.[178] Bertrand Russell presented the manifesto to the public on July 9, 1955 in connection with a big, well-attended conference at Caxton Hall, London. There was massive press attendance when the conference chairman, physicist Joseph Rotblat, gave the stage to Bertrand Russell, who talked about the genesis of the manifesto and went over its main points. The introduction reads as follows:

> In the tragic situation which confronts humanity, we feel that scientists should appraise the perils that have arisen as a result of the development of weapons of mass destruction, and to discuss a resolution in the spirit of the appended draft. We are speaking on this occasion, not as members of this or that nation, continent or creed, but as human beings, members of the species Man whose continued existence is in doubt. The world is full of conflicts; and, overshadowing all minor conflicts, the titanic struggle between Communism and anti-Communism. Almost everybody who is politically conscious has strong feelings about one or more of these issues; but we want you, if you can, to set aside such feelings and consider yourselves only as members of a biological species which has had a remarkable history, and whose disappearance none of us can desire.[179]

This was followed by an account of the recent development in the nuclear arms field, the scientists pointing out once more that just as one nuclear bomb could destroy a small city such as Hiroshima, one hydrogen bomb had the capacity to destroy metropolises like London, New York and Moscow. But even terrible destruction like this was something the world could come to terms with. "But we now know, especially since the Bikini tests, that nuclear bombs can gradually spread destruction over a very much wider area than had been supposed."

The manifesto continued by stressing that it was possible at the time to produce a hydrogen bomb that was 2,500 times more powerful than the nuclear bomb that destroyed Hiroshima. If such a bomb were to explode near the ground or under water, it would send radioactive particles high up in the atmosphere, from which "they would sink gradually and reach the surface of the earth in the form of a deadly dust or rain." It was exactly this type of dust that had infected the Japanese fishermen and their haul aboard the *Lucky Dragon*. "No one knows how widely such lethal radio-active particles might be diffused, but the best authorities are unanimous in saying that a war

Bertrand Russell and his wife Edith Russell spearheading an anti-nuclear protest march in London on August 6, 1961.

with H-bombs might quite possibly put an end to the human race." And it would not happen so that everyone died a sudden, merciful death; that would only happen for a small minority, while the majority would die slowly and painfully.

The manifesto thus addressed the increasing concern about radioactive fallout. The fallout issues conveyed a feeling that the entire humanity had been unwillingly dragged into a global experiment characterized by high unpredictability – or even ignorance – in terms of the extent and long-term effects of fallout.[180]

The manifesto ended with the optimistic prediction that humankind had the option of choosing a path on which nuclear energy was only used for peaceful purposes, bringing about "continual progress in happiness, knowledge and wisdom". On the other hand, if humankind were unable to leave behind mutual hostility and suspicion, it would probably mean mankind's "universal death". Russell and his fellow signatories finally compelled the Congress to support a resolution urging governments all over the world to acknowledge "that their purpose cannot be fulfilled by a world war, and we urge them, consequently, to find peaceful means for the settlement of all matters of dispute between them".[181]

The conference in London, and especially the Einstein-Russell Manifesto, received positive press coverage in much of the mainstream media. The *Bulletin of the Atomic Scientists* also covered the event intensively, and the manifesto became the starting point of one of the most successful peace initiatives ever: the Pugwash Conference on Science and World Affairs. Russell's idea behind the conference was to invite leading scientists from East and West to profound discussions of the problems connected to the use of nuclear energy for military and civilian purposes. The first attempts to organize the meeting came to nothing because Russell feared that his initiative was being taken over by the communist-dominated organization World Federation of Scientific Workers, which would cause a loss of legitimacy among governments in the West and most scientists in the Western democracies. However, he managed to engage his friend, physicist Joseph Rotblat, as a central figure in the group, and the efficient Rotblat arranged that the secretariat was placed at his own institute at Cambridge University so that he could steer the development. Despite the challenges, Russell and Rotblat's initiative led to a meeting that took place on July 6–10, 1957 in the small Canadian town of Pugwash. The organizers chose this remote location because a wealthy industrial magnate by the name of Cyrus Eaton, an enthusiastic backer of the ideas in the Russell-Einstein Manifesto, offered to pay the expenses for transport and lodging for most of the participants if the meeting was held at the conference center he had built in Pugwash, Nova Scotia.[182]

The meeting included 22 academics, 16 of whom were physicists, from countries including the USA, the Soviet Union, the United Kingdom, Australia, Japan and Austria. Several of the participants had previously appeared as experts in connection with years of futile negotiations on nuclear test bans and arms reduction in the UN. They had often experienced these negotiations as exercises in futility, but in Pugwash for once they had the opportunity to delve into issues such as the dangers of nuclear energy, nuclear arms control and the social responsibility of scientists. Afterward, they were surprisingly unanimous in stating that the meeting had been very productive because they had not had to discuss politics, and had not constantly been disturbed by sensationalist reporters. There was also a general consensus among the participants that the meeting should be followed up by a series of meetings or conferences based on the same format as the meeting in Pugwash. This was taken seriously: ever since, Pugwash conferences have been held at different locations around the world.[183] Some have been more successful than others, but it is a clear proof of the collective significance of the meetings that the Pugwash Organization and Joseph Rotblat, who was 87 at the time, shared the Nobel Peace Prize in 1995 "for their efforts to diminish the part played by nuclear arms in international politics, and in the longer run, to eliminate such arms".[184]

The First Popular Anti-nuclear Movements

The first American nuclear tests after the Second World War, and especially the hydrogen bomb tests at the Bikini Atoll, prompted both fascination and fear in the populations of the Western world. The fascination at the huge release of energy during a nuclear explosion was further stimulated by popular magazines that reveled in images of spectacular mushroom clouds and photos of beautiful young women wearing diminutive bathing suits. The women were called 'sex bombs', and the two-piece bathing suits were immediately named 'Bikinis'.[185]

However, the name Bikini also evoked fear because the *Lucky Dragon* affair was irrefutable proof that a hydrogen bomb can have grave consequences more than a hundred kilometers from the detonation site. This is because any test of nuclear or hydrogen bombs on or above the surface of the Earth creates a cloud of radioactive dust that – due to the generation of heat – is sent high up in the stratosphere from where strong winds can blow it far and wide. With one series after the other of atmospheric nuclear tests in both East and West, scientists could conclude that the fallout of radioactive isotopes from the tests – especially strontium-90, caesium-137 and iodine-131, which tend to lodge themselves into bones, muscles and the thyroid gland – were continually on the increase. People across the world were thus involuntarily exposed to additional radiation apart from the natural radiation from the environment.

The knowledge of these processes and their consequences grew gradually, which caused increased concern in the populations that had already come to know and fear the consequences of nuclear war. Since 1945, American and Japanese doctors and experts in radiation had monitored how the survivors from Hiroshima and Nagasaki were coping in terms of their health compared to a control group. By the middle of the 1950s, these researchers published material demonstrating that the survivors of the nuclear attacks (in Japanese they are called *hibakusha*) who had been within five kilometers of the center of the explosion had significant excess mortality due to leukemia, compared to a corresponding group of people from the same area of Japan who had not been exposed to radiation. More specifically, there were 10–15 cases of leukemia per 100,000 per year in the group close to the explosion compared to 2–3 in the control group.[186] A large-scale American-Japanese research project, Radiation Effects Research Foundation (RERF), has followed the survivors from the two cities ever since and came to similar conclusions: five times as many cases of leukemia and almost double the number of cancerous diseases in other organs. RERF has not yet been able to demonstrate genetic damage among the survivors, but that does not mean we can rule it out. Perhaps it is just not severe enough to be statistically significant.[187]

In the years following the *Lucky Dragon* incident, popular movements against nuclear weapons began to appear in one country after the other. Understandably, the protests began in Japan, but from there they spread to most countries in the Western world. In West Germany, the best-known organization was called Kampf dem Atomtod (*Fight nuclear death*). The leaders of the organization focused from its foundation in 1958 on agitating for a nuclear-free zone in Central Europe, and polls showed that it had backing from a sizeable part of the voting population. Most Germans were against nuclear weapons being placed in West Germany, which was what the USA was doing at the time. However, when the German Social Democrats (SPD), from the fall of 1958, decided to back the conservative Christian Democratic CDU/CSU-government's positive attitude toward nuclear weapons on German soil, as long as they were under American control, support for the movement against nuclear weapons waned. The SPD's sudden change of mind was a result of the Soviet Union's neutralization of the Hungarian uprising in 1956, and Nikita Khrushchev threatening in the fall of 1958 to hand over control of the access roads to West Berlin to the German Democratic Republic (DDR) if the Western powers refused to withdraw their troops from West Berlin.[188]

In the United Kingdom, a new and successful form of protest saw the light of day in 1958 when the Campaign for Nuclear Disarmament (CND) movement arranged a four-day march attended by a few thousand people. The 80-kilometer march started at Trafalgar Square in London and ended at the research center in Aldermaston, where the British nuclear weapons were developed. In subsequent years the route was reversed, so the march began at Aldermaston and ended at Trafalgar Square. The number of participants grew over the years, and British police estimates that no fewer than 100,000 people took part on the last day in 1960. Obviously, the organizers took this as a huge sign of success, not least because the media covered the march intensively, communicating the movement's messages to the entire British population.[189] The marches in the United Kingdom inspired similar initiatives against nuclear armament many other places in the Western world.

Apart from the specific demands in the individual countries, marchers everywhere wanted a ban on atmospheric nuclear tests because the radioactive fallout could be traced all over the planet, and they feared that within a relatively short time this would increase the incidence of various forms of cancer and cause genetic damage that would not show until the following generations. This demand evoked so much response in the general population, in the press, and among many politicians that in fact it did lead to a temporary nuclear test ban in the years 1958–61, which was joined by the USA, the United Kingdom and the Soviet Union. After that, tests were recommenced for a period of two years during which the Soviets detonated the hitherto most powerful hydrogen bomb – 50 megatons – on the island of Novaya Zemlya in the Arctic on October 30, 1961.

In 1963, the three nuclear powers finally entered into a permanent agreement, the Partial Nuclear Test Ban Treaty (PTBT), which obliged all signatories to refrain from testing nuclear weapons in the atmosphere and under water. Subterranean tests were exempted, partly because it was difficult at the time to distinguish the tremor from such tests from minor earthquakes. Nevertheless, many grassroot movements saw PTBT as proof that massive popular pressure can create political results – also at the international level.[190]

The reason the anti-nuclear movements' fight to achieve a nuclear test ban lasted so long was that – apart from the mutual suspicion among leading politicians in the East and the West that the opponent would try to cheat – influential weapon developers from both sides of the Iron Curtain wanted freedom to develop even more effective and lethal nuclear weapons than the ones that already existed: a process that, by the nature of things, is never-ending. One of the leading opponents of a nuclear test ban was Edward Teller, the man who was known in the USA as the father of the hydrogen bomb and one of the strongest voices in the successful attempt to remove Oppenheimer from any influence on American nuclear policy in the 1950s.

When Teller, who was director of the big Lawrence Livermore nuclear weapons lab in California at the end of the 1950s, predicted that atmospheric nuclear tests would soon be banned, he devised a plan to bypass this by promoting a project based on a non-military use of nuclear bombs. The project was called Project Chariot and entailed the establishment of a large artificial harbor at Cape Thompson in Alaska, created by blasting away millions of tons of rock by means of six hydrogen bombs placed at strategic spots in the area. This would be a simple matter, believed Teller, who at a conference joked that "if your mountain is not in the right place, drop us a postcard".

Teller promised that Alaska would come to experience a flourishing business community with prosperity both for the Caucasians in the capital of Fairbanks and the local Inuit people who lived traditionally from hunting and fishing. And in 1958 and the following years, funding did indeed come pouring in to the University of Alaska in Fairbanks, whose management was extremely positive toward Project Chariot.[191]

The project was intended as a form of showcase and pilot for far bigger plans that Teller and his peers had up their sleeves. One of them entailed blasting away entire mountains so that the shipping through the Panama Canal could avoid the many locks that make the traffic slow and expensive. Another idea was to establish an alternative Suez Canal that would go from Aqua Bay in the Red Sea through the Negev Desert to the Mediterranean – i.e., entirely through Israeli territory. The projects never came to anything, nor did Project Chariot. Independent geologists and biologists raised serious concerns about the purportedly minimal environmental impact of the projects, and, in the case of Project Chariot, the local Inuit people feared that their livelihood would be destroyed, based as it was on fish and seals. Eventually, opposition grew to the extent that Project Chariot was shelved in 1962.[192]

Difficult International Control

The Atoms for Peace program paved the way for peaceful utilization of nuclear energy. In 1959, the USA had thus already made bilateral agreements with 42 countries, promising assistance with building nuclear test facilities, while the corresponding number for the Soviet Union ten years later was 28.[193] In Denmark, the first decisive step in this direction was made when the government in 1955 set up a nuclear energy commission (AEK) with Niels Bohr as head. Thanks to technical and financial assistance from the USA and the United Kingdom in the years 1956–62, AEK built the nuclear test station Risø, which was equipped with three test reactors – two shipped from the USA and one from the United Kingdom. The British reactor's intensive neutron flux in particular was used to test the durability of various reactor components in the Danish reactor experts' unsuccessful attempts to develop two Danish nuclear reactors under the names DOR and DK-400.[194]

Regardless of whether nuclear reactors or fuel elements came from the USA, the United Kingdom or the Soviet Union, it was almost inevitably part of the contract between donor and recipient country that the recipient was obliged to use the nuclear facilities only for peaceful purposes and return the spent fuel to the donor. However, the USA's intention was, as time went by, to entrust the necessary control of the donor countries to the UN organization that Eisenhower had in mind – the International Atomic Energy Agency. In the beginning, the Soviet Union was against the idea, the Soviet Minister of Foreign Affairs Molotov arguing to his American colleague Dulles that the Atoms for Peace suggestion would result in potential stocks of highly enriched U-235 or Pu-239 in many countries, and that it would become very difficult – if not impossible – to prevent the proliferation of nuclear weapons. Dulles was skeptical in the beginning, but American nuclear experts convinced him that Molotov was right. The American government's reply to the Russian objection therefore was that "ways could be found"![195]

After the successful Geneva Conference in 1955, the Russians changed their attitude, and they engaged in the work of writing a draft for the statutes of the IAEA. A group of 12 countries that were either nuclear powers, had significant knowledge in the field, or had large deposits of uranium, which was still considered a rare element, worked on the statutes from the fall of 1955. These countries were: the USA, the Soviet Union, the United Kingdom,

Canada, France, Belgium, Portugal, Czechoslovakia, Brazil, India, Australia and South Africa.[196]

In April 1956 – surprisingly quickly – the 12 countries managed to reach an agreement on a draft for the statutes that were sent to all UN member countries. With minor changes, the statutes were passed at a founding conference including 82 member countries on October 23, 1956. The IAEA moved into interim headquarters in Vienna, which became the home of the IAEA immediately after the first general assembly of the IAEA had taken place there on October 1–23, 1957.

The IAEA's primary tasks can be summarized as follows:

- To initiate research in, and development of, practical utilization of nuclear energy for peaceful purposes;
- to deliver materials, services, and equipment for research, development, and practical utilization of nuclear energy with particular consideration of the needs of underdeveloped countries;
- to promote the exchange of scientific and technical information in the field;
- to establish safeguards to ensure that nuclear assistance or deliveries for which the IAEA were not responsible were not used for military purposes;
- to develop safety standards for the entire nuclear field.

A central aspect of the statutes was thus that the IAEA was to promote utilization of nuclear energy while at the same time ensuring that it was not used for military purposes. While it was easy to reach an agreement on the IAEA's objective, the structuring of the organization proved to be challenging until the members finally agreed on a system consisting of three layers: a Director General at the top, elected for a four-year period by a powerful Board of Governors consisting of 23 members, 12 of whom were permanent or semipermanent members while the rest of the board was elected via a cleverly devised system ensuring that all the different regions of the world were represented. At the bottom of the hierarchy was a General Conference to which all member countries could send a delegate. This organizational structure – just like the content of the statutes – broadly still exists today.

Because the USA had played such a central role in the formation of the IAEA and paid a large part of the costs of the preliminary meetings, the Americans insisted that the first Director General be American. The Soviet

Union and the other countries in the Eastern Bloc were not keen on the idea but eventually accepted Sterling Cole, former member of the American Congress and head of its nuclear energy committee, as Director General on the condition that Pavel Winkler from Czechoslovakia was made chairman of the board.

Sterling Cole's time as Director General proved to be anything but a walk in the park. This was first and foremost because the thawing relationship between the two superpowers in the years after Stalin's death in March 1953 had been plunged back into an ice age during and after the Suez and Hungary crises in October/November 1956. The Sputnik shock in October 1957, the Berlin Crisis in 1958–61, the failed American invasion of the Bay of Pigs in Cuba in 1961, and the building of the Berlin Wall in 1961 all became symbols of a series of agonizing defeats for American foreign policy during Eisenhower's second presidency and the beginning of Kennedy's. Unsurprisingly, these defeats and the simultaneous successes of the Soviet Union affected the USA's standing in various international organizations, including the IAEA. In this period, it proved almost impossible to find solutions to concrete problems because all meetings in the IAEA tended to deteriorate into political discussions between East and West, while the neutral countries were trying to navigate this political minefield. The respected UN Vice Secretary General, Dr Ralph Bunche, who represented the UN at several meetings in the IAEA during Sterling Cole's reign, commented at one of these occasions "that the Cold War raged more violently in the IAEA Board than in the UN itself".[197]

As a result of the tense atmosphere in the organization, Eisenhower's original plan of using the IAEA as a bank for fissile material, mainly U-235 and Pu-239, which the organization could lend out and monitor closely, never came to anything. In the end, it was only the USA that offered to make a large amount of enriched uranium available to the IAEA, and therefore the idea was quickly dropped. The USA grew impatient with the IAEA in this period, and instead of leaving the safety tasks to the organization in connection with the bilateral nuclear agreements that the USA made with a vast number of "friendly countries", the American nuclear authorities preferred to handle the tasks themselves.

In 1961, Sterling Cole, who was not known for his diplomatic skills, was replaced on the post by the Swede Sigvard Eklund, who was a highly experienced diplomat and also came from a neutral country.[198] The member countries soon acknowledged that he was the right person for the job, and when the relationship between the superpowers slowly started to improve after the Cuba Crisis in 1962, the collaboration in the IAEA also improved. The young organization thus came to play an important role in the development of the NPT (Nuclear Non-Proliferation Treaty) in 1968. The nuclear weapon states that have signed this treaty, which entered into force in 1970, are obliged to work toward phasing out their nuclear weapons, while non-nuclear weapon states that are party to it are obliged never to acquire such weapons. The IAEA's ardent effort to make the treaty a reality caused Professor Lawrence Scheinman, a recognized American disarmament expert, to emphasize that the NPT "gave IAEA a tremendous boost, making it the keystone of the non-proliferation regime, and catapulting it from the periphery to the centre of the international political system".[199]

Atoms against Peace

Even though Atoms for Peace attracted much attention from the mid-1950s, the nuclear armament race between the East and the West continued unabated. The race started, as mentioned, when the Soviet Union detonated its first nuclear bomb in 1949, and was intensified by the outbreak of the Korean War in 1950, ratcheting up further when the two superpowers almost simultaneously introduced hydrogen bombs into their weapons arsenal. The race was a competition both to produce a wide range of small and large nuclear weapons, and to develop delivery systems in the form of new aircrafts, submarines and missiles.

All through the 1950s, American nuclear armament proceeded in accordance with President Eisenhower's New Look strategy. Eisenhower had taken the oath on January 20, 1953, while the Korean War was still raging. He had won the election by promising peace in Korea and a cut in the huge military budget the war had necessitated in the USA. He could not ensure peace in Korea by dealing a decisive blow to the enemy, but the war was becoming so unpopular that the population was willing to settle for less: a ceasefire. This was settled via negotiation, coming into effect on July 27, 1953. Even though serious confrontations between North and South Korea have been brewing many times since, the ceasefire has more or less held since then, although it has never been replaced by a proper peace agreement.

An American caricature from the fall of 1962, reflecting the artist's view of the global situation during the Cuban Missile Crisis in October of that year.

President Eisenhower and his secretary of state, John Foster Dulles, were determined that the USA should never again be lured into a conventional war such as the Korean War, seeing that it had been immensely expensive in terms of the number of dead and wounded soldiers, as well as money that could have been spent on productive purposes. Therefore, they developed the New Look strategy which gave lower priority to the large, expensive American army. Instead, it prioritized the navy and, especially, the air force so that these forces at any time would be able to launch an obliterating nuclear attack on any enemy that dared to attack the USA or one of its allies. It was also part of the strategy that the USA might retaliate against communist aggression anywhere in the world "at places and with means of [our] own choosing", meaning nuclear weapons, even if the aggressor had not used such weapons. "Asymmetrical response", "massive retaliation" and "assured destruction" were the awe-inspiring terms the originators of the New Look strategy used to explain its purpose.[200]

The fact that military investments mainly went into nuclear weapons, which were cheap considering their immense efficiency measured by potential victims per bomb, ensured that Eisenhower throughout his presidency could keep his promise of reducing the defense budget. While the USA's total defense budget in 1953 made up 13.5 percent of the GDP, in the following years until 1960 it amounted to 9–10 percent.[201] However, the Democrats criticized Eisenhower harshly in his second presidency for having reacted too leniently to the Soviet challenge, considering that the Soviets did the same as the Americans: that is to say, they increased their nuclear arms production and development of means of delivery equipment – missiles as well as bombers – to such a degree that by the end of the 1950s, a myth took hold in the USA concerning a 'missile gap'. This myth, which has subsequently been revealed as a successful attempt by the American defense to secure additional funding, was propagated after the Soviet Union in October 1957 launched Sputnik, the world's first artificial satellite. According to the myth, the Soviet Union had surpassed the USA in regard to the number of operational missiles, but it is evident from a conversation between Secretary of State Dulles and the British ambassador on July 21, 1958, that the American government was well aware that the claim did not hold water. At this point, a serious crisis had broken out in the Middle East – a crisis that had prompted the USA to land 14,000 American soldiers in Lebanon. During the conversation, Dulles seemed almost "to lament that, although the current crisis in [the] Middle East might present a unique opportunity to achieve a definitive military victory over the Soviet Union, no one in Washington would dare to take advantage of it: According to Dulles, the Soviets were deeply concerned because they feared that US steps in the Middle East could leave them with the choice between accepting a major defeat in the region or facing the risk of a major nuclear war."[202]

Every year, the Soviet Union expanded its arsenal of nuclear weapons, and the impressive slogan of the New Look strategy, "assured destruction", was changed to the – in American ears far more ominous – "mutual assured destruction" (MAD). MAD became the commonly used term in the 1960s.[203] In this very tense atmosphere, the USA's three military forces each worked ardently on developing their weapons of deterrence using nuclear-armed, long-range missiles: the air force's Minuteman, which was installed in concrete silos in central USA, the navy's Polaris in nuclear submarines, and the army's Iceworm on railroads inside the ice cap in North Greenland. While the former two systems did in fact become operational and were deployed in the US military arsenal at the beginning of the 1960s, the latter system was scrapped for technical, financial and political reasons in 1962 before it was finished.[204]

It was becoming glaringly obvious that both superpowers were capable of destroying each other – and the entire world too – if the situation escalated to nuclear war. The New Look strategy had to be abandoned or at least modified to avoid the American president being forced to initiate massive retaliation regardless of the extent of potential provocations. The modified strategy, which was called the New New Look, and which Eisenhower founded in the last years of his presidency, became part of the bedrock of the American foreign policy when his successor, John F. Kennedy, took over the presidency on January 20, 1961.

The Kennedy administration's more cautious strategy was called Flexible Response, and proved its worth during the Cuban Missile Crisis in October 1962, when the world was probably closer to nuclear apocalypse than ever before or since. After the USA, in mid-October 1962, had found irrefutable proof that the Soviet Union was installing nuclear-armed medium-range missiles in Cuba, the Joint Chiefs of Staff (a body of the most senior personnel in the Department of Defense), recommended that the USA bomb these installations and occupy Cuba. But Kennedy turned down their advice because he was convinced it would lead to a third world war. Instead, he launched a naval blockade of Cuba, which allowed both parties time to think the situation through. This paved the way for an agreement in which Soviet Premier Khrushchev promised to withdraw all missiles and nuclear weapons from Cuba in return for the USA pledging not to attack Cuba and to remove some obsolete medium-range missiles from bases in Turkey. The world could breathe a sigh of relief.[205]

Dr. Strangelove – a Masterful Parody of the Nuclear Race

It was not only in geopolitics that nuclear weapons became a dominant theme. The Cold War arms race between East and West inspired many books, films and other popular cultural media of the era. There is no representation more masterful than Stanley Kubrick's *Dr. Strangelove* in terms of originality and impact. The film was originally scheduled to premiere on December 12, 1963, but because of the murder of President Kennedy on November 22, 1963, the premiere was postponed until the end of January 1964. When it finally premiered, the film was launched under the long and cryptic title *Dr. Strangelove or: How I Learned to Stop Worrying and Love the Bomb.* The film became a great success in the USA and many other countries.

Kubrick's film, which was immediately celebrated as a masterpiece, builds on the novel *Red Alert* by Peter George. But whereas the book is a rather conventional thriller revolving around the balance of terror between East and West, Kubrick was aiming for something different. He had from the outset intended to follow the book fairly closely, but during the writing of the script, it struck him that the story of the nuclear race was so absurd that no cinema audience would believe the film if he tried to present the case objectively. Instead, he went for the absurd humor that is the central element in the film – humor that draws parallels between the drivers behind the nuclear race and male sexuality.

The plot begins with US Air Force General Jack D. Ripper (played by Sterling Hayden) being convinced that the communists have secretly initiated a plan to make men in the West impotent by adding fluoride to the drinking water. In his state of growing madness, he orders his airbase to be hermetically sealed off from the surroundings and deploys his 34 B-52 bombers, each equipped with two hydrogen bombs in the megaton class, to attack their designated targets in the Soviet Union. The American president, Merkin Muffley (played by Peter Sellers), cannot call back the bombers without a specific codeword that he does not know. He therefore summons his crisis staff, including the war-crazy General Turgidson (played by George C. Scott) and the German-born scientific adviser Dr. Strangelove, aka Dr. Merkwürdigliebe (also played by Peter Sellers) to a crisis meeting at the War Room in Washington. He also summons the Soviet ambassador who, following a phone conversation with the intoxicated Soviet Premier, informs him that if the Soviet Union is attacked with nuclear weapons, it will automatically trigger a series of hydrogen bombs that together make up an apocalyptic cocktail and will eradicate all life on the planet. The doomsday device has been installed in all secrecy because the Russians could no longer afford to keep up with the USA in the armament race, but the existence of this ultimate weapon of deterrence was not planned to be revealed until the following week at a party congress.

The film takes place at three different locations, frequently cutting between them. The first is Burpelson Air Force Base, where General Ripper is together with a visiting English captain named Mandrake (also played by Sellers). When Mandrake realizes what is about to happen, he tries in vain to winkle the code word out of Ripper, but instead eventually guesses from scribblings on his desk that it is one of the six possible combinations of the beginning letters (POE) in two sentences "Purity Of Essence" and "Peace On Earth", which General Ripper keeps returning to before committing suicide.

The second location is the cabin of one of the bombers that are on their way to the target in the Soviet Union. Major Kong (played by Slim Pickens in great John Wayne cowboy style) is commander on the aircraft and thus responsible for dropping the bombs at the right location. He does so conscientiously, even though he has to release one of the bombs manually because of a faulty release mechanism and ends up leaving the aircraft riding the bomb as if it was a rodeo bull – or perhaps rather a giant phallus – swinging his cowboy hat in ecstatic triumph.

The third location is the War Room. Here, the plot threads are gathered as the discussion rages. The president receives a call with the code word from Mandrake but eventually has to face the fact that the disaster cannot be prevented because one of the 34 bombers (Major Kong's) does not respond to his order to abort the mission. It is in this final act that Dr. Strangelove finally shows up. Sitting in a wheelchair and with a prosthetic right arm that tends to raise itself in a Nazi salute, he dominates the scene completely. Extremely intelligent, charming, but also entirely devoid of empathy, he quickly calculates that when the doomsday device explodes, it will be approximately 100 days until the surface of the Earth is uninhabitable. But this does not make him despondent – on the contrary. He immediately develops a vision of a new, golden future for the elite: having a computer select perhaps 100,000 people, ten times as many women as men. These selected individuals will then seek cover in deep but pleasantly equipped mine shafts that radiation cannot reach. Obviously, the women need to be young and attractive, while the men will primarily be selected from the upper levels of government and the military. This selected population will, according to Dr. Strangelove's calculation, be able to propagate and achieve a GDP equivalent to the current level within only twenty years and thus be ready to reinhabit Earth when it is safe to leave the mine shafts again.

The film ends to the sound of Vera Lynn's famous Second World War song, "We'll meet again, don't know where, don't know when", while one mushroom cloud after the other appears and vanishes as testimony to the detonation of the doomsday device and the farce that has turned into chilling reality.

Dr. Strangelove is obviously a parody – exaggerating the characteristics of a phenomenon to achieve a satirical effect – but the absurdity of the escalating arms race between the superpowers was very real. In the period 1953–55 alone, the American defense doubled its nuclear weapons arsenal, and many of the new weapons were hydrogen bombs. In these two years, the destructive force of the arsenals was multiplied by 40, from 73 megatons TNT – equivalent to 4,867 Hiroshima bombs – to 2,880 megatons TNT – equivalent to 192,000 Hiroshima bombs. Measured in megatons, this number dropped significantly in the 1960s as the largest bombs were replaced by smaller but more accurate types. Still, the capacity was based on scenarios entailing the use of nuclear weapons against all cities in the Soviet Union with more than 25,000 inhabitants. The first American Single Integrated Operation Plan (SIOP) from 1961 on how a nuclear war was to be fought also included the bombing of China, even if the country had not taken active part in the aggression against the USA.[206] The military's own estimate was that 285 million people would be killed in the Soviet Union and China alone if the Americans went through with an attack. This astronomical figure by far surpassed the casualties of all wars in the first half of the 20th century. Still, it was a conservative estimate as it only included those who would be killed by the explosions themselves and not those who would be killed by firestorms, radioactive fallout and other secondary effects.[207] On top of this comes the fact that both Washington and Moscow knew that even the most full-blown attack would never fully prevent the enemy from returning fire with nuclear weapons, be it with bombers, submarines, land-based missiles or low-flying cruise missiles. Ultimately, they could only fall back on the threat of 'mutual assured destruction'.

There were several factors behind this situation. Historian Richard Rhodes summarizes these in his book *Arsenals of Folly*, including factors such as struggles for prestige and funds between army, navy and air force, which led to armament in all sections of the American defense, as well as the fact that on both sides of the Iron Curtain, there was a consistent tendency to view nuclear weapons on a par with conventional weapons. The ruins of Hiroshima and Nagasaki resembled the ruins of the conventional air raids on Tokyo and Dresden, and the casualties were comparable. What was overlooked or ignored was the new possibility of deploying thousands of aircrafts, each with a nuclear bomb, or, alternatively, fewer aircraft armed with thermonuclear megabombs. Physicists Enrico Fermi and Isidor Rabi – one conservative, the other liberal, both Nobel laureates with experience in developing nuclear weapons – pointed out as early as 1949 in a report developed for the American nuclear energy commission that a hydrogen bomb "goes far beyond any military objective and enters the range of very great natural catastrophes. By its very nature it cannot be confined to a military objective but becomes a weapon which in practical effect is almost one of genocide."[208] The distinction between civilian and military targets – which had already been blurred during the Second World War – would become meaningless in a war fought with powerful nuclear weapons. Nevertheless, the strategic plans still operated with the distinction.

The realization that the very nature of war was changing came slowly. The above factors were to some extent linked to the specific historical period, but it was – and still remains – an additional factor that the nature of atoms makes it relatively inexpensive to produce great forces of destruction. Rhodes writes:

> It was quite simply the fundamental physical fact of nuclear energy that such energy is relatively cheap to generate and essentially unlimited. Nuclear warheads cost the United States about $250,000 each; less than a fighter-bomber, less than a missile, less than a tank. Each one can destroy a city and kill hundreds of thousands of people. 'You can't have this kind of war,' Eisenhower concluded. 'There just aren't enough bulldozers to scrape the bodies off the streets.' It followed, and follows, that there is no military solution to safety in the nuclear age: There are only political solutions. As the Danish physicist and philosopher Niels Bohr summarized the dilemma succinctly for a friend in 1948, 'We are in an entirely new situation that cannot be resolved by war.'[209]

Dr. Strangelove is an artistically elegant pillorying of the absurdity of military solutions and their insufficiency in the nuclear race. Behind the satire, the film is also a very somber piece, as the director did not leave cinema-goers with much faith that either politicians or scientists would be able to provide the necessary solutions.

Fortunately, Kubrick's prediction only partly came true. The second half of the Cold War may have been marked by accelerating armament and proliferation of nuclear weapons, but also by the most comprehensive disarmament agreements in the field of nuclear weapons thus far. As we will see in the next chapter, the scientists played a central role in this contradictory development.

CHAPTER 5

The Role of Science During the Cold War

Physicists Between Science and Politics

The Manhattan Project and the ensuing nuclear arms race created an entirely new situation for science and – especially – many academically trained physicists. They found themselves in a world of big corporations, interdisciplinarity and project-based research in large teams. Contrary to classical academic research, the organizational reality included almost unlimited resources, but correspondingly tight deadlines. Scientists entered into close collaboration with commercial, military and political stakeholders, and nuclear physics and technology became *big science* – a framework for science that science historian Jon Agar characterizes with the five Ms: Money, Machines, Men, Military, Media. Large budgets, huge instruments and machines, thousands of people organized hierarchically, massive military attention and extensive propaganda were central components of the new conditions.[210]

As described in Chapter 4, leading scientists had different attitudes toward the new situation. Arthur Compton's ideas of science as a universal human activity built on the conception that science – despite the rapid growth in government-funded *big science* projects – incarnated a particular ethos that gave hope for peaceful coexistence. This stance in some respects echoed the idealistic internationalism expressed in Niels Bohr's open letter to the UN. However, Bohr's point of departure was different in that his internationalism was influenced by his experiences of scientific work in the war-torn Europe of the interbellum period. In Bohr's view, scientific internationalism required pervasive openness and an ongoing diplomatic effort driven by the scientists themselves.[211]

The American scientists who engaged actively in the struggle against the nuclear arms race during the Cold War did so in different ways. Some refused point blank to have anything to do with nuclear weapons. Nobel laureate chemist Linus Pauling belonged to this group. In 1958, he published the book

No more war! and argued in newspapers, radio and TV that any development and test of nuclear weapons was a crime against the moral principles of science and against the next generations who would have to live with the health-related consequences.[212] Pauling also acted as expert witness in legal proceedings taken by individuals or their next of kin in connection with illness or death that could be linked to radioactive leaks from the American nuclear arms production or tests. His scientific activism was grassroots-based and directed at the public sphere. Other scientists tried to achieve more direct influence by moving closer to political power and the government offices. These nuclear weapons opponents had to accept the fact that their efforts took place within a framework dictated by the president, military and state, which in practice entailed an acceptance of the deterrence rationale and thus of nuclear weapons in some form being part of the long-term defense strategy. Within this framework, they could try to influence the development in a slightly less militarized direction – i.e., by advocating test bans, increased international efforts to prevent the proliferation of nuclear weapons, and limited funding to develop new offensive and defensive nuclear arms technologies. In practice, this meant that scientists with an anti-nuclear agenda in many cases had a limited role as technical experts in the security state – a problem that was acknowledged among nuclear arms opponents but nevertheless was difficult to circumvent.[213]

In any case, there were great differences in comparison with, e.g., Edward Teller, the father of the hydrogen bomb. In his own time, Teller was criticized for being a cynic, although he perceived himself as a proponent of a form of realism that in his view was the best safeguard against war: "I don't like weapons. I would like to have peace. But for peace we need weapons and I do not think my views are distorted. I believe I am contributing to a peaceful world," as he wrote in 1954.[214] Teller also warned against what he perceived as his colleagues' misconceived moralism, and he maintained that political decisions lay with the democratically elected leaders and should remain there. Nevertheless, this did not keep Teller from being a very active political scientist throughout his career, which lasted all the way until the end of the Cold War. Teller was inherently suspicious of communists, which in his autobiography he attributed to his experiences as a child in Hungary, where communist troops led by Béla Kun had invaded the country, closed down his father's legal practice, and billeted soldiers in his childhood home.[215] Teller had influential allies in the Republican Party and was a driving force in the large Lawrence Livermore arms lab that was founded in California in 1952. His supporters included physicists and nuclear arms expert Albert Latter and Lewis Strauss, who became head of the United States Atomic Energy Commission (AEC) in 1954. The group fought several test bans successfully (see the mention of Project Chariot in Chapter 4), non-proliferation agreements, and other disarmament initiatives, arguing that the Soviet Union would not respect the agreements anyway, and their only effect would therefore be to set back the USA in the arms race.

Historians have demonstrated that Teller, on several occasions, in his political work sowed doubts about technical matters despite knowing that his claims were unfounded.[216] For instance, he claimed that the radioactive fallout from nuclear tests did not exceed the cosmic background radiation people were exposed to in big cities, and that it could even be healthy for an organism to be exposed to some level of human-produced radiation. More successfully, Teller and his supporters in the 1950s and 1960s managed to question whether the Americans would be able to discover any Soviet transgressions of test bans against subterranean test explosions without manned measuring stations in Soviet territory. Later during the Cold War, Teller played a similar role in relation to the so-called Star Wars Program that the Reagan administration was planning as a space-based defense against attacking missiles. Unlike most other scientific experts, Teller described the project as both realistic and effective.[217] Contrary to the liberal Pauling and other left-wing scientists, Teller and his peers spoke the language of the Cold War state, and there is no doubt that their effort contributed to dragging out various disarmament agreements and making them more toothless. Overall, scientists in the West often appeared divided in regard to technical questions that were vital to their nation, which made it possible or convenient for the politicians to ignore scientists they did not agree with or disliked.

It is difficult to assess how widespread Teller's views were, but science historian Steven Shapin point out that it is first and foremost the idealists and doubters among the scientists who have received attention among historians. Shapin also notes that the American Cold War state never had any problem finding skilled scientific staff for Los Alamos, Livermore or other centers for nuclear arms production. There are several possible explanations to this. Shapin concludes:

> Several of the more influential, if less oratorically gifted, atomic scientists enthusiastically endorsed weapons work, either because they agreed with Teller that scientists had no moral right to refuse their democratically elected government's legitimate wishes, because they found the work interesting, or because they considered the nation under imminent threat from Godless communism, against which winning the arms race was the only conceivable defense.[218]

The overall picture is further complicated by the fact that many scientists changed their views over the course of their life and career. We generally know less about what Soviet scientists thought and believed, but Andrei Sakharov is an exception. He achieved status as a hero in his homeland for his crucial contribution to equipping "the Soviet man" with the hydrogen bomb. In his large autobiography, Sakharov wrote that the major reason why he and his physicist colleagues worked so hard on the project at the beginning of the 1950s was that they viewed this work as necessary to ensure that no enemy would attack the Soviet Union. He continues:

> I understood, of course, the terrifying, inhuman nature of the weapons we were building [...]. Over the course of time we devised or borrowed a number of principles, including strategic parity and nuclear deterrence, which even now seem to justify intellectually, at least to some extent, the creation of thermonuclear weapons and our role in the process. Our initial zeal, however, was inspired more by emotion than by intellect. The monstrous destructive force, the scale of our enterprise and the price paid for it by our poor, hungry, war-torn country, the casualties resulting from the neglect of safety standards and the use of forced labor in our mining and manufacturing activities, all these things inflamed our sense of drama and inspired us to make a maximum effort so that the sacrifice – which we accepted as inevitable – would not be in vain.[219]

However, during the 1970s, Sakharov became an increasingly outspoken critic of the Soviet system. He was ordered to keep away from political involvement, but when in 1980 he took the liberty of openly protesting against the Soviet war in Afghanistan, it became too much for the Soviet authorities. He was taken to court and sentenced to live in internal exile in the city of Gorky (present-day Nizhny Novgorod) some four hundred kilometers east of Moscow. Gorky was a 'closed city' meaning that it had military installations and was off-limits to foreigners. The exile lasted until 1986. Sakharov passed the time writing his memoirs, although he had to start over several times because the Soviet authorities confiscated the material when they found it. In 1986, the new president Mikhail Gorbachev finally allowed Sakharov to return to Moscow.

Sakharov was awarded the Nobel Peace Prize in 1975, but the Soviet leaders reacted with fury, and refused Sakharov permission to travel to Oslo for the award ceremony. His wife, Jelena Bonner, received it on his behalf in Oslo on December 10. At that point, he had long since made the transition from a central figure in the development of the Soviet hydrogen bomb to an icon of the international peace movement on both sides of the Iron Curtain. He died in 1989, and the following year his memoirs were published in a number of Western countries.[220] It took many years before permission was given to publish them in Russian.

Oppenheimer's story shares certain similarities with Sakharov's. As described earlier, Oppenheimer felt guilty after the Manhattan Project, and the father of the atomic bomb was left to watch the dramatic nuclear race of the 1950s from the sidelines. As a publicly known scientist who was on countless government-appointed boards regarding nuclear questions and still allowed himself to have communist friends and voice left-wing views, he was bound to eventually become a person of interest to US intelligence. In fact, he had been so for some time, but General Groves's unconditional support had ensured that he had peace to work, until 1950 when he directly opposed the development of the American hydrogen bomb. This opposition, and a growing FBI file with his name on the cover, meant that he was summoned to a meeting in 1954 with an AEC security board that had been set up by one of his enemies, the powerful head of the AEC, Lewis Strauss. After lengthy proceedings, which we can follow in detail in a document named the *J. Robert Oppenheimer Personnel Hearings Transcripts*,[221] Oppenheimer was deprived of all access to confidential documents and membership of the many committees in which he had thus far played a central role. This was an immense fall from grace, which many of his friends and colleagues bemoaned, while it was celebrated on the opposite side of the political spectrum, not least by the many who were influenced by the infamous Senator Joseph McCarthy, Staff Director of the House Committee on Un-American Activities, who saw communists and traitors everywhere.

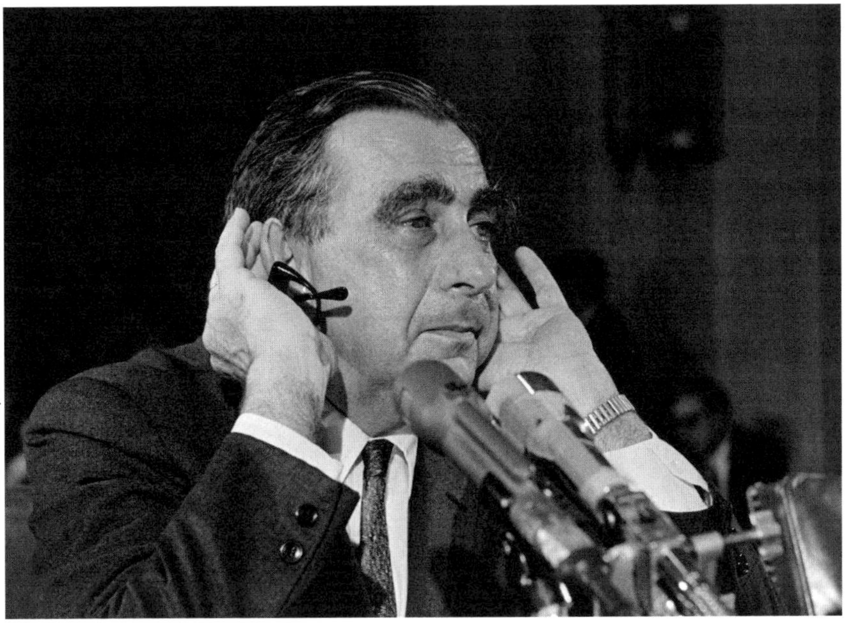
© Uncredited / AP / Ritzau Scanpix

The ever-flamboyant nuclear physicist Edward Teller testifies before the Senate Foreign Relations Committee on the Non-Proliferation Treaty (NPT), in Washington D.C., on July 17, 1968.

After that, Oppenheimer continued to work as Director of the Institute of Advanced Studies at Princeton University, where he maintained the board's backing even though Lewis Strauss tried several times to have him removed. Oppenheimer refrained from getting involved in security policy issues, but was pleased to see how popular American opinion slowly swung toward his side. In Europe, he had been a hero all along who had been treated unfairly by the shrill American anti-communists. In the last year of John F. Kennedy's presidency, he received the prestigious Enrico Fermi Award as proof that his time as a pariah in the American political establishment was over for good. However, he did not receive the prize money of $50,000 until December 4, 1963, after Kennedy had been murdered. It was therefore his successor, Lyndon B. Johnson, who presented it in the White House. Strauss, who had not buried his old hatred of Oppenheimer, boycotted the ceremony, whereas Teller showed up and even shook hands with the man of the hour.[222]

On the occasion of the 20th anniversary of the bombings of the Japanese cities of Hiroshima and Nagasaki, the TV company NBC produced a documentary titled *The Decision to Use the Atomic Bomb*. A number of the people who had contributed to the decision took part, and obviously Oppenheimer was one of them. He talked about the Trinity Test and how, immediately after the explosion, he had recited the *Bhagavad Ghita* passage, "Now I am become Death, the Destroyer of Worlds". When the interviewer asked him his opinion about Senator Robert Kennedy's recent proposal that President Johnson initiate negotiations with the Soviet Union on stopping the proliferation of nuclear weapons, he replied crisply: "It's twenty years too late ... it should have been done the day after Trinity."[223]

In February 1966, Oppenheimer, who had been a heavy smoker all his adult life, was diagnosed with throat cancer. Even though he was immediately taken into medical care, his health quickly deteriorated and he died on February 18, 1967. At that time, Bohr, Einstein and most of the other iconic physicists who had established the theoretical foundation of nuclear physics and technology had also passed away. Due to their personalities and history, they had enjoyed a special impact and influence while they lived – also in the public sphere. The impact of this generation naturally waned as time passed, but some milestones remained, among them the Pugwash Conferences. The most lasting and direct mark on the disarmament efforts was made by Polish-British physicist Joseph Rotblat. Rotblat took part in the Manhattan Project, which he – as the only scientist – left at the end of 1944 when it became clear that the nuclear bomb was no longer needed to defeat Nazi Germany. As mentioned in Chapter 4, he was one of the signatories of the Einstein-Russell Manifesto and served for a number of years as secretary of the Pugwash Organization. He subsequently continued his ardent pursuit of disarmament until his death in 2005, 50 years after the manifesto had been written.[224] His work remained highly relevant for many decades, which may have been characterized by several disarmament agreements, but also – and ironically even more so – by ever-growing nuclear arsenals in an increasing number of nuclear arms-producing countries.

A Stop to the Proliferation of Nuclear Weapons

The Cuban Missile Crisis in 1962 had made the leaders of the two superpowers, the USA and the Soviet Union, more aware that in the future they had to avoid direct confrontation, which might get out of hand and result in a devastating nuclear war. Nevertheless, both countries continued to expand their arsenals of nuclear weapons and delivery systems such as aircrafts,

Andrei Sakharov first became famous in the Soviet Union as the father of the Soviet hydrogen bomb, but subsequently in the West as a critic of the Soviet government. He was awarded the Nobel Peace Prize in 1975.

nuclear submarines and missiles. In 2010, the two prominent nuclear experts Robert S. Norris and Hans M. Kristensen published in the *Bulletin of Atomic Scientists* an overview of nuclear weapons that the nine nuclear powers had each had at their disposal since they became nuclear weapon states. The list estimates that the USA in 1960 had more than 18,638 nuclear warheads and no fewer than 26,008 in 1970, while the equivalent numbers for the Soviet Union were, respectively, 1,605 and 11,643.[225]

The arsenals of both countries were still growing, even though almost all experts agreed that the existing arsenals were more than enough to kill all humans on Earth several times over if it came to an ultimate nuclear conflict between the two superpowers. Over the course of the 1960s, both countries developed still more precise IRBMs (intermediate-range ballistic missiles) and ICBMs (intercontinental ballistic missiles), which could convey nuclear weapons and hit predetermined targets with ever-growing precision. The political-military establishments of both countries were dominated by the MAD mentality and they were ready at any given time to launch an eradicating retaliatory attack – also called a *second strike* – against the enemy, if the enemy had started the conflict with a nuclear *first strike*.

The ongoing nuclear armament in the two superpowers was far from the only thing threatening world peace. For example, it was alarming that the number of countries with nuclear weapons at their disposal continued to grow. As mentioned, the United Kingdom became a nuclear weapon state as early as 1952, and France followed suit in 1960 when the country tested its first nuclear bomb in the Algerian desert. From an American point of view, it was obviously a greater cause of concern when Mao's China joined the nuclear weapons club in 1964, and the CIA was in possession of intelligence indicating that the number of nuclear states might grow to 15–25 by the middle of the 1970s.[226] It is in light of this we should consider Oppenheimer's comment from 1965, "It should have been done the day after Trinity", expressing his frustration that the USA had not done anything drastic to diminish the risk of nuclear proliferation.

Oppenheimer did not live to see the result, but in the years 1964–68 negotiations did in fact take place in the UN for a treaty regarding the preventing of proliferation of nuclear weapons and the associated technologies beyond the current nuclear club of five countries – aka the five great powers that were also permanent members of the powerful UN Security Council. However, most UN countries agreed that the treaty must not prevent but rather encourage collaboration on the peaceful utilization of nuclear energy. The two aims were difficult – not to say nearly impossible – to achieve at the same time because a nuclear project can both provide power for consumers in a peaceful country and produce plutonium for the military industry of that same country. As a consequence, the negotiations were complicated and protracted.

In the mid-1960s, the USA and the Soviet Union therefore agreed to boost the formerly under-prioritized IAEA with technical knowledge and nuclear experts, which would allow this neutral UN organization to manage the monitoring of nuclear facilities in all the countries that joined the planned non-proliferation treaty. This marked the return to one of the cornerstones of Eisenhower's Atoms for Peace plan from December 1953. Obviously, it was crucial for the realization of the treaty that the IAEA be willing to take on this difficult task, which it did in September 1967. The final version of the Treaty on the Non-Proliferation of Nuclear Weapons (NPT) was ready to be signed on July 1, 1968. By March 5, 1970, the USA, the Soviet Union, the United Kingdom and 40 other UN member states had ratified the treaty – the number required for the treaty to come into force.[227]

From Seven to Ten Minutes to Midnight (the 1960s)

After the Doomsday Clock had been set forward all the way to two minutes to midnight in September 1953, following the hydrogen bomb tests in both the USA and the Soviet Union, the minute hand had stayed in this position until January 1960. The editors of the *Bulletin* could easily have found reasons to set the time even closer to midnight as the years after 1953 saw several upsetting events including the Suez and Hungary crises, the new Berlin crisis triggered by Khrushchev in 1958, and the French colonial wars in Vietnam and Algeria. Nevertheless, the editors had decided that the clock should not react to a single event unless they were convinced that this event would have long-term consequences for the entire world and decisively shift the global strategic security situation. The journal has generally stuck to this approach ever since. As British researcher of international security at Cambridge University Simon Beard has pointed out in a discussion of the Doomsday Clock, most single political events have appeared as fluctuations in the geopolitical system and diplomacy. The strategic security situation, on the other hand, is more about which weapons might be used in the conflicts and which institutions and means are available to stop the conflicts. The problem of strong weapons and weak institutions, states Beard, "are not created by individual global crises, they are systemic in nature and this is what the Doomsday Clock is trying to measure."[228]

It was January 1960 before the editors moved the minute hand again – this time five minutes back – so that it showed the same time as in 1947: seven minutes to midnight. But why? In his editorial, Eugene Rabinowitch admitted that the adjustment happened "with a hesitant hand" because the reasons he stated were not very concrete. He did mention the establishment of the IAEA and Pugwash as good news, even though the two institutions did not have many positive results to show for themselves thus far. He also mentioned that the USA, the Soviet Union and numerous other countries had collaborated on achieving scientific results at the International Geophysical Year 1957–58 and promised each other that the Antarctic would be exempt from superpower conflicts. In summary, he concluded that the movement of the minute hand expressed the *Bulletin*'s "belief that a new cohesive force has entered the interplay of forces shaping the fate of mankind, and is making the future of man a little less foreboding".[229]

After this, the Doomsday Clock remained set until the October 1963 issue of the *Bulletin*, when the editors once again set the minute hand back – this time to 11 minutes to midnight. This may seem surprising considering that, during the Cuban Missile Crisis from October 16 to 28, 1962, the world had probably never been closer to nuclear war. But firstly, the crisis had been so brief that the monthly journal had not had time to react, and secondly, the brief crisis was soon replaced by significant relaxation of the tension between the two superpowers. Rabinowitch also justified the new setting in that both countries had shortly before agreed to a partial cessation of nuclear testing that entailed a ban on atmospheric and underwater tests. Underground tests were still excluded, among other reasons because it had been brought into question whether their seismological effect could decisively be distinguished from the effects of an earthquake. The editor-in-chief of the *Bulletin* emphasized that the test ban was not equivalent to nuclear disarmament – quite the opposite. The arms race between the USA and Soviet Union was still raging, France had become a nuclear weapon state in 1960, and China seemed to be heading in the same direction. But at least the nuclear test ban would reduce the widespread fear of radioactive fallout and the potential consequences in the form of cancer and genetic damage. This fear had, as mentioned, grown since atmospheric nuclear tests began shortly after the end of the Second World War.[230]

The next adjustment of the Doomsday Clock was made in January 1968, but this time it went the other way, so that the clock once more showed seven minutes to midnight. This was an indication of the editors' frustration that the promise of further détente between the two superpowers, heralded by the nuclear test ban in 1963, had not been met in the intervening five years.[231] According to Rabinowitch, the superpowers seemed again to be returning to the old nationalist positions where spectacular – and extremely expensive – space projects, not least the moon landings, demanded resources that could have been used for other purposes. The facts that the USA under Lyndon B. Johnson had gotten itself into another hopeless war in Vietnam, and that China was now in possession of nuclear weapons, were also steps in the wrong direction.

Fortunately, the minute hand would be set back again the following year, so that the Doomsday Clock from April 1969 showed 10 minutes to midnight. In the editorial of the *Bulletin*, Rabinowitch argued that it was because the American Congress – despite the war in Vietnam – had ratified the UN's Non-Proliferation Treaty the previous year. This was promising and worth celebrating, even though Rabinowitch also stressed that the superpowers had only taken the first tentative step toward true détente:

> They must proceed without delay to the next one – the dismantling, gradually, of their own oversize military establishments. Otherwise, the hope raised by the treaty will prove futile. The treaty has cleared the way for future, more substantial steps on mankind's painful path towards security in a nuclear age. This security cannot be based on a competitive rush towards more and more apocalyptic weapon systems. Its only realistic foundation lies in all nations recognizing that their political and ideological self-interests must be subordinated in the future to mankind's common concern with survival.[232]

According to the *Bulletin*, humankind could thus step into the 1970s with a bit more optimism than 10–15 years previously, when everything had looked hopeless after the development of the hydrogen bomb, its deployment in the arsenals of both superpowers, and the countless atmospheric nuclear tests that alarmingly quickly polluted the atmosphere across the globe.

Bilateral Disarmament Agreements

All through the 1960s and 1970s, the number of nuclear weapons kept rising. The medium-sized nuclear weapon states of the United Kingdom, France and China gradually built arsenals of a few hundred weapons each – a level at which they remained for decades. The superpowers – the USA and the Soviet Union – on the other hand, had reached 23,000 and 30,000 nuclear weapons respectively by 1980.[233] It was no less alarming that the number of intercontinental missiles (ICBMs) and medium-range missiles (IRBMs) was also on the rise, and that each type of missile was gradually replaced by more advanced types that could carry several nuclear weapons and even guide each of them to separate targets. These advanced missiles, called MIRVs (MIRV = Multiple Independently Targetable Reentry Vehicle), in reality rendered all planned anti-missile defenses, called ABMs (Anti-Ballistic Missile), obsolete before they were even made operational. It was as if humanity found itself on a train whose drivers constantly increased the speed even though everyone knew that it was approaching an abyss at a dizzying speed.

Maybe this prospect started to dawn on the leaders of the two superpowers by the end of the 1960s. In any case, they realized that it would be a clever move to try to contain this insane – and insanely expensive – nuclear arms race, which did not make anyone safer. In 1967, the USA and the Soviet Union began bilateral negotiations aimed at limiting the number of strategic delivery systems and anti-ballistic missiles for each country. Starting in 1969, these talks alternated between Helsinki and Vienna and concerned the capping of the number of strategic means of delivery as well as the number of anti-ballistic missiles for each of the two countries. The negotiations led to two agreements in 1972. First, the ABM Treaty, which limited each side to no more than 100 anti-ballistic missiles to protect its capital and one of its ICBM sites. Second, the SALT I Treaty (Strategic Arms Limitation Treaty), which set a cap on the number of deployed long-range missiles – whether intercontinental ballistic missiles (ICBMs) or submarine-launched ballistic missiles (SLBMs) – at the levels they were at in 1972. Short-range, tactical missiles with nuclear warheads were not covered in the agreement. Both agreements were signed in Moscow on May 26, 1972 by US President Richard Nixon and USSR General Secretary Leonid Brezhnev.[234]

SALT I from 1972 was by no means an ambitious disarmament agreement, so later that same year the USA and the Soviet Union commenced a new series of bilateral negotiations about stricter limits for delivery vehicles. These negotiations were, logically, called SALT II and stretched over a seven-year period. On June 18, 1979, the SALT II negotiations were concluded, resulting in an agreement to limit the number of ICBM silos, SLBM launch tubes and heavy bombers for both the United States and the Soviet Union to 2,250 each by January 1, 1981. Additionally, the number of ICBMs equipped with MIRVs and having a range greater than 5,500 kilometers was capped at 1,320. The SALT II Treaty was signed in Vienna by American President Jimmy Carter and Soviet General Secretary Leonid Brezhnev. Missiles with shorter range, including submarine-launched nuclear-armed cruise missiles and tactical nuclear-armed missiles with a range up to 500 kilometers, were not included in the agreement.[235]

A Temporary Détente

The SALT II agreement was never ratified by the American senate because of the Soviet Union's decision in December 1979 to send troops into the neighboring country of Afghanistan to aid the communist president's fight against Muslim rebels who were trying to seize power. However, the Western countries did not accept this, resulting in the Cold War, which had been relatively mild since the Cuba Crisis in 1962, turning relations between East and West ice-cold again by the beginning of the 1980s.

But the situation in Afghanistan was not the only reason for the deteriorating relationship between East and West. In the years after 1976, the Soviet Union had started to replace its outdated medium-range missiles in Eastern Europe with new SS-20 missiles equipped with three individually guided nuclear weapon modules, each with an explosive force of approximately 150 kilotons of TNT. The range was just under the SALT II limit of 5,500 kilometers, which meant that they could hit any target in Western Europe. Further, they were mobile because each missile was mounted on a large cross-country vehicle that could be hidden in a forest or other hiding place and made operational in a matter of minutes. The NATO countries perceived this as a breach of SALT II, which led to NATO's double decision, passed on December 12, 1979 in Brussels. This entailed that the Soviet Union would be offered an agreement on a drastic limitation of medium-range missiles on European soil with a range between 500 and 5,500 kilometers; if they refused, 572 new American Pershing II medium-range missiles and cruise missiles would be installed in West Germany, Italy, the Netherlands, Belgium and the United Kingdom from December 1983.[236]

In the summer of 1981, the USA and the Soviet Union, both with ageing presidents at the helm – the newly-elected, 70-year-old Ronald Reagan and the seasoned, 75-year-old Leonid Brezhnev, initiated negotiations on high-tech missile limits. However, these negotiations, which became known under the acronym START (Strategic Arms Reduction Treaty) turned out to be fruitless and came to an end when the Soviet negotiators left the table as the first Pershing II missiles arrived in Western Europe, ready to be installed.[237]

The negotiations recommenced three years later, but much had happened in the meantime. In the West – starting with the Freeze Movement in the United States – there were large-scale protests against the ongoing arms race in general and the new medium-range missiles in particular.[238] In the East, the authorities were more or less free from that sort of disturbance because protests and other demonstrations against the governments' politics were not tolerated. On the other hand, it was becoming increasingly clear – not least to the populations in the Eastern Bloc – that the Moscow-dictated, communist regimes simply did not work. Everything seemed stagnated, no decisions could be made locally, and life expectancy and the standard of living were not improving, and were even dropping in several Eastern European countries, including the Soviet Union itself. Only the military was usually provided for. There was a dire need for renewal. But even though the Soviet Union had three different presidents during the 1980s, this renewal only happened during the last presidency – when it was already too late.

When Brezhnev died at the age of 76 in 1982, he was replaced by the former KGB boss Yuri Andropov, but even though he was only 62 at his accession, he only lasted a little over a year before he was laid to rest. His successor was another elderly gentleman, 73-year-old Konstantin Chernenko, but he too died less than a year after taking office, in March 1985. Now, the Soviet elite finally agreed to appoint a young, dynamic politician to lead the colossal country. His name was Mikhail Gorbachev and he was only 54 years old when on March 12, 1985, he was appointed General Secretary of the Soviet Communist Party. He did not waste any time and immediately began to implement his ambitious plans of *glasnost* (openness) and *perestroika* (renewal) in Soviet society. His plans soon proved unattainable because the communist party reigned supreme and had people at all government levels who would do anything to prevent Gorbachev from succeeding.

All this, however, is beyond the scope of this book, and we will focus on the nuclear disarmament that was taking place in the years Gorbachev held power in the Soviet Union. In the beginning, the Western leaders were rather skeptical toward the new, strong man in the Kremlin. But even Reagan, who concurrently with the START negotiations challenged the Soviet Union by launching a new, extremely expensive arms race in space – the so-called Strategic Defense Initiative (SDI), also known as the Star Wars Program – was soon convinced that Gorbachev was serious about disarmament. The Soviet Union simply could not afford to raise the military budget any further; on the contrary, it had to be cut if Gorbachev was to have any hope of ensuring the increased standard of living that his people dreamed of. Experts have estimated that while the USA in the mid-80s spent approximately 5 percent of its GDP on defense, the corresponding number for the Gorbachev Soviet Union was at least 20 percent – but measured in absolute terms, the USA was still investing far more because the US GDP was much bigger than that of the Soviet Union.[239]

The negotiations for the START technical disarmament agreements therefore went faster than this type of negotiation usually did. On October 11, 1986, Reagan and Gorbachev met face to face in the Icelandic capital of Reykjavik to confirm their agreement on a part of START, the so-called

Intermediate-Range Nuclear Forces (INF) Treaty, regarding the removal of all land-based American and Soviet medium-range missiles from Europe. The two heads of state came a long way but not all the way to the finishing line because Reagan was not willing to give up the American Star Wars Project, which Gorbachev had as a precondition for accepting the INF. However, on February 28, 1987, Gorbachev stated that he was prepared to separate the negotiations about the Star Wars Project from INF. The reason for this about-turn was probably that prominent American politicians and scientists had convinced Gorbachev that if an INF agreement came into place, Reagan would have no chance of ensuring the necessary funding for the Star Wars Project in the American Congress. Furthermore, most Russian and American experts – Teller, unsurprisingly, being an exception – agreed that the complicated Star Wars defense system would never come to work as intended. The idea that the USA would be able to develop space weapons capable of shooting down all missiles and other objects that a potential attacker were to launch against the USA in a surprise attack was a castle in the air according to the experts. The attacker would always manage to make a proportion of their nuclear armed missiles hit their targets, and at a fraction of the resources it would cost to build the Star Wars defense system.[240]

Meetings in Moscow in February 1987 between high-ranking scientists from the USA and the Soviet Union appear to have been crucial. The meetings were attended by two American nuclear weapon experts, Jeremy Stone and Frank von Hippel, who met with two Soviet experts at the same level, Evgeny Velikhov and Andrei Sakharov.[241] Their discussions focused on the opportunity to utilize nuclear arms reductions as a means to undermine American Congress members' support for the Star Wars Project. The Soviet intelligence service KGB recorded the meeting on a tape that was sent to Gorbachev on February 23. Three days later, the Soviet Politburo gave its consent to Gorbachev continuing the negotiations with Reagan on the INF Treaty without demanding that the USA give up the Star Wars Project.[242]

Gorbachev's offer in February 1987 kickstarted the INF negotiations again. A number of smaller and larger technical problems needed to be solved via direct negotiations between disarmament experts from the two countries. They managed this task successfully, and on December 8, 1987, Reagan and Gorbachev signed the INF Treaty at a formal event in Washington. The treaty included the destruction of 843 American medium-range missiles and 1,842 Soviet ones before June 1, 1991. This took place under mutual control, ensuring the hitherto most substantial nuclear arms reduction treaty between East and West. It was settled only half a year before the collapse of the Soviet Union, so Mikhail Gorbachev missed the opportunity to continue the disarmament process and renewal of Soviet society that he had worked so hard for during his five-year reign. Before he had to step down and leave the post as Russian president to Boris Yeltsin in June 1991, he did manage to land an expanded disarmament agreement, called START I, with the new American president, George Bush, who had succeeded Reagan in January 1989. This bilateral agreement set an upper limit of 1,600 ICBMs armed with a maximum of 6,000 nuclear weapons for each of the two superpowers.[243] It is worth noting that the American Congress in 1990 had already made significant cuts to the funding for the Star Wars Project, as Jeremy Stone and Frank von Hippel had predicted three years earlier.[244]

The political détente did not stop here. After the collapse of the Soviet Union in December 1991, there was much concern, especially in the USA, about what Secretary of State James Baker called "loose nukes" in Russia and the other former Soviet republics with nuclear weapons, namely Ukraine, Belarus and Kazakhstan. Some American nuclear experts had foreseen the problem, however, and one of these, Tom Neff, who headed the MIT's International Energy Studies Program, came up with a very bright idea: the USA should offer to buy most of the highly enriched uranium (HEU), which would become 'waste', when thousands of warheads were to be dismantled as a consequence of the NPT and SALT II agreements. Or rather, the USA should buy from Russia low enriched uranium fuel (LEU) for its approximately one hundred civilian American light water reactors – the LEU (3–4 percent U-235) being obtained by mixing 1 kg of Russian HEU (90 percent U-235) from the dismantled uranium bombs with approximately 30 kg of natural uranium (0.7 percent U-235). Neff's idea was a win-win deal for the USA as well as Russia, because it would keep the extremely dangerous Russian HEU off the black market, and it would boost the Russian economy at a time of desperate need due to the low global market prices of oil and natural gas – Russia's main source of income – during most of the 1990s. According to Frank von Hippel, the USA ended up buying 500 tons of HEU from Russia, enough to build 20,000 warheads of the size of *Little Boy* that destroyed Hiroshima in August 1945.[245]

Russia – the largest of the former Soviet Republics – took over responsibility for all the Soviet nuclear weapons in 1994. But Russia was in a fragile

© National Archives and Records Administration / Wikimedia Commons

Ronald Reagan and Mikhail Gorbachev signing the INF Treaty in Washington on December 8, 1987.

position, and even though there were people in the Kremlin fighting tooth and nail against it, President Yeltsin managed to force through large cuts in the defense budget. Among various consequences, this made way for the START II agreement, which he co-signed with President Bush on January 3, 1993, regarding further reductions in the number of operational strategic nuclear weapons for each party down to between 3,000 and 3,500. "A major step towards fulfilling mankind's century-old dream of disarmament," said Yeltsin to the world press on the occasion.[246] However, this optimism proved unrealistic. Although the U.S. Congress ratified the agreement in 1996 and the Russian parliament, the Duma, followed suit in 2000, the momentum for nuclear disarmament was lost. This became evident soon after the September 11, 2001 terrorist attacks on Washington and New York. President George W. Bush informed Russia that the United States would withdraw from the ABM Treaty, arguing that the treaty would prevent the U.S. from deploying anti-ballistic missile systems to defend against 'rogue states', wherever they might be. The new Russian president, Vladimir Putin, responded by withdrawing Russia from the ABM Treaty in 2002, signaling the end of the era of the détente between the two nations.[247] The United States and Russia did agree to further reductions in their nuclear arsenals, with the SORT Treaty in 2002 and the New START Treaty in 2010. Under these agreements, each country reduced its stockpile of operational strategic nuclear warheads to around 1,900 and 1,550, respectively. However, the key point is that even these reduced numbers are more than sufficient to cause an apocalyptic disaster for humanity, especially since the nuclear powers have never ceased improving the quality of their warheads and the accuracy of their delivery systems.

Scientific Activism Against Nuclear Weapons

There is hardly any doubt that without the *Zeitgeist* that the powerful international movement against nuclear weapons contributed to in the 1980s, also among people who would not dream of marching in large protests, Reagan and Gorbachev would not have been able to dislodge themselves from the habitual mindset that dictated ever-stronger defense and more effective nuclear weapons. Testimony to this can be found in the letter that Gorbachev, after signing the INF Treaty, sent to Bernard Lown, leader of the organization International Physicians for the Prevention of Nuclear War. In the letter, Gorbachev thanked Lown "for your enormous contribution to preventing nuclear war. Without it and other powerful anti-nuclear initiatives, it is unlikely that this treaty would have come about."[248] Matthew Evangelista's book *Unarmed Forces* provides many other examples of the so-called "transnational movement" of physicists, physicians and other scientists from both sides of the Iron Curtain gaining significant influence – especially in the 1980s and particularly in the Soviet Union – on the détente efforts that led to the end of the Cold War in 1989.[249]

In a more indirect way, the transnational movements and the nuclear arms race also had a lasting impact on the perception of the relationship between science and politics. In their opposition to nuclear weapons, scientists tried to gain influence, both via grassroots activism and as advisers to governments and state organizations. In both contexts, their authority relied on a combination of technical expertise in nuclear questions and the way they, as scientists, embodied virtues of international collaboration and open exchange of viewpoints, and the idea that they safeguarded a responsibility to use science for the benefit of humankind. The tension between technical expertise and moral activism could be observed in many of the physicists who got involved in the struggle, but also at state level. In an in-depth study on the American state during the Cold War, historian Paul Rubinson has

The organization International Physicians for the Prevention of Nuclear War (IPPNW) was founded in 1980 by medical doctors and researchers from both sides of the Iron Curtain joining forces to prevent a nuclear war. The organization received the Nobel Peace Prize in 1985.

demonstrated that the American state had a great need – and to a large extent also the power – to decide which scientists were credible experts in the nuclear question and who could be written off as moral activists. Rubinson argues that a distinction between the neutral scientific expert, whom the state will listen to, and the scientific activist, whom the state can ignore, is a product of the Cold War when the states had to handle carefully their relationship with scientific expertise regarding nuclear issues. A paradoxical result of this inheritance today is that science's room for maneuver has gradually diminished as scientists have had to put up with the status of technical experts – nothing more or less than that.[250] This development is perhaps also part of the reason why the subsequent generations of prominent scientists in the decades after the end of the Cold War have occupied a less central – or at least less visible – position in issues regarding nuclear weapons, compared to their predecessors.

CHAPTER 6

Four New Nuclear Weapon States – and Several Candidates

The Proliferation of Nuclear Weapons Continues

So far, we have focused on the five world powers – in particular, the two superpowers, the USA and the Soviet Union. They were the first nations with nuclear weapons at their disposal – first fission bombs and subsequently hydrogen bombs – but as time passed, more states joined them. This is in accordance with the Acheson-Lilienthal Report from 1946. As described in Chapter 3, the authors of this report predicted only a year after the end of the Second World War that "a system of inspection superimposed on an otherwise uncontrolled exploitation of atomic energy by national governments will not be an adequate safeguard".[251] It was exactly this type of system that saw the light of day as a result of the Atoms for Peace agreements in the 1950s to the 1970s. As Soviet Minister of Foreign Affairs Molotov pointed out to his colleague Dulles in 1954, 'peaceful' and 'un-peaceful' nuclear energy are intimately linked because any nuclear reactor that uses uranium as fuel produces plutonium, which can be used in a civilian nuclear power plant but also as a central component in nuclear weapons.[252] The fundamental problem remains to this day.

Skeptics may object that the USA and a number of other countries – today especially China and India – have operated with a very different type of test reactor. Here, the fuel is not uranium but the element thorium, and this type of reactor produces far less radioactive waste and almost no plutonium. On the other hand, it produces large quantities of the fissile uranium isotope U-233, which contributes significantly to energy production but also, albeit with some difficulty, can be extracted and used as an 'explosive' in a nuclear bomb. It is therefore uncertain whether thorium reactors in reality entail less risk in terms of the proliferation of nuclear weapons than uranium reactors, and in any case, it is a fact that thorium reactors are still in their early development phase and therefore a long way from being able to contribute substantially to the world energy supply.[253]

Since 1970, no fewer than 191 countries have signed and ratified the Non-Proliferation Treaty (NPT), but this has not prevented Israel, India, Pakistan and North Korea, who have not signed the treaty, from becoming nuclear states. This chapter explains how these countries acquired nuclear weapons despite the NPT. Focusing on this worrying fact, critics of the NPT have often claimed that the treaty is useless because any country that wishes to become a nuclear power can do so. Obviously, it can only be done if the country is willing to sacrifice the required resources and conceal its intentions when acquiring the necessary components and technical assistance from countries with more nuclear expertise. Proponents of the NPT, on the other hand, claim that the number of nuclear powers in the world would have been much larger if the treaty had not been in place.

As mentioned earlier, the CIA estimated during Kennedy's presidency that there could be as many as 15–25 nuclear powers in 1975 if the nuclear arms race were allowed to continue at the current rate. However, the actual number in 1975 was six, even though the IAEA at that point was not sufficiently prepared to effectively solve the colossal task it had taken on. Hence, the IAEA cannot take all the credit for preventing a number of other countries outside the nine current nuclear states from developing nuclear weapons. We will see several examples of this in the present chapter, looking at three countries – Iraq, Libya and South Africa – that made it a long way in their attempts to procure nuclear weapons, but either gave up themselves or were prevented by stronger states that would not accept their crossing the threshold to the exclusive club of nuclear weapon states.

Israel: "We shall never again be as lambs led to the slaughter"

The state of Israel was founded in the wake of Hitler's holocaust, during which approximately six million Jews were killed in the German death camps, most of which were located in the part of Poland occupied by the Germans in 1939. In the years after the Second World War, thousands of Jews traveled to Palestine, where a small Jewish colony had resided since the 16th century, living relatively peacefully with the predominantly Muslim population in the territory. The growing influx to the Jewish settlements after the First World War and, in particular, the Second World War soon gave rise to a series of conflicts, some of them bloody, between Israelis and Palestinians. After a majority of UN member countries on November 29, 1947 had recommended a two-state solution for Palestine, the tension grew so widespread that the leaders of the Jewish people in Palestine on May 14, 1948 announced the establishment of the state of Israel with David Ben-Gurion as Prime Minister. The declaration resulted in war between the Israelis and the Palestinians, who received military assistance from some of the surrounding Arab states. After a few months of fighting, Israel came out of the war victorious in the fall of 1948. By then, hundreds of thousands of Palestinians had been driven away from their homes within what became the Israeli borders until 1967.[254]

Most Israelis, not least Ben-Gurion, anticipated that the war in 1948 was just the beginning of a long-term conflict with the Arabs in the Middle East, who would not continue accepting the humiliating defeat by this small, recently established state in their midst. Therefore, it was the paramount responsibility of the Israeli government and the Prime Minister himself to provide security for the state of Israel. From the outset, Ben-Gurion focused on arms deliveries and security guarantees from the great Western powers – the USA, the United Kingdom and France – but also on boosting science in Israel. This applied not least to nuclear science and technology, which toward the end of the Second World War had proved its formidable potential to radically change the power relations between nations. Ben-Gurion referred repeatedly to the fact that Albert Einstein, Robert Oppenheimer and Edward Teller all had Jewish ancestry, and in 1948 he wrote in a pamphlet to the employees at the Armaments Development Authority:

> We are inferior to other people in our numbers, dispersion, and the characteristics of our political life, but no other people is superior to us in our intellectual prowess. Until now we have disseminated our intellectual capital in foreign lands, and helped many nations in the great scientific achievements of the nineteenth and twentieth centuries [...]. There is no reason why the genius of science would not blossom and flourish in this native land.[255]

Whether Ben-Gurion at this early stage was dreaming of an Israeli nuclear bomb is unclear. What we do know is that before "the War of Liberation", as many Jewish Israelis favor calling the 1948 conflict, a scientific corps (HEMED) was set up under the armed forces, which from 1948 became the Israeli army. We also know that Ben-Gurion in 1948 appointed Ernst David Bergmann, who worked as a chemist at the Hebrew University in Jerusalem and had extensive knowledge of nuclear physics, as leader of HEMED. It was Bergmann who, more than anyone else, had sparked Ben-Gurion's interest in nuclear research and technology, and he also in 1949 convinced HEMED to fund six young, promising Israeli physicists' studies over several years with prominent researchers at American and European universities. In 1952 Bergmann was employed as Ben-Gurion's personal adviser and that year he also persuaded the prime minister to establish an Israeli Atomic Energy Commission (IsAEC) inspired by the American, British and French models. Finally, it was Bergmann who made Ben-Gurion set up a secret Israeli nuclear energy project tasked with building a nuclear reactor because "I am convinced that the State of Israel needs a defense research program of its own, so that we shall never again be as lambs led to the slaughter."[256]

Thus, from the beginning of the 1950s, Bergmann focused on utilizing nuclear energy for military as well as peaceful purposes. Many Israeli scientists, led by the internationally recognized Amos de-Shalit, took exception to these plans, which they viewed as overly ambitious for such a small country. Instead of being employed at what they saw as a precarious and inferior research and development center under the IsAEC, they preferred careers at traditional university institutes, especially the famous Weizmann Institute in Rehovot, south-west of Tel Aviv.[257] However, this did not make Ben-Gurion and Bergmann change their minds. Together with Shimon Peres, who shared their views and at the time was the highest-ranking official in the Ministry of Defense, they initiated in 1955 a fusion of all application-oriented nuclear research units under the Ministry of Defense. Then, in the years 1955–60, a particular international situation occurred, which the trio of Ben-Gurion, Bergmann and Peres decided to exploit.

Firstly, from 1955 it had – as a result of Eisenhower's Atoms for Peace initiative – become possible for many countries to receive American support in the form of test reactors and reactor fuel. The Israelis made use of this opportunity and by 1959 Israel had a small but operational test reactor of the 'swimming pool' type. The fuel consisted of highly enriched uranium that was immersed in a tank of heavy water functioning as a moderator. The USA provided everything and insisted on the uranium fuel being returned when it was spent. The reactor was constructed by the American company American Machines and Foundry Atomics, and installed in a prepared building at Soreq, a town close to Rehovot. The Americans donated 350,000 US dollars to cover most of the expense of procuring and establishing the reactor.

Israeli researchers used the Soreq reactor for research purposes, and American reactor specialists monitored it routinely. Everything went by the book at the Soreq Nuclear Research Center.[258]

Secondly, Ben-Gurion, Bergmann and Peres cultivated their connections with the French government and the French nuclear energy commission, CEA. Over the course of 1955–56, the governments of France and Israel reached a mutual understanding that the Egyptian President Gamal Abdel Nasser was the root of all problems in the Middle East and North Africa. Egypt posed a constant threat to the state of Israel while France was losing the colonial war against an increasingly strong rebel movement in Algeria, which received significant support from Egypt. France therefore signed a contract with Israel on speedy delivery of large quantities of French weapons, including advanced fighter aircraft and tanks that would make the Israeli military strong enough to pressure Egypt from the east in the event of a serious crisis.

The impending crisis came sooner than expected. On July 26, 1956, Egyptian President Nasser announced that Egypt would seize the Suez Canal with immediate effect. This was unacceptable to the two former colonial powers, France and the United Kingdom, who had vital interests in maintaining control of this means of access to the massive Middle Eastern oil reserves. They decided to occupy the Suez Canal zone, but France in particular wanted to bring Israel on board in the potential war alliance because the French general staff assumed that the modern, well-trained Israeli army would be able to quickly reach the Suez Canal through the Sinai Desert. When the French Minister for Defense and the Armed Forces, Bourgès-Maunoury, contacted Peres regarding the matter, Peres replied that Israel might be willing to enter into alliance with France and the United Kingdom, but on the condition that another agreement be made at the same time. Whether it was a direct precondition for Israel taking part in the war is unclear, but in any case, Israel wanted the French government to guarantee that France would secretly provide blueprints and components for a nuclear reactor of unspecified size at Dimona in the Israeli Negev Desert. According to Peres's autobiography from 1995, he quickly secured verbal guarantees at a confidential meeting with Prime Minister Guy Mollet and Bourgès-Maunoury on October 23–24, 1956.[259]

A mere five days later, on October 29, 1956, the war began when Israel occupied the Sinai Peninsula.[260] The Israeli army soon proved to live up to the French general staff's expectations. During a week of intense fighting, the Israelis neutralized the Egyptian forces in Sinai and reached the Suez Canal, where they joined French and British paratroopers. However, because the USA was very critical of this British-French neocolonial project, and the Soviet Union, then in the process of crushing a civilian uprising in Hungary, was threatening to use nuclear weapons against the three attacking countries, they had to pull out before achieving their goal. On top of that, Nasser gained much backing in the Arab populations in the Middle East.

The failed Suez action irrevocably triggered France and Israel's decisions to pursue the development of nuclear weapons. Ben-Gurion and Peres must have realized at that time that it presented a unique opportunity for Israel to procure a reactor capable of producing large quantities of plutonium – and without the USA, the Soviet Union or the newly-established IAEA knowing about it, because as long as France was not a nuclear power, the French were not interested in dealing with the IAEA.

The Suez Crisis had encouraged Peres and his companions to ramp up their ambitions with regard to the type and the size of reactor. Now, they insisted on a reactor about the same size (40 MW thermal effect) as the first Marcoule-reactor (G1) and an accompanying reprocessing plant that could separate plutonium from the spent fuel. Like G1, the Dimona reactor should use natural uranium as fuel, but instead of graphite, it must be designed to use a more effective moderator such as heavy water. Finally, the French technicians must take part in the construction of the large facility from start to finish – i.e., until the plant was fully functional. The French government was not happy to be reminded of its promise, but after lengthy negotiations the final contract was signed on October 3, 1957 by Peres and Bourgès-Maunoury, a few hours before the latter's government was overthrown in the National Assembly.

As described earlier, France became the world's fourth nuclear state in 1960, but in addition to this, France clandestinely transferred nuclear technology to the secret Israeli nuclear facility in the Negev Desert in the years 1957–63. Shortly after the contract between France and Israel had been signed on October 3, 1957,[261] extensive construction work commenced in an area of the Negev totally sealed off from the public. French and Israeli technicians collaborated closely to realize the so-called Dimona Project, naturally with the French in the role as instructors and the Israelis in the role as eager and able trainees.

The process was not straightforward. In 1958, de Gaulle returned to power, and when he learned that France was helping Israel acquire nuclear weapons, he wanted to put a stop to the collaboration, partly because he wished to establish a better relationship with the Arab states, and partly because he was intending to join the IAEA as soon as France had become a nuclear state. However, a large part of the nuclear collaboration between France and Israel was organized through the relatively autonomous CEA, an arrangement that allowed the Dimona Project to continue relatively unchanged until the Israelis were able to take over management from the end of 1963 when the reactor at Dimona had been taken into use.[262]

During the process, Israel received valuable help from Norway, which supplied 20 tons of heavy water, which was needed as a moderator but which neither France nor the USA were willing to deliver without control of its use. The Norwegians did not express the need to control anything; they just requested a signed declaration from Israel that the heavy water would be used only for peaceful purposes. Once this was in place, the Norwegians would sell the heavy water. But as Israel and Norway were both interested in keeping the transaction secret, Norway bought back 20 tons of heavy water in 1960 that it had previously sold to the United Kingdom, and shipped it in secret from the UK to Israel.[263]

There were also problems in relation to the USA. American U-2 spy planes had already observed in 1958 that a large-scale construction project was underway in the Negev, but even though several American experts interpreted the photo evidence as proof that Israel was building a nuclear facility, the American government refrained from taking action. Nothing was certain at that time. Two years later the American embassy in Tel Aviv picked up rumors that the construction work was in fact part of a French-Israeli nuclear energy project. Now, the ambassador made inquiries. Initially, the Israelis responded that the facility in question was a textile factory, but he did not buy it, and at the beginning of August 1960, he reported to Washington to confirm the suspicion: Israel was building a large, French reactor at Dimona, and the project had been going on for three years.[264]

This made Eisenhower and the American government very worried. With his Atoms for Peace initiative, Eisenhower had hoped to prevent the proliferation of nuclear weapons to other states than the three that already had them at their disposal – the USA, the Soviet Union and the United Kingdom – in addition, possibly, to the two other great powers, France and China, whom it might prove impossible to prevent from developing nuclear weapons. Now, reports stated that the reactor under construction at Dimona was

5 OCTOBER 1986 No 8,461 Price 50p

THE SUNDAY TIMES

Revealed: the secrets of Israel's nuclear arsenal

INSIGHT

THE SECRETS of a subterranean factory engaged in the manufacture of Israeli nuclear weapons have been uncovered by The Sunday Times Insight team.

Hidden beneath the Negev desert, the factory has been producing atomic warheads for the last 20 years. Now it has almost certainly begun manufacturing thermonuclear weapons, with yields big enough to destroy entire cities.

Information about Israel's capacity to manufacture the bomb comes from the testimony of Mordechai Vanunu, a 31-year-old Israeli who worked as a nuclear technician for nearly 10 years in Machon 2 – a top secret, underground bunker built to provide the vital components necessary for weapons production at Dimona, the Israeli nuclear research establishment.

Vanunu's evidence has surprised nuclear weapons experts who were approached by Insight to verify its accuracy because it shows that Israel does not just have the atom bomb – which has long been suspected – but that it has become a major nuclear power.

Vanunu's testimony and more than 60 photographs he secretly took inside have been scrutinised by nuclear experts on both sides of the Atlantic. They show that Israel has developed the sophisticated and highly classified techniques needed to build up a formidable nuclear arsenal. They confirm that:

● Israel now ranks as the …

Pictured for the first time in detail: Israel's nuclear bomb plant is built deep beneath the Negev desert and has been secretly operating for more than 20 years

… beneath an innocuous, little used building.

● The plant is equipped with French plutonium extracting technology, which transformed Dimona from a civilian research establishment to a bomb production facility. Plutonium production rates amount to 40 kilograms a year, enough to build 10 bombs. In the past six years Israel has added further equipment to make …

… have been assembled – 10 times the previously estimated strength of Israel's nuclear arsenal.

The scientists include Theodore Taylor, one of the world's most experienced nuclear weapons experts. He was taught by Robert Oppenheimer, the father of the atomic bomb, and worked on America's first bomb designs. He later went on to head the Pentagon's atomic weapons …

… testimony was entirely consistent with an Israeli capacity to produce 10 nuclear weapons a year that are significantly smaller, lighter and more efficient than the first types of weapons developed by Russia, America, Britain, France or China.

Another scientist who authenticated the evidence uncovered by Insight is Dr Frank Barnaby, a nuclear …

… the flow rates through the plant which he quotes exactly confirm the quantities of plutonium that were being made."

Vanunu says that, despite tight security, he was able to smuggle a camera into Machon 2. Insight debriefed him for four weeks and invited Barnaby to interview Vanunu in an attempt to find scientific flaws in his story. "His testimony is totally …

… Atomic Energy Commission in Dimona. He was made redundant last November with 180 other Dimona workers during a cost-cutting drive by the establishment. Security men had grown concerned about Vanunu's developing political contacts with West Bank Arab students during a part-time philosophy degree course he was taking at Beersheba University.

… though never proved, that when Israel was in danger of losing the Yom Kippur War in 1973 after the initial Egyptian attack, the then prime minister, Golda Meir, ordered nuclear devices to be moved to air bases.

Last Thursday, a senior US government source at the time, now retired, confirmed the incident to The Sunday Times.

Inside Dimona: full story pages 4 & 5

On October 5, 1986, the *Sunday Times* revealed Israel's secret nuclear program in the Negev Desert, at a time when Israel had already been producing nuclear weapons for nearly 20 years.

an advanced French 24 MW, heavy-water moderated reactor built to use natural uranium as fuel. This reactor would, according to experts, be able to produce 10–15 kilos of plutonium a year – enough for 2–3 nuclear bombs – when it was up and running. However, this was not what the Israelis intended, declared Ben-Gurion in a speech to the Knesset on December 21, 1960, when the Israeli public learned about the Israeli plans for the first time. In the speech, Ben-Gurion said:

> We are also engaged at this time in the construction of a research reactor with a capacity of 24,000 thermal kilowatts, which will serve the needs of industry, agriculture, health and science. This reactor will also be used to train Israeli scientists and technologists for the future construction of a nuclear power station within a presumed period of 10 to 15 years.

He added that the reactor would be another 3–4 years underway, and that it "like the American reactor, is designed exclusively for peaceful purposes".[265]

The American government was convinced that Ben-Gurion was not telling the truth about Dimona on this and subsequent occasions when he was being pressed for answers. The Eisenhower administration was on its way out and therefore did not have time to do much about the matter. But the Kennedy administration, which took over on January 20, 1961, did. It was paramount for Kennedy to prevent the Israelis from acquiring nuclear weapons. He feared that if it were to happen, several of the Arab states in the Middle East would contact the Soviet Union to acquire similar weapons, which would trigger a lethal nuclear arms race in the Middle East. Therefore, Kennedy tried to convince Israel to permit inspections of the Dimona facility twice a year, either by IAEA specialists or American reactor experts. But Israel managed repeatedly to drag out the process by claiming that the visits – as they insisted on calling the inspections – were inconvenient. Thus, under neither Kennedy nor his successor Johnson was there more than one annual visit, which arms experts were well aware was not enough. When a visit finally took place, the experts were allowed such a short time at the facility itself that they were prevented from doing the inspection properly. The experts never managed to uncover the fact that irradiated uranium rods were being removed from the reactor and taken to a plutonium reprocessing facility. The Americans suspected that it was happening but could not prove it, and every time the question was brought up, the Israeli government replied that Israel would not be the first country to "introduce nuclear weapons to the region [the Middle East]."[266]

On October 5, 1985, the British newspaper *The Sunday Times* was finally able to reveal that the world had been misled for more than 20 years. The newspaper published the story of a technician from Dimona, Mordechai Vanunu, documenting in text and images that under the Dimona reactor building there was a large reprocessing facility and an actual bomb factory which the Israelis had kept hidden from the American inspectors by camouflaging the elevator that led from the ground floor to the basement.[267] On March 27, 1988, Vanunu was sentenced in Jerusalem to 18 years in prison for treason and espionage.

In 1965 and 1966, Edward Teller visited Israel's Prime Minister Levi Eshkol and several high-ranking members of the Israeli nuclear energy commission.

Teller made no attempt to conceal his support for Israel becoming a nuclear weapon state, and many years later he admitted that he had been convinced during the visits that Israel already possessed nuclear weapons or was very near the goal. The same conclusion appears in a secret CIA report from the beginning of 1967, which was to become a dramatic year in the Middle East.[268]

The drama began when Egypt's President Nasser in May 1967 requested that the UN withdraw its peacekeeping forces from Sinai, where they had been deployed since the Suez Crisis in 1957. The withdrawal happened surprisingly fast, after which Nasser sent his army to the Sinai Peninsula, where some units took position close to the Israeli border. Egyptian spy planes flew over the Dimona facility and other locations in Israel several times, which Israel perceived as a precursor to an imminent Egyptian attack on the reactor which had been running for four years. This threat made the Israeli government start the war on June 5, 1967, which has since become known as the Six-Day War. That was how long it took Israel to crush the Egyptian, Syrian and Jordanian armies and air forces, which were ready to attack Israel but were caught unawares by the Israeli surprise attack. Israel did not use nuclear weapons on that occasion, but we now know that the country already had some untested, but likely fully functional, nuclear weapons at its disposal, and that the Israeli government intended to use them against its enemies if the nation's survival was compromised. However, it was the absolute last resort, later referred to as "the Samson option" with reference to the Old Testament story about the strong Israelite leader Samson, whose eyes Israel's mortal enemy, the Philistines, gouged out. Doomed to be a slave and submitted to humiliating treatment by the Philistines in their great temple, Samson took revenge by bringing down the pillars of the temple, with the result that the building collapsed and killed everyone inside, including himself.[269]

Today, the general view is that Israel possessed fully developed nuclear weapons from 1969 or 1970, and that some of them were deployed in ballistic missiles during the Yom Kippur War against Egypt and Syria in 1973, ready to be fired if the existence of the state of Israel was threatened.[270] Currently, Israel probably has approximately 100 nuclear weapons at its disposal, possibly even hydrogen bombs.[271] Still, the Israeli government has never admitted that this is the case, and Israel's policy has consistently been to neither deny nor confirm the existence of Israeli nuclear weapons.[272]

India: "Smiling Buddha"

India had a long and winding path to becoming a nuclear weapon state. The young nation was an early mover in terms of utilizing nuclear energy; as early as April 1948, less than a year after the independence celebrations and the division of the country into a mainly Muslim Pakistan and a mainly Hindu India, the Indian parliament passed a law to establish an Indian nuclear energy commission (InAEC) after the British model. India's political and scientific elite, and not least Prime Minister Jawaharlal Nehru, were convinced that modern technology was the answer to creating progress in this economically underdeveloped country with a large and poor population – and the state of the art was nuclear technology; hence, India needed to embark on the nuclear journey from the beginning. This paved the way for the rapid establishment of the InAEC, which Nehru's close friend, nuclear physicist Homi Bhabha, had recommended. After long debates in the parliament, Nehru recommended that members vote yes to the new law, which would require a significant part of the state budget in the following years. In the speech, Nehru said:[273]

> Consider the past few hundred years of history, the world developed a new source of power, that is steam – the steam engine and the like – and the industrial age came in. India with all her many virtues did not develop that source of power. It became a backward country in that sense; it became a slave country because of that. [...] Now we are facing the atomic age; we are on the verge of it. And this is obviously something infinitely more powerful than either steam or electricity. [...] The point I should like the House to consider is this, that if we are to remain abreast in the world as a nation which keeps ahead of things, we must develop this atomic energy quite apart from war – indeed I think we must develop it for the purpose of using it for peaceful purposes. Of course, if we are compelled as a nation to use it for other purposes, possibly no pious sentiments of any of us will stop the nation from using it that way.[274]

Considering that Nehru until his death in 1964 was known and recognized across the world as a statesman who was consistently pro-disarmament and opposed to nuclear weapons, it is noteworthy that on several occasions, as in the speech above, he did not preclude the possibility that even India might feel pushed to develop such weapons – and use them.

The parliament passed the law on the Indian Atomic Energy Commission (InAEC) on April 15, 1948, and the commission started work on August 10 of the same year. InAEC's management, with Bhabha as director, was powerful because the law prescribed that the research and development activities be kept secret at the same time as making all the country's uranium and thorium deposits the property of the state. This meant that Bhabha could almost single-handedly design grandiose, expensive plans for nuclear research and development activities in India, present them during his regular conversations with Nehru, and be almost sure to receive funding for most of them from the parliament. Nehru and Bhabha were both from wealthy Indian families, both had studied at Cambridge University, and both had an extensive network of influential people in Europe and the United States who were willing to help the young nation move forward after more than a century under imperial rule.

Bhabha's and Nehru's ambitions of employing nuclear energy as a central element in the Indian modernization process gained further impetus after Eisenhower's *Atoms for Peace* speech in 1953. At a conference in New Delhi in November 1954, Bhabha presented a grand plan for the Indian energy supply, called "The Development of Atomic Energy for Peaceful Purposes". The plan divided India's energy development into three phases. The first phase entailed building, with Canadian assistance, a small number of reactors that used natural uranium as fuel and heavy water as moderator and coolant. Canadian assistance was mentioned in this context because Canada had most experience with this type of reactor. CIRUS is the name of the first reactor of this type in India. These first-generation reactors could supply a small quantity of electricity, but their primary function was to produce plutonium for the next two phases. The second phase entailed building reactors that ran on fuel consisting of a mix of plutonium (Pu) and thorium (Th). India had thorium in abundance, whereas not much uranium had been found within the country's borders at this point. As a by-product, these second-generation reactors, which no one in the world had much experience with, would produce a new, fissile uranium isotope – U-233 – which was heralded as something of a philosopher's stone for the even more advanced nuclear reactors of the third phase. According to Bhabha's plan, the third-generation reactors would be so-called breeder reactors in which the fuel consisted of U-233 and Th-232. Such a reactor would – provided that the considerable technical issues connected with this type were solved – produce more fissile U-233 from thorium nuclei than is used for the fission processes that keep the reactor running.[275]

Today, we know that Bhabha's project was unrealistic. No one has succeeded even to this day in making such third-generation reactors operational beyond the experimental stage. But in the mid-1950s, when faith in peaceful and inexpensive nuclear energy in large quantities peaked, Bhabha's plan sounded very attractive, and he got almost anything he asked for. In the years 1954–56, the funding for India's nuclear energy research increased by a factor of 12, and in the following years the money kept pouring in. Huge amounts were allocated to build a large research center, the Atomic Energy Establishment (AEET), in Trombay near Bombay (now Mumbai). This center, of which Bhabha was director, employed more than a thousand scientists and engineers in 1958, and the number kept rising in the following years.

The extensive funds also went into equipping the AEET with two reactors and a reprocessing plant to extract plutonium from the spent fuel. The first reactor was a small, 1 MW test reactor built with British assistance in 1955–56 and made critical for the first time in 1956. According to the political scientist Itty Abraham, this reactor, called Apsara,[276] was hailed as a purely Indian achievement, fulfilling the young postcolonial state's promise of modernity. He wrote:

> Through demonstration, the production of the technological artefact which would stand in for development (or national security as the case may be), the state sought to produce a modern fetish. Inscribed with all the accoutrements of the postcolonial state's desire – science, modernity, indigeneity, the technological artefact was meant to stand out from the landscape of Indian History and tradition, bearing no trace of its origins, embodying the future, situated only in relation to other fetishized objects like dams, railways, steel mills and jet aircraft, aesthetically and practically the new face of India. The special, even sacred aura of the state fetish produced through the difference it embodied, affirmed through its particular rituals of achievement and status, monitored by the high priests of the modern state (in this case the atomic scientists) was the demonstration, and, by displacement, the proof, of the postcolonial.

Being unable to fulfil the high promises generated by the Apsara fetish, "the state's only available response was to conceal, even more than before, the institution of atomic energy behind the barrier of state secrecy in order to postpone the emerging public denouncement of unfulfilled modernity".[277]

For many years to come, India had to rely heavily on imported nuclear technology, i.e. the Canadian 40 MW reactor CIRUS, which InAEC commissioned from Canada in 1955. As described in Bhabha's 1954 plan, this reactor used natural uranium as fuel and heavy water as moderator. It was implied that the reactor had only peaceful objectives, but neither the Canadians, who provided the drawings and contributed to the construction, nor the Americans, who subsequently provided the 20 tons of heavy water needed, insisted on inspecting the facility once it was operational. When in 1959–60 the time approached when the reactor needed to be loaded with uranium fuel, the Indian nuclear authorities insisted on providing it themselves, arguing that a proud, independent nation like India could not accept having to import fuel that it could provide itself. This was the argument, and the decision stood.

CIRUS was made critical in 1960, and from the beginning of the 1960s India began to build up a stock of plutonium that could be used for peaceful purposes in second-generation reactors, as well as for Indian nuclear weapons if and when the government decided to produce them. From the mid-1950s, many Indian scientists and politicians argued that India needed to develop nuclear weapons to earn the international respect that they believed the large country deserved. But the government and the majority of the parliament opposed this for a long time.[278]

Without doubt, a main reason for the government's reluctance was that independent India as one of the world's most populous nations pursued the role as leader of the so-called 'alliance-free countries', countries that had not formally chosen a side in the Cold War division of East and West. The group of alliance-free countries quickly grew after 1960 as an increasing number of African countries achieved independence. The group gained a large influence in the UN when the countries managed to stand together, which they often did, not least on nuclear issues. In these cases, India favored maintaining a high moral stance by persistently proclaiming that the country did not wish to have nuclear weapons, while at the same time hinting that it could easily produce some within 1–2 years – a very optimistic estimate. Precisely because India rode on a high horse was it in a position to reproach countries with this type of weapons for acquiring them. On the other hand, if India developed nuclear weapons, it could no longer continue in its role as moral beacon that suited Nehru so well.

However, there were also external circumstances which, in the minds of many Indians, pulled in the opposite direction, including serious conflicts with the country's two closest neighbors, China and Pakistan. In the northeast where India borders China, from the day India was founded the People's Republic of China challenged the nation's right to the border region. In 1962, it culminated in a war between the two countries – a war that India lost, but after which China nevertheless chose to vacate part of the occupied territory. The shameful defeat made the most bellicose members of the Indian parliament demand rearmament, and with nuclear weapons. Their demand was not met at the time, but when the news of the first Chinese nuclear test at Lop Nor in 1964 reached New Delhi, the Indian government sensed that the tides were changing. It was time for India to make the long overdue decision to develop nuclear weapons to deter China from attacking India, no matter the cost, they argued. Prime Minister Lal Bahadur Shastri, who had succeeded Nehru upon his death in 1964, was very partial to the argument. The Indian defense budget was already a whopping 28 percent of the state budget, which meant that investments in e.g., agriculture, lagged behind, with the inevitable consequence that the general population experienced a drop in the standard of living. This situation was untenable. But developing nuclear weapons as well as reliable missiles – and both were necessary if the project was to make any sense – would be far too expensive if India wanted to avoid escalating social unrest.[279]

However, Bhabha had considered other possibilities. According to him, it would be inexpensive for India to prepare a peaceful nuclear test, termed PNE (peaceful nuclear explosion). Such an explosion would bring prestige to India, not least the scientific elite, without ruining the country's reputation as a principled opponent of nuclear weapons, argued Bhabha. Shastri believed that a majority in the parliament would allow the nuclear researchers to prepare a PNE, but the final approval for the test would only be granted by the prime minister when everything was ready. On November 27, 1964, Shastri said to the Indian parliament:

> Dr. Bhabha has made it quite clear to me that as far as we can progress and improve upon nuclear devices, we should do so as far as development is possible, we should resort to it so that we can reap its peaceful benefits and we can use it for the development of our nation. Just assume that we have to use big tunnels and we have to clear huge areas,

> we have to wipe out mountains for development parks, and in this context if it is required to use nuclear devices for the good of the country as well as for the good of the world, so then our Atomic Energy Commission is pursuing the same objectives.[280]

Today, the PNE phenomenon sounds contradictory, but the fact remains that others had similar ideas. Edward Teller, for instance, argued in writing and speech in the USA in the 1950s that nuclear bombs could and should be used in the construction of harbors and canals to blast away, e.g., mountains that were in the way. In the USA, explosions of this type were known under the name of Project Plowshare – a name that refers to a manner of speech often used in connection with peace agreements, namely that the parties are reforging their swords into plowshares.[281] In Chapter 4, we described an example of such a project in the Teller-inspired Project Chariot, which aimed to create a large artificial harbor in Alaska by detonating six hydrogen bombs. The project was never realized.

Shastri's comments to parliament on November 27, 1964 may come across as a rather ambiguous consent to Bhabha's plans, but in any case, Bhabha interpreted the statement to mean that his staff could start working on the many large and small problems that needed to be solved before India could perform a nuclear test. The plutonium in the bomb would consist almost entirely of Pu-239 and the required amount of Pu-239 needed to be calculated precisely; the focused detonation of conventional explosives to compress the Pu-239 into supercritical size had to be tested; and a suitable initiator had to be invented. All this had to work. Finally, they needed to find and prepare a subterranean test station. Given that in 1963 the USA, the Soviet Union and the United Kingdom had agreed to ban all atmospheric tests, India wanted to mitigate the risk of incensing the world community with this type of detonation. Neither Shastri nor Bhabha lived to witness the realization of these plans as they both died in January 1966. Shastri presumably died from natural causes on January 11, while Bhabha died dramatically when the Air India flight he was on hit a mountain near Mont Blanc on January 24. Nehru's daughter Indira Gandhi took over the position as prime minister, while Vikram Sarabhai became director of InAEC.

India's relationship with Pakistan was no less volatile than that with China. When the states of India and Pakistan were founded in 1947, the main part of the northern region Kashmir became part of India, even though the majority population was Muslim. It was clear from the outset that this might cause problems in the long term – and it did. In addition to many armed border conflicts, it led to outright war between the two countries in 1965 and 1971. On both occasions, India was victorious and the question of Indian nuclear weapons came up again. During renewed political unrest in many Indian provinces in 1972, the pressure on Prime Minister Indira Gandhi grew so intense that she finally gave in and authorized a PNE explosion that was given the code name "Smiling Buddha".[282]

On September 7, 1972, Gandhi gave her consent to the test to Raja Ramanna, Sarabhai's successor as director of Bhabha Atomic Research Center in Trombay (the former AEET).[283] The long-awaited test took place in May 18, 1974 in a subterranean cave near the village of Pokhran in north-western India, approximately 150 kilometers from the Pakistani border. The force of the explosion was similar to that of the Hiroshima bomb. It flung the soil above high up into the air and left a crater that is still visible. The crater was intended to prove to the national and foreign press that a nuclear explosion had in fact been performed, and that such explosions could be used for peaceful purposes. The majority of the Indian press was excited. For instance, the headline in *The Sunday Standard* read, "Monopoly of Big Five Broken"; the *Indian Express* claimed that "India's nuclear blast has catapulted her into the front rank of nations", while the *Motherland* drily concluded that "India goes nuclear at last".[284]

A few other Indian newspapers were less enthusiastic, while most foreign media were cautious or negative. The same applied to the official government statements from many countries, because they perceived India's nuclear test as a serious challenge to the non-proliferation treaty (NPT) that came into effect in May 1970. India had not joined the NPT, and the IAEA therefore had not had access to the key Indian nuclear facilities such as the CIRUS reactor and the plutonium reprocessing facility in Trombay. India's argument for not joining the NPT was the refusal to be constrained by an unequal and unjust world order – sometimes called 'nuclear apartheid' – as long as the existing superpowers could not agree on a binding plan for nuclear disarmament.[285]

It remains unclear whether it was due to the lukewarm foreign reaction to the news of the 'peaceful' Indian nuclear test in 1974, or the Indian government's ambition to maintain the country's role as the unfailing watchdog in relation to the nuclear powers, that made India refrain from further nuclear tests for 24 years. In any case, it is a fact that India 'made do with' continuing

Indian Prime Minister Indira Gandhi visiting the site where India's so-called "peaceful nuclear explosion" took place on May 18, 1974.

the development of nuclear weapons and means of delivery in the form of Agni missiles, which burned solid fuel, had a range of some hundred kilometers and were made operational in 1998. That year, a nationalistic Hindu government seized power in India, and one of its first actions was to permit the Defense Research and Development Organization to carry out the nuclear tests they had requested for so long. No fewer than five subterranean nuclear tests were performed in the days between May 11 and 13 in the old test area in north-western India – and the reaction from the rest of the world was even more critical than in 1974.[286]

At the very end of his 1998 book, Itty Abraham characterized India's current nuclear politics succinctly:

> The Indian atomic energy programme continues to be out of time. Even as the Indian state has now abjured the original position on the peaceful uses of atomic energy and fully accepted the anarchic norms of the international system, the world has not remained in the same place. International ideas about nuclear power have come full circle. Atomic energy no longer has the significance it once had. A country acquires neither international respect nor prestige by developing, or continuing to hold, nuclear weapons. The latest movement against nuclear weapons is not led by the superpowers eager to monopolize atomic energy for themselves and to prevent other countries from obtaining them, but rather by non-nuclear countries. International public opinion, to the extent that there is such a thing, is now where India was nearly half a century ago. But India has moved on from its lofty, idealistic standpoint. India has demanded its right to become a nuclear power just when the atomic age has come to an end, and thus remains an outsider, a spoiler, but for reasons completely opposed to its original purpose.[287]

Abraham's remarks reflect opinions that were quite common in American academic circles around the turn of the millennium: in the future, nuclear power would be phased out and substituted with other sources of energy, not least renewables like wind and solar power. Not so in India, where the elite's plans for massive investments in nuclear energy have survived to the present day. Since India has never signed the NPT, the nation has been largely excluded from trade in nuclear plants and material, and thus has had to develop its own reactor technology, including a thorium nuclear fuel cycle. Nevertheless, it is clear that India's ambitious goal of generating 63 GW of electricity from nuclear power by 2032, set in 2011, is far from being realized. Recent estimates now suggest that the actual capacity will likely fall short, not exceeding 27 GW.[288]

Pakistan: "We will eat grass or leaves"

"If India builds the bomb, we will eat grass or leaves, even go hungry. But we will get one of our own. We have no alternative."[289] These are the words of Pakistani Minister of Foreign Affairs, Zulfikar Ali Bhutto, in 1965, after his country had been defeated in the war against India that year, and after he had received intelligence that India had started a nuclear project that would probably make Pakistan's great neighbor the world's sixth nuclear power within a few years. But Bhutto failed to convince his Prime Minister, Ayub Khan, that it would be rational to spend lots of money – money the country did not have – on developing a nuclear bomb. Khan would rather try to acquire conventional weapons for the Pakistani army by maintaining a good relationship with the USA and China. However, only six years later, Bhutto eyed a new chance to realize his dream of procuring the ultimate weapon of deterrence for his country.

Pakistan was founded in connection with India's foundation as an independent state in August 1947 and consisted of two parts – West Pakistan and East Pakistan (also known as Bengal), which were more than a thousand kilometers apart. Even though the population of East Pakistan was larger than that of West Pakistan, the entire country after independence was dominated politically and financially by a West Pakistani political and military elite. This situation was challenged in the 1960s by a Bengali independence movement led by politician Sheikh Mujibur Rahman, who pursued autonomy for East Pakistan.

At the first relatively free elections in 1970, Rhaman's independence party won absolute majority in the Pakistani parliament, but West Pakistan was unwilling to accept this. The West Pakistani army marched into East Pakistan in 1971, where it committed massacres in many Bengali villages. Millions of Bengalis fled across the border to India, from where they started guerilla warfare against the occupiers. Because they also received massive support from the well-equipped Indian army, which attacked the Pakistani forces in both east and west, the Pakistanis soon had to admit that they were thoroughly beaten. On December 17, 1971, a truce agreement was made, and East Pakistan became an independent state under the name of Bangladesh.

West Pakistan was left morally and economically defeated after the war. Neither the USA nor China had come to the country's aid when it was most needed, and the population's trust in the Pakistani politicians hit rock bottom. However, the wealthy Zulfikar Ali Bhutto, with his academic degrees from prestigious American and English universities, and with close ties to the military, had received most votes at the election in West Pakistan in 1970. The army chief appointed him president of the amputated country until he could assume the position as prime minister with increased powers following a constitutional amendment in 1973.

Bhutto instantly began to pursue his visions revolving around the plan to become the first Muslim leader in the world with nuclear weapons at his disposal. In 1977 he was removed by the military, and in 1979 he was executed for corruption and other alleged crimes. Before this happened, however, he had managed to take big steps to fulfill his dream in ways that remained a mystery for many years, until the truth was revealed by BBC journalists in 1979–80. Based on years of thorough investigation in a number of countries the BBC published the shocking result of this investigation in a documentary called *Project 706 – the Islamic Bomb*, and the following year in the book *The Islamic Bomb: the Nuclear Threat to Israel and the Middle East*. The book was written by Steve Weissman and Herbert Krosney, who received help from a number of leading news media in Europe and the USA. The highlights of the dramatic story follow here.

At the beginning of January 1972, around 50 of Pakistan's leading scientists received an invitation from their new leader to a secret meeting at a grand estate in the city of Multan.[290] There were many excellent Pakistani scientists at the time because rich Pakistani families for generations had encouraged their sons to study political science and natural science at high-ranking Western universities. Three of the scientists at the meeting in Multan were Professor Abdus Salam, who seven years later would receive the Nobel Prize in Physics, Dr Ishrat Usmani, who was director of the Pakistani nuclear energy commission, and Dr Munir Ahmad Khan, who for several years had been employed at the IAEA in Vienna and therefore knew all about the safety measures the organization used in countries that had entered the NPT. He would soon put this knowledge to good use.

Bhutto began the meeting by reminding the participants of the country's recent ignominious defeat by India. According to him, it had resulted from the fact that the former president, Ayub Khan, had failed to understand that Pakistan needed to acquire nuclear weapons to be able to deter their far larger and more populous neighbor India from attacking. It was naïve to believe, as Khan had, that the USA or China would come to Pakistan's aid. It had not happened this time, and it would not happen next time either. But now he, Zulfikar Ali Bhutto, was president and de facto prime minister, and he would make sure that Pakistan acquired nuclear weapons. Money was no issue, he promised. With his good connections to wealthy, oil-producing countries in the Middle East and North Africa, he was convinced that these countries would be willing to pay large amounts to ensure that Pakistan came to possess 'Islamic nuclear bombs'.

"How long will it take?", Bhutto asked the assembly. Abdus Salam, Usmani and a few others advised against Pakistan embarking on such a project, which they believed was beyond the financial and technical capacity of the country, while others were more positively inclined. One scientist ventured to claim that it could be done in five years. "Three years. I want it in three years," declared Bhutto with assertion that prompted great enthusiasm among most of those present.[291] Now they knew that Bhutto was serious, which made one of the youngest participants, Dr S.A. Butt, promise that the nuclear project could be completed in three years if the scientists and technicians were given all necessary resources and facilities. The promise was madly unrealistic, but Bhutto appreciated it and promised that he would secure the necessary funding. This turned out to be an easy task. The money came, among others, from Bhutto's good friend Muammar Gaddafi in Libya, who was willing to finance the Pakistani nuclear venture with hundreds of millions of dollars in cash in return for unlimited access to the nuclear technology that Pakistan developed with his investment.

After the groundbreaking meeting in Multan, Bhutto replaced skeptics with enthusiasts in all important posts. The director of the Pakistani Atomic Energy Commission (PAEC), Ishrat Usmani, was replaced by Munir Ahmad Khan, who would do anything to procure nuclear weapons for Pakistan. It also meant that young Butt was employed directly under Khan and – as a highly trusted chief buyer – tasked with traveling to numerous national nuclear energy institutions and private suppliers of components for the nuclear industry in Western countries. Usually, Butt and Khan were received warmly. There might be a ban on exporting facilities to extract plutonium from spent nuclear fuel and uranium enrichment plants to countries which did not allow the IAEA to supervise facilities in accordance with the NPT – which Pakistan had never signed – but the IAEA's list of banned export articles did not include the components for such facilities. Also, the Pakistanis knew how to play the game in relation to their contacts in Western governments and private companies, who were first and foremost interested in securing lucrative nuclear technology deals and far less in preventing the proliferation of nuclear technology to more countries. Anyway, potential problems in that connection would not surface for years.

© Arif Ali/AFP/Ritzau Scanpix

Pakistani activists from the Islamic organization Islami Jamiat Tulba during a protest in the city of Lahore in 2007, celebrating Dr A.Q. Khan as a hero for his role in securing nuclear weapons for Pakistan. This is in stark contrast to photos in Western media such as *Time Magazine* and the *Atlantic*, featuring A.Q. Khan on their covers as the ultimate nuclear villain.

From the outset, Pakistan wanted a French plant to extract plutonium from the uranium fuel that had been used in the so-called CANDU reactor, which had been provided by Canada to ensure the power supply in the vicinity of Karachi. There was nothing strange about this; ever since the final years of the Second World War, it had been a broadly accepted fact among experts that the easiest path to a nuclear bomb went via plutonium. Pakistan did in fact manage to purchase and receive a large plutonium plant, the Chasma plant, from France, but before it was finished, the French government tightened security measures so severely that the construction almost came to a stop.[292]

Munir Ahmad Khan had predicted that this might happen, so he was testing the uranium path as well. This had become a feasible option because a group of companies in Germany, the Netherlands, Switzerland, Italy and the United Kingdom in the 1970s had collaborated on developing ultracentrifuges from high-tech steel alloys that rotated at more than 100,000 rotations a minute. Such centrifuges made it possible to produce highly enriched uranium at a price that could compete with the price of plutonium. The Pakistanis wanted to get their hands on some of these ultracentrifuges, but because it was out of the question to buy them as DIY-kits, they had to find out exactly which components they needed, the correct dimensions and which companies could deliver the different parts. The task seemed almost insurmountable. However, this changed when the mysterious Dr Abdul Qadeer Khan took nuclear spying to a level perhaps only paralleled by Klaus Fuchs when he spied for the Soviet Union during the Second World War.[293]

Abdul Qadeer Khan was born in 1936 in Bhopal in the former British India. Around 1960, he arrived at the Technical University in West Berlin to study materials science. A couple of years later, he went to the Netherlands, where he studied metallurgical engineering at Delft University of Technology and went on to do a PhD at the Catholic University of Leuven in Belgium, graduating in 1972. Khan was brilliant at languages and picked up new ones easily. He could communicate fluently in English, German, French and Dutch and, combined with his natural charm, this earned him friends wherever he went. This came in handy in 1972, when he landed a job at the Physical Dynamics Research Laboratory (FDO) in Amsterdam.

FDO was not an ordinary lab but a high-tech subcontractor of the Dutch partner of URENCO, a consortium of British, German and Dutch companies, which was established in 1971 to develop ultracentrifuges for the nuclear industry in Europe. Obviously, this was a secret project that only trusted employees knew about, but for some reason – probably his natural charm again – no one ever did much to check Khan's background. He was soon regarded as one of the participants in the secret centrifuge project, which gave him access to all relevant documents and experimental designs. He could come and go almost as he pleased and he made good use of this position. He translated documents from German to Dutch to gain detailed insight into the construction of the centrifuges and from this he picked up which companies delivered which parts for the different types of centrifuges.[294]

In September 1974 – a few months after India had performed its first nuclear test – A.Q. Khan wrote a letter to Pakistan's Prime Minister Bhutto, offering his help in procuring fissile material for nuclear weapons. Bhutto gratefully accepted, which meant that Khan, from the fall of 1974 until he left the Netherlands with his wife and two children in late 1975, photographed countless documents and drawings, which he passed on to contacts from Pakistani intelligence. This was high-quality material and URENCO has subsequently admitted that Khan probably stole drawings for all the centrifuges the consortium worked on while he was employed at FDO.[295]

After his return to Pakistan, Khan became a highly trusted employee on the Pakistani nuclear bomb project that Prime Minister Bhutto was hell-bent on completing. First, Khan was hired in the PAEC, but because he thought the work progressed far too slowly under the management of Munir Ahmad Khan, he was – with Bhutto's support – made head of a newly established independent lab, Engineering Research Laboratories (ERL), set up to focus solely on the centrifuge project. From that point, he and his rapidly expanding staff contacted the relevant companies in the United Kingdom, Germany, and the Netherlands with exact orders on the thousands of components needed to build ultracentrifuges to produce enriched uranium in Pakistan. A brand new, secret uranium enrichment plant was built in several stages in the city of Kahuta, but it remains a well-kept secret when the first Pakistani nuclear bombs, using U-235 from this plant, were ready to serve as weapons of deterrence. What we do know is that A.Q. Khan announced in 1981 that the plant in Kahuta was now capable of providing a "considerable amount of [enriched] uranium", and that as a reward he was allowed to rename ERL Khan Research Laboratories (KRL).[296] He had achieved a high status in Pakistan, but that was not all: the rumors of his successful KRL corporation spread effectively via a ramified secret network of contacts and middlemen with connections to countries and organizations that had ambitions of gaining access to advanced nuclear technology. We will encounter the name A.Q. Khan several times in the following subchapters, because in the 1980s and 1990s he and his international network were behind numerous attempts – some successful, others less so – to proliferate nuclear weapons to countries that the old nuclear powers and the IAEA did not wish to see armed with the ultimate weapons of mass destruction.[297]

To conclude the A.Q. Khan story, it is appropriate to recall that in 1976, the same year he wrote the decisive letter to Prime Minister Bhutto, he made the often-quoted comment that when all great civilizations – Christian, Jewish, Hindu and Communist – had the bomb, Islamic civilization had to have it too. In that connection, it was of little consequence that Bhutto was removed from power in 1977 and executed for corruption and a contract killing of a political opponent. His successor, General Zia-ul-Haq, was just as keen to procure nuclear weapons as Bhutto had been. In July 1978, Zia-ul-Haq thus made a statement that echoed A.Q. Khan's comment above: "China, India, the U.S.S.R. and Israel in the Middle East possess the atomic arm. No Muslim country has any. If Pakistanis had such a weapon, it would reinforce the power of the Muslim world."[298]

Some of A.Q. Khan's old European friends met him in his home near Islamabad sometime at the end of the 1970s, and he struck them as the same friendly man they had known in the Netherlands and Belgium. But when a BBC reporter wanted to visit him after the news of his role in the transfer of advanced nuclear technology from the West to Pakistan had started to leak in 1979, the reporter was beaten up by security officers guarding Khan's house. In a letter to the editor in the German weekly *Der Spiegel*, Khan accused Western journalists of "false and malicious reporting" when writing about developing countries – especially Muslim countries. He also had harsh words to say about how the Americans and the British viewed themselves:

> These bastards are God-appointed guardians of the world to stockpile hundreds of thousands of nuclear warheads and have the God-given authority of carrying out explosions every month. But if we start a modest program, we are the Satans, the devils, and all the journalists consider it a crusade to publish fabricated and malicious stories.[299]

It remains uncertain when Pakistan became a de facto nuclear state with nuclear bombs ready to be used, but the respected International Institute for Strategic Studies in London estimates that it happened around 1985.[300] However, Pakistan did not perform 'hot' tests of nuclear weapons until May 28 and 30, 1998, in the form of five or six subterranean nuclear explosions as a direct response to the Indian nuclear tests earlier that month. It seems unquestionable that Pakistan at that time – with the help of North Korea – was also far along in the process of developing two-stage Ghauri missiles that could carry nuclear weapons more than 2,000 kilometers. All this played out in the framework of Khan Research Laboratories – another testimony to the role that A.Q. Khan played in the Pakistani endeavors to achieve nuclear parity with India.[301]

The story of Pakistan's path to the nuclear bomb is testament to the fact that even though the five great nuclear powers – the USA, the United Kingdom, the Soviet Union, France and China – may have believed that the NPT from 1968 would prevent the proliferation of nuclear weapons to smaller countries, especially 'unstable' countries in the third world, the existing agreements and security measures were far from sufficient. They simply cannot have been when it was possible to buy vital components on the free market, and when the sellers – be they national institutions or private companies – could earn large sums from selling the requested products. It is a matter for debate how much this situation has changed since the disclosure in 2002 of the international A.Q. Khan network, which we shall encounter again in the next subchapter.

North Korea: "A great leap forward"[302]

North Korea established a nuclear energy commission while the Korean War was still raging and in 1956 things picked up pace with regard to nuclear energy in the poor, war-torn country. From this point, many promising young North Korean students were sent to study at leading technical and scientific institutions in the Soviet Union. In 1959, the Soviet Union and North Korea signed an agreement that obliged the Soviet Union to assist North Korea in establishing a center for the peaceful utilization of nuclear energy in the city of Yongbyon, approximately 100 kilometers north of the capital Pyongyang.

While Soviet support for the Chinese nuclear program dried up completely after 1960, the opposite happened in North Korea. Through the 1960s, the nuclear research center in Yongbyon grew into a large institution that housed, among other facilities, a Soviet IRT-2000 test reactor, which was used both to produce radioactive isotopes and to train North Korean reactor engineers. North Korea for many years depended on Soviet technology transference and nuclear experts, but the country's supreme leader, Kim Il-Sung, consistently insisted that he was in charge of what happened in Yongbyon and the other nuclear institutions that gradually sprung up in the regimented and closed country. He also insisted that North Korea could continue cultivating a positive relationship with China even though the relationship between China and the Soviet Union cooled further during the 1960s. The Soviet Union reluctantly accepted this because North Korea was perceived as an indispensable bulwark against American influence in South and East Asia. After China had performed its first nuclear test in 1964, Kim Il-Sung allegedly tried to exploit his – real or imagined – position to request access to China's nuclear weapons technology, which, however, Mao Zedong refused.[303]

Despite this setback, the North Korean leaders did not give up on their ambition of becoming a nuclear state. At the end of the 1960s, the country expanded its nuclear research program to add a military branch to its civilian nuclear program. Thanks to the ample transfer of technology from the Soviet Union and China in the 1960s, and the many fully trained North Korean nuclear physicists and technicians, North Korea was now able to take the development of nuclear weapons further. And when they needed something, they had supporters willing to help.

Over the course of the 1970s, they received help from the Soviet Union to build a reprocessing facility in Yongbyon to extract plutonium from spent reactor fuel. However, this came at a price, as North Korea in 1977 had to sign a tripartite agreement with the Soviet Union and the IAEA, obliging the country to allow inspections of the nuclear facilities in Yongbyon by the IAEA. Kim Il-Sung accepted this.[304] Now, the North Koreans could take their time to build a much bigger nuclear reactor than the almost 20-year-old test reactor IRT-2000, as well as a facility to produce nuclear fuel for future North Korean reactors. In 1985, Kim Il-Sung also signed the NPT in return for Soviet assistance in building four light water reactors of Soviet design.[305] Based on subsequent developments, it is fair to assume that Kim Il-Sung from the very outset calculated that North Korea could withdraw from the NPT if the country experienced problems with the IAEA inspectors. And this was exactly what happened later.

When North Korea was still bound by the NPT, the IAEA had in 1992–93 made a number of inspections in Yongbyon and found that its engineers had apparently extracted far more plutonium than the 100 grams officially recorded, allegedly derived from some damaged fuel for the 5 MW reactor in Yongbyon. The IAEA's nuclear experts therefore demanded access to inspect a couple of locations where North Korea, by its own admission, stored spent reactor fuel. But the demand was refused because these locations were military areas closed to the public. In the following years, the USA in particular tried hard to make North Korea stay in the NPT collaboration, after it had threatened several times to leave.[306] In a 2018 paper, three American inspectors published a detailed account of what they had found and reported back to IAEA year-by-year from 1992 to 2018 and combined this with a review of the literature and expert analysis of diplomatic and political developments.[307]

The decisive break occurred in 2001 as a result of the CIA picking up clear indications that the father of the Pakistani nuclear weapons – the mysterious A.Q. Khan from the previous subchapter – had sold advanced uranium enrichment equipment in the form of ultracentrifuges, via his smuggling network, to North Korea, Libya, Iran and possibly other countries during the 1990s.[308] Khan received various favors in return. For example, he was allowed to buy some of the newest North Korean missiles, which had longer range and were more precise than the ones Pakistan had at the time. The intelligence, which Khan later confirmed, made the USA adopt a hard line towards North Korea, with the result that Kim Jong-Il, who had succeeded Kim Il-Sung after his death in 1994, finally pulled North Korea out of the NPT in January 2003.

Since 2001, the USA had tried to press Pakistani President Pervez Musharraf to arrest and prosecute A.Q. Khan. Musharraf did remove Khan as director of Khan Research Laboratories, which had developed into a multimillion dollar business, but for months he refused to take further action against Khan, who retained a role as the Prime Minister's 'special adviser'. The game continued until the American and British intelligence agencies managed to redirect a suspicious cargo ship, *BBC China*, headed for Tripoli in Libya, to the Italian harbor city of Taranto. Here, some of the containers were inspected and proved to contain all the parts for more than a thousand ultracentrifuges that the A.Q. Khan network had secretly sold and tried to deliver to Muammar Gaddafi in Libya.[309]

Confronted with this irreputable proof and the USA's threat to publicly expose Pakistan's tacit acceptance of Khan's illegal nuclear proliferation activities, Musharraf was forced to act. This was inconvenient for him as he wanted to maintain positive relations with the USA, while at the same time he was well aware that Khan was a national hero in Pakistan. Caught between a rock and a hard place, Musharraf opted for a compromise he hoped would appease both parties: on January 31, 2004, he fired Khan as special adviser and put him under house arrest. But instead of prosecuting him, Musharraf quickly granted him amnesty after he had admitted his crimes.[310] A.Q. Khan's international network had been discovered, and because Musharraf was convinced that the USA would from now on watch Khan's activities closely, there could be no harm in allowing the people's hero to remain a free man in Pakistan. As reported in the *New York Times*: "On Thursday, February 5, Pakistan's president, General Perez Musharraf, granted a full pardon to Abdul Qadeer Khan, the founder of Pakistan's nuclear weapons program, a day after Dr. Khan appeared on television and confessed to sharing nuclear technology with Iran, North Korea and Libya. As a result, Dr. Khan, 67, will not face prison, fine or any other punishment. Explaining his decision to pardon the scientist, Gen. Musharraf said that Dr. Khan 'is still my hero; he is still high in the sky for me'."[311]

Although North Korea from that point on could no longer make use of Khan and his network, the country shocked the world two years later with the announcement on October 2006 that it had performed its first successful underground nuclear test at Punggye-ri in the north-eastern part of the country. This had happened at "a stirring time when all the people of the country are making a great leap forward in the building of a great prosperous powerful socialist nation", as the North Korean news agency declared in a press release on the test.[312] Obviously, this message mentioned nothing about Khan's network and the invaluable help it had provided to the North Korean nuclear arms development program.

Almost There: Iraq

Late in the afternoon on Sunday June 7, 1981, eight Israeli F-16 aircraft took off from an airbase in Sinai and set a course east over Jordan toward a target north of Baghdad, the Iraqi capital. Apart from extra fuel tanks, each aircraft was equipped with two bombs, each weighing approximately a ton, which naturally lowered the maximum speed. To compensate for this, they were accompanied by six F-15 fighters ready to combat any hostile aircraft they might encounter on their way. The distance from the base to the target and back was 1,800 kilometers, which was at the limit of the range of the aircraft. It was therefore crucial that they not be caught by surprise before reaching their target.[313] But everything went according to the plan devised by the Israeli military command following Prime Minister Menachem Begin's order. The mission was to destroy the Iraqi Osirak nuclear reactor before it was made critical and could start producing plutonium for Iraqi nuclear weapons.

The fighters flew very low to avoid detection by Jordanian, Saudi or Iraqi radar. When the eight bombers closed in on Osirak, they formed a line west of the target so they could attack with the sun behind them. In the preceding months, the pilots had performed numerous bombing exercises on a dummy of the Osirak reactor, situated in the Sinai Desert. This paid off now. Most of the bombs hit the target – the base of the reactor dome where the construction was weakest. The reactor was totally destroyed and, according to the Israeli army command, all aircraft made it safely back to their base. We cannot be sure this is correct, but it is beyond any doubt that the mission was a success for the Israeli military and contributed significantly to ensuring Begin's right-wing Likud Party victory over Shimon Peres's liberal Kadima Party in the Israeli parliamentary election on June 30, 1981.

The Osirak reactor had long been a thorn in Israel's side. Many Israelis saw Iraq's President Saddam Hussein as a ruthless dictator who would not hesitate to eradicate the state of Israel if he had the chance. The political and military leadership in Israel was convinced that the Osirak reactor was built to produce nuclear weapons for Saddam Hussein. The reactor had been provided by France, and the Israelis knew from experience with their own Dimona facility in the Negev Desert that French reactors were an effective means of producing plutonium once they were up and running. They also knew that France at the time had a very lenient attitude toward the safeguards that could have prevented Israel from secretly producing plutonium for nuclear weapons. Therefore, they did not buy the French assurances that French nuclear experts kept the security in Osirak under control and that the Iraqis would not be able to extract plutonium without being discovered.

The Israeli attack on the Osirak reactor was denounced by the IAEA's Director General Sigvard Eklund, who assured the governors that the IAEA "had inspected the Iraqi reactors and had not found evidence of any activity which was not in conformity with the Non-Proliferation Treaty".[314] Eklund described Israel's action as an attack on the NPT itself, which was meant to underpin the development of civilian nuclear energy across the world at the same time as preventing the proliferation of nuclear weapons to more countries than those that had them already. The case was therefore brought before the UN Security Council, which on June 19, 1981 unanimously passed Resolution 487 which supported Eklund's view that the Israeli attack con-

IAEA weapons inspectors arriving on December 12, 2002 at a military facility west of Baghdad suspected of being involved in the development of nuclear weapons.
© Karim Sahib/AFP/Ritzau Scanpix

stituted "a serious threat to the entire safeguards system". In line with the NPT, the resolution confirmed the "inalienable sovereign right of Iraq and all other states, especially the developing countries" to use "nuclear technology for their economic and industrial development".[315]

However, Resolution 487 was a diluted version of the original text proposed by Iraq. This was because the USA had threatened to veto the resolution, because among other reasons one of the IAEA's inspectors, the American Roger Richter, had handed in his resignation a few days after the Israeli attack on the grounds that the IAEA's inspections were not sufficiently thorough. For instance, inspections had to be announced several weeks in advance, and the country in which the inspection was taking place had the right to exclude specific countries from sending inspectors. In the case of Iraq this had meant that the country's nuclear facilities had only been inspected by experts from the Eastern Bloc and so-called alliance-free countries.[316]

As it turned out later, Israel's reluctance to accept the French assurances was well-founded. Shortly before the Israeli attack in the Osirak reactor, the socialist François Mitterrand had replaced the conservative Giscard d'Estaing as president of France. During the presidential election, Mitterrand had brought up the question of the Osirak reactor several times, criticizing the French-Iraqi agreement that the reactor was to run on enriched uranium – a material that the Iraqis could convert almost directly into primitive nuclear bombs if they extracted it from the fuel elements.[317]

One of Mitterrand's first initiatives on May 21, 1981 when he moved into the presidential office in the Élysée Palace was thus to ask his Foreign Minister Claude Cheysson to prepare a report on all details of the French contract with Iraq on the Osirak reactor. It turned out the Cheysson report contained several examples of what the writers of the report characterized as 'loopholes' – vague points that the Iraqis could potentially exploit. These included how long the French technicians were allowed access to the facility after it had become operational, and what was to be done with the spent fuel after it was removed from the reactor. All this needed to be tightened up. The previous *laissez-faire* French nuclear policy, which allowed French companies to sell nuclear reactors and facilities for plutonium extraction to any country that could pay, was to be replaced by a more responsible policy obliging the receiving countries to allow the IAEA to monitor the French facilities.[318] But it was too late in relation to Iraq. The Israelis pre-empted the implementation of the new French government's plan when they destroyed the Osirak reactor on June 7, 1981.[319]

Saddam Hussein considered the Israeli attack to have been beneficial, because his country won international sympathy while Israel was condemned by almost all UN member states.[320] Consequently, due to the new, cautious French policy regarding nuclear technology, Iraq did not try to rebuild the reactor. Instead, the Iraqi military focused on producing large quantities of chemical weapons of mass destruction, which Hussein used against the external enemy Iran as well as the internal enemies, the Kurds, in the northern provinces of Iraq during the ferocious Iran-Iraq War 1980–88. But in the 1980s, Saddam Hussein and his companions also secretly bought advanced nuclear uranium enrichment equipment from obliging Western European companies that were happy to earn money at the same time as helping Iraq defeat its mortal enemy Iran.[321] The Iraqi nuclear technicians did not have time to develop nuclear weapons before Saddam Hussein made the biggest mistake of his life by occupying Kuwait in August 1990 – an act that prompted almost unanimous condemnation among UN member countries.

With the looming threat of a US-led invasion, in the fall of 1990 Saddam Hussein ordered a crash program called Project 601, which entailed the development of a primitive uranium bomb by extracting highly enriched uranium from the fuel of two Iraqi test reactors that had been provided by the USA and the Soviet Union.[322] He failed in this endeavor too. In the spring of 1991, the occupying Iraqi army in Kuwait was vanquished by a US-led UN operation and Saddam had to accept the destruction of his weapons of mass destruction under UN inspection.[323]

Yet after this, questions concerning Iraq's nuclear ambitions would shape the history of the country and indeed much of the region. In 2003, dubious American and British intelligence reports were used as proof that Iraq was in possession of weapons of mass destruction, and thus to establish a rationale for the USA, the United Kingdom and a number of other countries to invade Iraq and force through a regime change in the country. It subsequently turned out that Iraq in fact did not have any of these weapons in 2003, and that the invasion had taken place on false pretenses.

Almost There: Libya

It came as a huge and positive surprise when Libya's dictator Muammar Gaddafi on December 19, 2003 announced to the world that his country would discontinue all work on the development of weapons of mass destruction, and that all international specialists would be welcome to witness the destruction of relevant arsenals and facilities. Having been viewed as a pariah in large parts of the world, Gaddafi suddenly became a celebrity, with whom many Western state leaders were ready to build relationships – until 2011 when Gaddafi's ruthless crushing of an internal rebellion made his newly won friends turn against him and bring his reign to an end through military intervention.[324]

Libya's nuclear adventure dates back to 1975 when the country ratified the NPT, accepting IAEA inspection of the country's nuclear facilities. This was relevant at a time when the Soviet Union was building a 10 MW test reactor at Tajoura, about 25 km from Tripoli. The reactor was finished in 1979 and the entire facility inspected by the IAEA.

On the surface everything appeared to be in perfect order, but that was not the case: Gaddafi, who had already been accused of financing international terrorism, also wanted nuclear weapons – presumably to match Israel's de facto nuclear status. The ratification of the NPT can thus best be described as a cloak behind which Gaddafi was trying by various means to procure nuclear weapons for his country.[325] For instance, in the 1970s, Libya imported more than one thousand tons of uranium oxide from Niger without the IAEA knowing about it. The aim was for the oxide to be part of a secret program and converted into undeclared nuclear fuel in the Tajoura reactor (or some other reactor) with an eye to producing plutonium. The plan never materialized – probably because Libya did not have sufficiently qualified technicians.

Instead, Gaddafi allegedly tried in the 1970s to convince both China and India to allow Libya to buy ready-made nuclear weapons, but they refused. For some years it looked as if Gaddafi might benefit by helping Pakistani Prime Minister Bhutto with funding for Pakistan's nuclear program. However, this plan failed too when Bhutto was removed from power in 1977 and his successor, Zia-ul-Haq, did not trust Gaddafi. This resulted in a temporary postponement of Gaddafi's nuclear ambitions, but in the 1990s he tried once again. This time, the skilled and industrious A.Q. Khan, played a key role as the puppeteer in the network of experts, politicians and European companies that were willing to sell all the ultracentrifuges Libya desired for uranium enrichment.[326] This project would probably have been successful if Khan and his network had not – as mentioned earlier – been exposed by the American and British intelligence services in connection with the inspection of the cargo ship *BBC China* in October 2003. The revelation put a spotlight on Khan and his wealthy clients, including Gaddafi, who had to acknowledge that Libya's secret nuclear activities had become a heavy burden. This led to his surprising message in December 2003, which for some years improved his reputation in the West, albeit not enough to prevent his ultimate fall from grace in 2011.

Over the Threshold and Back Again: South Africa

Ten years before Libya gave up on its nuclear ambitions, another African country, South Africa, had done the same. In South Africa's case, the decision constituted an even more radical break with previous nuclear weapons ambitions. In fact, the country had for some years owned six uranium bombs, each with an explosive force of approximately 17 kilotons of TNT, when President Frederik W. de Klerk in 1993 announced to the South African parliament in Pretoria that these weapons had indeed existed but had now been destroyed under the control of the IAEA.[327]

But how had South Africa, viewed by most countries as a pariah due to the despicable apartheid system, managed to become a nuclear power without the world noticing? The first step in that direction was taken as early as the 1950s when South Africa, like many other countries, received nuclear technology from the USA via the Atoms for Peace program. South Africa was already on the way to earning its bad reputation in the Western democracies, but the country had access to easily accessible uranium deposits, which made the USA turn a blind eye to South Africa's race policies. In 1963, the Kennedy administration did introduce a hesitant arms embargo against the apartheid rule, but the embargo did not include collaboration on nuclear development. As Gabrielle Hecht notes, this is a striking example that "in a time and place where the Cold War trumped racial injustice, South African 'source materials' made the country nuclear enough to drown out the increasingly vocal opposition of postcolonial nations to the apartheid state".[328] The USA provided South Africa with its first test reactor, called Safari-1. All the way up until 1975, the Western superpower also provided heavy water – and probably also enriched uranium – to South Africa with the aim of training the country's nuclear technologists in the most recent technology.

The work took place near the capital of Pretoria, where the state-owned company Atomic Energy Corporation began the construction of a large nuclear research facility in 1960. The center was located at a place called Pelindaba, taken to be isiZulu for 'We don't talk about this anymore'. In the 1960s, focus was almost entirely on developing nuclear reactors for future energy supply, and in that connection the technicians performed preliminary tests of uranium enrichment, which were surprisingly successful. From around 1970, the Atomic Energy Corporation also launched military projects at a new facility close to Pelindaba that was named Valindaba, taken to mean 'we don't talk about this at all'.[329] These placenames are worth noting because they indicated secrecy and at the same time made it clear to those in the know that South Africa was doing something that only a technically evolved and modern state was capable of.[330] The South African Atomic Energy Corporation received a good deal of assistance from Israel, but the details are unknown. What we do know is that in 1965 South Africa, circumventing the IAEA, sent 10 tons of yellowcake, a concentrate made from uranium ore, to Israel. This marked the beginning of a secret collaboration between the two countries on nuclear technology – a collaboration that grew increasingly vital to South Africa as it became marginalized in the international community.[331]

The reason that the Atomic Energy Corporation engaged in military activities was precisely the country's increasing international isolation due to the apartheid laws, as well as the fear among the white minority, who held on to power but at the same time witnessed the black militant rebel movement growing ever stronger. The increasingly unstable political situation in the region also affected the white South African politicians. They reasoned that the possession of nuclear weapons would make South Africa better able to deter the neighboring countries of Angola and Mozambique, where rebel movements had just fought their way to independence from Portugal.

In 1974, Prime Minister John Vorster issued a secret order to work determinedly on developing a South African nuclear bomb. The key scientific figure in the South African nuclear program was the highly competent nuclear physicist, engineer and writer of short stories Pierre C. Haarhoff. Having assessed which path would be the easiest, the South African experts chose the uranium path. This choice implied that they would have to build a facility to produce highly enriched uranium from the natural uranium that South Africa possessed in abundance. The facility, which was built with help from Germany, was named the Y plant. It was operational as planned from 1977, and the first uranium enriched to contain more than 80 percent U-235 was extracted the following year. The first nuclear test was scheduled to take place in the Kalahari Desert, but was cancelled after pressure from the USA and France.[332] The first fully functional nuclear weapon was ready in 1981, and over the course of the 1980s, South Africa's production of enriched uranium was sufficient to build the six uranium bombs mentioned above. The bombs constructed were similar to *Little Boy* – the American nuclear bomb that demolished Hiroshima on August 6, 1945. In a speech to his countrymen, Prime Minister P.W. Botha, who was closely associated with the military, did not hesitate to compare the South African achievement with the Manhattan Project.[333]

Historians William Beinart and Saul Dubow conclude that the six nuclear bombs – apart from the strategic advantage they gave South Africa in the region – also served to demonstrate the technological and scientific capacity of the republic, both internally in the conflict-ridden country and externally in its relationship with the surrounding world, which was becoming ever more critical of the regime.[334] The development of the nuclear bombs was part of a wide-scale militarization of the apartheid state which gained impetus in the 1970s. However, it is not possible to identify a specific point in time or a specific historical decision that marked the transformation of South Africa's nuclear program from a civilian to a military undertaking.[335] As mentioned earlier, quite generally civilian and military technologies and motives have been intertwined in the global history of nuclear technology. The case of South Africa further accentuates how the balance can shift to military considerations in response to unexpected and unpredictable political developments.

South Africa's nuclear bombs were never used, as the challenges of keeping up the apartheid rule by the 1980s had become so insurmountable that the white majority government was compelled to terminate apartheid rule. In February 1989, de Klerk was elected with this as his declared goal, and over the following two years he took a series of important steps that gradually changed the perception of South Africa as a pariah state. First, de Klerk put an end to South Africa's long-standing occupation of the neighboring country of Namibia; second, he released lifelong prisoner Nelson Mandela; and third, he ordered the destruction of all the South African nuclear weapons and closure of the Y plant. De Klerk's decisions were facilitated by the sweeping geopolitical changes that started in 1989, and which led to the end of the Cold War and the ensuing nuclear disarmament. This meant that the world's 'material interest' in South Africa's uranium occurrences shrunk in comparison to the situation during the Cold War. Gabrielle Hecht has argued that the international nuclear arms race underpinned the apartheid regime and most probably prolonged it. This is evident from the fact that apartheid continued many years after both superpowers had declared forms of government based on formal racial segregation unacceptable, and after these forms of government had been abolished in other parts of Africa following decolonization.[336]

It would still be some years before Nelson Mandela could take office as president of South Africa in 1994, and before the six nuclear weapons plus a seventh, which had not been completed, were destroyed. But in 1993, the process was concluded and the IAEA confirmed that it had been carried out satisfactorily. The good news is thus that we have an example of a nuclear state – South Africa – realizing that nuclear weapons did not provide more security, and that security was better achieved by getting rid of nuclear weapons and working toward making Africa a nuclear arms-free zone. South Africa did so by initiating a conference in 1996, where 47 out of the 53 independent African states signed a treaty that committed them to remain free of nuclear arms.

The bad news is that the now-retired head of South Africa's nuclear bomb project, Waldo Stumpf, has said that it is much cheaper to build uranium bombs than most people believed, because uranium enrichment since 1945 was believed to be immensely costly – at least without modern, high-tech ultracentrifuges. Whether this is correct is still contested, but according to Stumpf, South Africa's highly enriched uranium only cost a fraction of the staggering amounts that, for example, Pakistan sacrificed to acquire the coveted but lethal material.[337]

For the record, it should be noted that South Africa is in fact not the only country that has unequivocally relinquished its right to possess nuclear weapons. This applies to the former Soviet republics of Ukraine, Belarus and Kazakhstan, which all chose to become independent nations when the Soviet Union ceased to exist in 1991. Three years later, at the OSCE 1994 conference in Budapest, they agreed to hand over all nuclear weapons in their respective territories to Russia in return for security assurances from Russia, the United States and the United Kingdom. This outcome has been the subject of renewed attention in light of the war between Russia and Ukraine, which began in February 2022. We will return to a further discussion of the decision and its consequences in Chapter 7.

From Twelve to Nine Minutes to Midnight (1970–2000)

The 1970s started out well, as seen from Rabinowitch's editor's chair. In 1972, he thus moved the minute hand on the Doomsday Clock another 2 minutes back on the occasion of the SALT I agreement between the USA and the Soviet Union – a small but important step despite all its shortcomings.

The following year, the passionate Rabinowitch died aged 72, and so this tireless advocate for the non-proliferation of nuclear weapons and nuclear disarmament under international control was spared from experiencing the many setbacks in the following years for his and the *Bulletin*'s primary hope since the journal was first published in 1947. Over the next 12 years, the board of the *Bulletin*, who managed the Doomsday Clock after Rabinowitch's death, felt compelled to set the time forward no fewer than four times.

In 1974, the board set the clock to nine minutes to midnight for two reasons. One was that India had just tested its first nuclear bomb. The Indian leaders may have promised that the bomb would only be used for peaceful purposes, but the board had its doubts. In fact, they saw the test as a glaring setback for the NPT even though India had consistently refused to ratify it. The other reason was that both superpowers were now modernizing their nuclear weapons with associated delivery systems, which was completely against the declaration of intent regarding nuclear disarmament when they entered the NPT in 1968 and ratified it in 1970.[338]

In 1980, the board set the clock to seven minutes to midnight because the USA and the Soviet Union continuously perceived growing numbers of nuclear weapons of deterrence as indispensable to their security. The editorial in the *Bulletin* described the countries' behavior as an ongoing downward spiral: "Both nations [The United States and the Soviet Union] have been behaving like 'nucleoholics' – drunks who continue to insist that the drink being consumed is positively 'the last one' but who can always find a good excuse for 'just one more round'."[339]

The following year saw the third adjustment of the minute hand in 12 years: after the Soviet invasion of Afghanistan and the ensuing sudden deterioration in the relationship between East and West, the board set the Doomsday Clock to four minutes to midnight. Also, the new American president, Ronald Reagan, refused to negotiate with the Soviet Union about arms control and nuclear disarmament. In his opinion, the USA should instead rearm with an eye to winning the Cold War.[340]

But the situation got even worse. The long series of leaps toward midnight reached a climax in 1984 because the Cold War at that point became more intense. The two superpowers appeared to have given up completely on negotiations: "Every channel of communication has been constricted or shot down; every form of contact has been attenuated or cut off. And arms control has been reduced to a species of propaganda," stated the editorial in the *Bulletin*. It also highlighted the intensified arms race between East and West, including President Reagan's plans for the so-called Star Wars Project, as a reason for the decision to set the clock forward to three minutes to midnight.[341]

After that, the hands of the Doomsday Clock time moved slowly away from midnight. A couple of years after the ominous 1984 editorial in the *Bulletin*, an unexpected era of political relaxation between the two superpowers began – as described in Chapter 5 – lasting from around 1986 until shortly before the turn of the millennium. Obviously, this development was reflected in the Doomsday Clock. In 1988, the minute hand was set back to six minutes to midnight, in 1990 to 10 minutes to midnight, and in 1991 – when the Cold War was declared over – the longest the Doomsday Clock had been from nuclear apocalypse since its introduction in the *Bulletin* in June 1947: 17 minutes to midnight.[342]

The many adjustments in these years illustrate that the editors of the *Bulletin* reckoned that the strategic security situation regarding nuclear weapons had improved significantly. We may note that the editors of the *Bulletin* are thus not natural born pessimists or doomsday prophets. Unfortunately, the developments in the following decades have not given the editors much reason to view the global security situation with the same level of optimism as in 1991.

Even before the present millennium, the minute hand on the Doomsday Clock was set forward again twice. In 1996, a slight adjustment was made because the USA and Russia in the *Bulletin*'s opinion did not follow up quickly enough on the strategic nuclear arms reductions that had been negotiated in START II between presidents Bush and Yeltsin in 1993. The fact remained, emphasized the journal, that "although the possibility of a global holocaust is remote, as was true four years ago, some 40,000 [nuclear] weapons remain in the world's arsenals", and this entailed a risk of terrorists getting their hands on weapons from poorly protected arsenals in the former Soviet Union. In 1996, the clock was therefore set to 14 minutes to midnight.[343]

This setting lasted two years. The year 1998 saw the last adjustment in the 20th century, and once again in the wrong direction: when the Doomsday Clock entered the new millennium, it showed nine minutes to midnight. There were several reasons for this, not only the old nuclear states' reluctance to significantly reduce nuclear arms, but also the many demonstrative nuclear tests by India and Pakistan in 1998. The *Bulletin* deemed these tests "a symptom of the failure of the international community to fully commit itself to control the spread of nuclear weapons – and to work toward substantial reductions in the numbers of these weapons".[344] Among those who followed the development closely, the optimism at the end of the Cold War had been quenched quickly and replaced by the realization that the clock in the new millennium would still be close to midnight.

CHAPTER 7

Nuclear Hotspots in the New Millennium

From a Bipolar to a Multipolar World Order

In the years around the end of the Cold War, American political scientists and public intellectuals Francis Fukuyama and Samuel Huntington each published a bestseller in which they – from different perspectives – argued that in the year 1991 a crucial shift in human history occurred.[345] Fukuyama claimed in *The End of History and the Last Man* (1992) that the end of the Cold War marked the conclusion to the century-old struggle between different societal ideologies. The Western democracies, based on capitalist, liberal economic models, had definitely triumphed, and in future the rest of the world would gradually move in the same direction, thus bringing the conflicts of ideologies to an end. The cornerstone of Samuel Huntington's *The Clash of Civilizations and the Remaking of World Order* was the theory that while the world during the Cold War had been split according to societal ideas – Communism in the East and Capitalism in the West – the world after the end of the Cold War was shifting toward a situation in which the most important divisions between people were no longer ideological, political or economic ones, but rather rooted in cultural factors such as language, history, religion and tradition.[346]

Fukuyama and Huntington each presented in his own way a powerful story of rupture. The world of the future would be different from the one previous generations had experienced, argued the authors. However, things turned out differently than they imagined. At the end of the millennium, it was becoming increasingly clear that these stories did not hold water. The consequences of the Cold War in particular persisted and therefore cast shadows far into the new millennium.

A major aspect of this continuation was the nuclear arms predicament, which remained unsolved by the end of the millennium. As we have seen, it was not just the two superpowers, the USA and the Soviet Union, that had nuclear weapons at their disposal by the end of the Cold War. Nuclear weapons were also present – or being developed – close to what we will term the world's 'nuclear hotspots'. We use the term to denote a long-standing conflict, regardless of whether it is of an ideological, political, economic or cultural nature, between two or more countries, where at least one is a state with nuclear weapons capabilities.

Rather than a powerful story of rupture or "the end of history" in the style of Fukuyama and Huntington, nuclear arms and security policy experts today speak of a shift from the First Nuclear Age (1945–91) to a new situation sometimes labelled the Second Nuclear Age (1991–), in which nuclear weapons are still a crucial geopolitical factor in terms of ideology, culture and military strength, but in a different geopolitical context.[347] As described in previous chapters, the primary characteristic of the First Nuclear Age was that the Cold War constituted the strategic framework for the huge arsenals of tactical and strategic nuclear weapons that the two superpowers had built,

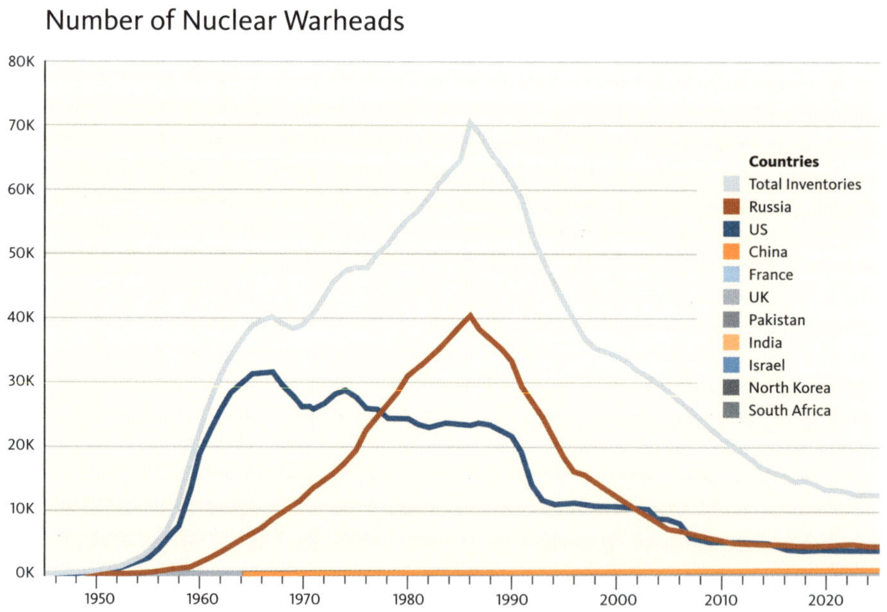

Estimated Global Nuclear Warhead Stockpiles, according to Kristensen et al. (2025) in https://fas.org/initiative/status-world-nuclear-forces/. The reduction in the estimated global nuclear stockpiles from their peak is due to decreases by the United States and the USSR/Russia, which still remain by far the largest possessors of nuclear weapons. In contrast, the stockpiles of other nuclear-armed states are relatively small, as shown by the line near the bottom of the graph. However, they are expected to grow in the coming years.

World Nuclear Forces, January 2025

Country	Year of first nuclear test	Number of deployed nuclear warheads	Total inventory
United States	1945	1770	5177
USSR/Russia	1949	1718	5459
United Kingdom	1952	120	225
France	1960	280	290
China	1964	24	600
India	1974	??	180
Pakistan	1998	??	170
North Korea	2006	??	50
Israel	n.a.	??	90
Total		**3912**	**12241**

"Number of deployed nuclear warheads" in column 3 includes warheads placed on missiles (ICBMs, SLBMs) or located on bases with operational forces. "Total inventory" in column 4 also includes warheads in central storage that could potentially be deployed after some preparation plus retired warheads that have not yet been dismantled. (The figures in this table are taken from Kristensen and Korda, "World Nuclear Forces", Chapter 7 in SIPRI Yearbook 2025.)

based on the logic of 'mutual assured destruction' (MAD) – i.e., that a nuclear attack by one superpower would inevitably be met by a corresponding, devastating attack by the other. In comparison, the Second Nuclear Age is marked by significant reductions in the nuclear arsenals of both the USA and Russia, resulting in a much lower total number of nuclear weapons compared to the peak levels of the Cold War.

Still, both countries have more than sufficient nuclear weapons and delivery systems – and now much more advanced ones – to keep the world in the deadlock of the MAD rationale. In fact, extensive modernization of and investment in the nuclear arsenals is taking place in the old nuclear weapon states, as we shall show in this chapter. Moreover, the Second Nuclear Age is characterized by an increased number of nuclear hotspots in the multipolar world we inhabit after the collapse of the Soviet Union and China's growing geopolitical influence. The new strategic context entails, according to many experts, an increased risk of proliferation of nuclear weapons to more states than the existing nine nuclear powers.[348] More recently, several experts argue that the growing geopolitical volatility after 2020 signals the onset of a Third Nuclear Age, a topic we will revisit in our final chapter.

Whether the security logic of the First Nuclear Age regarding mutual deterrence can be transferred to the current geopolitical situation is an open question to which we will return later in this chapter. First, over the following pages, we will look at five current interstate conflicts that have the potential to lead to wars involving nuclear weapons for the first time since August 1945. Apart from recent developments in the permanently troubled relationship between the neighboring nuclear powers India and Pakistan, the 2010s were dominated particularly by three other nuclear hotspots: USA–North Korea–South Korea, USA–Iran–Israel and USA–Russia, all of which appear more menacing now than they did fifteen years ago. A fifth nuclear hotspot that attracts growing attention is the strained relationship between the USA and China in regard to Taiwan. (This chapter covers the development until January 2025. In our final chapter we discuss the most significant development from February to July 2025 in the hotspots).

It is important to stress that the five hotspots discussed below are not the only ones that could potentially lead to the use of nuclear weapons. The selected hotspots unquestionably belong to the most dangerous and unpredictable today, but overall, the fact is that every time a nuclear power gets into conflict with another country, nuclear power or not, there is a small risk that the conflict will escalate into nuclear war. That is why it is so important that the world not only prevent further proliferation of nuclear weapons but also reduce their number.

India–Pakistan

On February 14, 2019, more than 40 Indian paramilitary security staff were killed in the city of Lethpora in Kashmir, when their military convoy was attacked by a suicide bomber who detonated the bomb when his vehicle passed the convoy. A Pakistani-based, Islamist terror group called Jaish-e-Mohammed took responsibility for the attack that marked the beginning of another chapter in the decades-long conflict between the nuclear-armed neighbors India and Pakistan.[349]

Since India and Pakistan became independent states in 1947, they have been engaged in conflicts over Kashmir. With assistance from the UN, the two nations in 1949 agreed that Kashmir should be divided into a south-eastern, Indian-controlled part and a north-western, Pakistani-controlled part with a border between the two termed the Line of Control (LoC). As described in

The map shows Kashmir, consisting of a part controlled by India, a part controlled by Pakistan and a part annexed by China. The so-called Line of Control is also shown.

© Finn Petersen

Chapter 6, Kashmir was the scene of devastating wars between India and Pakistan in 1947–49 and 1965, and also a brief border war in 1999, while the war in 1971 resulted from East Pakistan's successful attempt to achieve independence from West Pakistan. The periods between these wars, however, have not been peaceful but have been marked by frequent riots and violence, especially in the Indian-controlled part of Kashmir where the majority population is Muslim. Some rebel movements in this part of Kashmir fight for Kashmir to become an independent state, while others want Kashmir to become part of Pakistan. Indian government estimates – which should be taken with some caution – are that 47,000 people in the Indian-controlled part of Kashmir died as a result of terror and violence between 1989 and 2008, and that the number for the following ten years is at least 4,000.[350]

After the last, albeit brief, border war between India and Pakistan in 1999 there was hope that the relationship between the two countries would improve. Once again, they agreed on a truce: Pakistan promised to stop supporting the rebels in the Indian-controlled part of Kashmir, and India offered amnesty to captured rebels who agreed to renounce the armed struggle. Even though neither of these promises was kept, a period with less violence followed – until the conditions deteriorated again in 2016 when India accused Pakistani-supported rebels of having orchestrated the attack on an airbase in northern India. New violent confrontations followed in Kashmir, including the terror attack on February 14, 2019 on Indian security forces.

Less than two weeks later, on February 26, India retaliated when 12 Indian Mirage jets attacked a number of Jaish-e-Mohammed training camps in Pakistan, according to Indian sources killing around 350 militant terrorists. Pakistan admitted that the attacks had taken place, but the Pakistani government-controlled media claimed that the Indian aircrafts had been forced to retreat and that their bombs caused no damage to people or infrastructure in Pakistan. Contradictory claims were made from both sides, once again confirming the ancient saying that truth is the first casualty of war. The following day, Pakistani fighters bombed what were claimed to be military targets in the Indian-controlled part of Kashmir, and the Pakistani military displayed the remains of a shot-down Indian aircraft and the captured pilot to the world press. The pilot, Abhinandan Varthaman, was subsequently returned unharmed to India as a gesture to demonstrate Pakistan's willingness to avoid an escalation of the conflict. That was badly needed as it was, as far as we know, the first time that two nuclear powers had carried out air raids in enemy territory. Both the Indian and the Pakistani political and military leadership must have been in the highest state of emergency in those days, as neither side could be certain how the other side would react to the air raids.[351]

The new conflict between India and Pakistan has not been resolved after the dramatic events in the beginning of 2019. On the contrary, tension has built up after the Indian parliament in August that year passed Hindu National Prime Minister Narendra Modi's suggestion to revoke the partial self-government of the Indian-controlled part of Kashmir. This self-government agreement had been in place since the UN negotiated a plan for the division of Kashmir in 1949. In the future, the region that has been divided in two will be governed directly from New Delhi. This decision prompted the Pakistani Prime Minister at the time, Imran Khan, to vow that he would bring the case before the UN and the International Court of Justice in The Hague, while also issuing a cryptic warning: "If the world does not react today" [...] "if the developed world does not uphold its own laws, then things will go to a place that we will not be responsible for."[352] Since then, tensions have remained high, with frequent exchange of grenades between Indian and Pakistani army units across the LoC, which have almost invariably resulted in the loss of both civilian and military lives.

For each new round of the India-Pakistan conflict, the danger of things getting out of hand increases. Pakistan blinked first during the confrontation in February 2019. The question is whether India can afford to assume that the same will happen next time. How will Pakistan's political and military elite react if they feel that their country is being humiliated by India once more? Both countries are nuclear powers, and each country is estimated to have more then 170 nuclear warheads at its disposal in 2025, cf. table p. 193.

After numerous border skirmishes across the LoC in 2020, a series of peace talks took place between "the Director Generals of Military Operations in India and Pakistan" from November 2020 to February 2021. According to a joint statement, dated February 25, 2021, the two parties had discussed "the established mechanism of hotline contact [and] reviewed the situation along the Line of Control and all other sectors in a free, frank and cordial atmosphere".[353] The two parties

> agreed for strict observance of all agreements, understandings and cease firing along the Line of Control and all other sectors with effect from midnight 24/25 Feb 2021. Both sides reiterated that existing mechanisms of hotline contact and border flag meetings will be utilised to resolve any unforeseen situation or misunderstanding.[354]

Overall, in the four years since then, both parties appear to have honored their commitments under the agreement. No reports of major border skirmishes between India and Pakistan have reached the headlines in international media, which in itself is very positive news. But that is only one side of the coin. The other side is that both countries are expanding and modernizing their nuclear striking force. A *Bulletin* report from May 2024 notes, for example, that "On March 11, India successfully tested a new multiple independently targetable reentry vehicle (MIRV) on its Agni-V medium to intercontinental-range ballistic missiles, sparking concerns about the country's strategic ambitions".[355] The report continues:

> The technological gap between China and India and the asymmetry in technological capability between Pakistan and India are driving each state's current strategic posture. While the improvements and upgrades in defense inventory have raised significant concerns in the regional dynamics, potentially destabilizing technologies like MIRVs now risk fueling a full-scale arms race between China, India, and Pakistan.

This assessment points out the emerging contours of a tripartite arms race between three of the world's most populous countries.

In an extensive study from 2019, an international team of experts estimated that India and Pakistan would have approximately 500 nuclear warheads in total in 2025. These warheads could range in explosive force from 10–45 kilotons – the size of those the two countries tested in 1998 – to several hundred kilotons, more than 10 times the force of the Nagasaki bomb. They were also expected to have missiles capable of delivering these weapons up to 3,000 kilometers.[356] The same study made calculations for a scenario in which India fires 100 of these nuclear weapons against Pakistani population centers, and Pakistan retaliates with 150 nuclear weapons against similar population centers in India. The estimate is that this scenario would result in the instant death of around 150 million people. This is beyond frightening, but apart from these instant effects, the researchers estimate that firestorms in cities would release between 16 and 36 million tons of carbon which, in the form of smoke, would rise up to the stratosphere and spread across the planet. The particles in the smoke would prevent a large part of the sun's radiation incident on the Earth's atmosphere from reaching its surface, a phenomenon called "nuclear winter". For this particular theoretical scenario, the researchers calculate that the solar radiation on the surface of the planet would be reduced by 20–35 percent and would result in a drop in the surface temperature of 2–5 degrees Celsius and a drop in precipitation of 15–30 percent over a ten-year period. This would lead to widespread crop failure and famine across most of the planet. The conclusion is that a regional conflict with mutual nuclear attacks would have terrible consequences not only in that region but most likely also worldwide in the form of famines, destroyed social structures and mass deaths.

U.S. President Trump and North Korean leader Kim Jong-Un shake hands during their meeting in Hanoi on February 27, 2019. Trump sought an agreement to remove all nuclear weapons from the Korean Peninsula, but the negotiations broke down.

© Saul Loeb/AFP/Ritzau Scanpix

USA–North Korea–South Korea[357]

In retrospect, the period from 2006, when North Korea conducted its first nuclear test, to the start of Donald Trump's first presidency in 2016 can be likened to a drama, with North Korea playing the role of the villain. Following North Korea's withdrawal from the NPT, the militarized and authoritarian country broke agreements on nuclear disarmament time and time again, despite having co-signed them ceremoniously at the six-nations talks together with the USA, China, Russia, Japan and South Korea. Every time North Korea had detonated a nuclear bomb in the subterranean test area at Punggye-ri (which happened in 2006, 2009, 2013, twice in 2016, and 2017 – the last one with a yield of well over 100 kilotons of TNT), or performed provocative tests with missiles of increasing range, new negotiations began and new agreements were made, only to be broken again, usually because

North Korea, according to its opponents, denied the IAEA inspectors access to all nuclear facilities within the country's borders. North Korea, on the other hand, claimed that the USA was to blame for not honoring the promise to lift all the sanctions imposed on North Korea.

During Trump's first presidency, the ongoing play turned into an absurd drama in which the two main adversaries threatened each other with fire and brimstone in a tone more reminiscent of a school playground than discussions between leaders of two sovereign nations. Immediately after a North Korean nuclear test in August 2017 of a Hwasong missile, which American experts described as an intercontinental ballistic missile, the country's supreme leader, Kim Jong-Un, bragged that North Korea was now able to hit targets even in the USA. This comment infuriated Trump who warned the North Koreans that at if they continued making such threats, they would face "fire and fury like the world has never seen". And on September 19, 2017, a few days after North Korea had tested its hitherto most powerful nuclear weapon, which Kim Jong-Un claimed was a hydrogen bomb, Trump responded on the social media platform Twitter (now called X) that "Rocket Man is on a suicidal mission". This made Kim Jong-Un retort by describing Trump as "a mentally deranged" person.[358] The mutual insults and threats came to a head after Kim Jong-Un, in his New Year's speech on January 1, 2018, told his fellow countrymen (and the rest of the world): "The nuclear button is always on my desk." This comment prompted a tweet from Trump the following day reading: "Will someone from his depleted and starved regime please inform him that I too have a Nuclear Button, but it is a much bigger & more powerful one than his, and my Button works!"[359]

But what seemed to be turning into an ever-escalating series of insults nevertheless marked the beginning of a remarkable turnaround. Over the following year and a half, the two heads of state met three times – first on June 12, 2018 in Singapore, second on January 27, 2019 in Hanoi, and third on June 30, 2019 at the demarcation line in Panmunjom.[360] Trump particularly highlighted the first meeting as a great success. He talked about Kim Jong-Un as his good friend and predicted a speedy solution to the more than 70-year-old conflict between North and South Korea – a solution that would make the entire Korean peninsula nuclear arms-free. Things did not turn out this way. Kim Jong-Un walked out of the second meeting when Trump let him know that the USA knew about the existence of more North Korean nuclear facilities than the country had told the IAEA. And the meeting in Panmunjom was merely a ceremonial meeting intended to show the world that the two leaders were on speaking terms and mutually respected each other. Over the next months the unpredictable drama continued, but little happened. This is probably due to the fact that President Trump spent much time defending his *laissez-faire* attitude to the rampant Covid-19 epidemic that hit the USA extremely hard over most of 2020, and because he was completely engrossed in the electoral campaign he ended up losing.

After Joe Biden moved into the White House in 2021, the public drama of the relationship between the USA and North Korea was less pronounced. On April 30, 2021, the Biden administration revealed the policy it intended to pursue in regard to North Korea, a mix between President Obama's patient, gentle pressure and Trump's attempt to strike a quick, all-encompassing deal with Kim Jong-Un.[361] Predictably, North Korea reacted negatively to Biden's initiative, but the escalated rhetoric characteristic of the first Trump presidency was toned down by both sides. However, on March 24, 2022, North Korea tested its longest-range intercontinental ballistic missile so far, which traveled 1,000 kilometers before landing approximately 150 kilometers from the Japanese peninsula of Oshima. The missile test was likely intended to send a clear message to the world about the credibility of the North Korean nuclear threat.[362]

The test in March 2022 was just the beginning. It was followed by many more over the next months and years. Perhaps the most alarming to Americans were the tests conducted on April 13, July 12 and December 17, 2023, of the solid-fuel ICBM, Hwasong 18, which has an estimated range of 15,000 km. This means the missile could potentially reach any location in the USA. However, less sophisticated short and medium ranged ballistic and cruise missiles, armed with nuclear warheads, probably pose the most serious near-term threats to North Korea's neighbors, South Korea and Japan, and to American bases in South-East Asia.[363] But missiles alone do not constitute a threatening military arsenal; the number and size of nuclear warheads is even more important. The Notebook concerning North Korea, published July 2024 by The Federation of American Scientists (FAS) in the *Bulletin*, estimates that North Korea may have produced sufficient fissile material to build up to 90 nuclear weapons but has probably only assembled around 50. The Notebook also estimates that North Korea could have enough fissile material to produce up to 130 weapons by the end of the decade.

The increased tension in East Asia is partly a result of the war in Ukraine, to which North Korea has contributed significant amounts of ammunition and over 10,000 soldiers on the Russian side, and partly due to the rapid expansion of North Korea's nuclear arsenal in recent years. Also, whereas Kim Jong-Un in 2020 stated that North Korea's nuclear weapons "will never be used preemptively", North Korea's parliament in September 2022, passed a law which allowed the country "[the] right to launch nuclear weapons preemptively" if Kim Jong-Un and his government in Pyongyang feel threatened.[364] These developments increase the risk of the proliferation of nuclear weapons to countries in the region that have until now harbored few ambitions in this direction. On January 11, 2023, South Korean President Yoon Suk-Yeol thus stated that if North Korea were to continue its nuclear threats, the USA would have to deploy nuclear weapons in South Korea again or, alternatively, his country would develop nuclear weapons of its own.[365] However, Yoon's new course runs against American interests in the region. Therefore, to stabilize the situation, South Korea and the USA in April 2023 signed a bilateral agreement, obliging South Korea to refrain from developing nuclear weapons in return for the USA periodically deploying nuclear-armed submarines to the area and allowing South Korea more influence on the nuclear strategy on the Korean peninsula.[366]

Still, nothing indicates that North Korea will stop the expansion of its nuclear arsenal. According to U.S. government officials, North Korea has conducted over 80 ballistic missile tests capable of delivering nuclear weapons since 2022.[367] Also, according to other American sources, there is good reason to expect more North Korean nuclear tests before long in continuation of the recent intensification of a nuclear strategy that allows preventive use of nuclear weapons.[368]

In this situation it is not unlikely that South Korean leaders will be induced to launch an independent nuclear program. In fact, on December 3, 2024, the 'lame duck' president Yoon Suk Yeol, with less than 20 percent approval rating and an opposition-controlled parliament, declared martial law in South Korea in a televised announcement "to protect the country from 'antistate' forces that sympathize with North Korea".[369] A few hours later, a sufficient number of lawmakers – a majority from opposition parties but also a few from Yoon's own party – voted to block the martial law, which would have given Yoon absolute power and put an end to South Korea's democracy. Yoon is now impeached by parliament, a process that may answer the question many people in Korea and abroad are asking: Did Yoon impose martial law to enable the nuclearization of South Korea? This cannot happen as long as the country is under obligation by the NPT, but for precisely this reason it may put the UN non-proliferation treaty from 1968 under significant pressure.

USA–Iran–Israel[370]

Iran's nuclear ambitions date back to before the Islamic Revolution in 1979.[371] In 1974, the country's Western-oriented absolute monarch, Shah Muhammad Reza Pahlavi, introduced an ambitious nuclear project that, over the next decades, was intended to result in 20 large Iranian reactors, a reprocessing facility for spent nuclear fuel and an enrichment facility to produce enriched uranium. Iran was a rich country, but its wealth rested on large oil reserves that the shah wished to stretch as far as possible by investing massively in nuclear energy for power production. He was probably also planning to use the peaceful nuclear energy production as a cloak for developing Iranian nuclear weapons, but we cannot know for certain.

Pahlavi never saw his project come to fruition; while it was still embryonic, he was forced to flee Iran when Ayatollah Khomeini returned from exile in France in 1979 to lead the Islamic Revolution. Khomeini immediately stopped the nuclear program, which he declared to be 'un-Islamic'. However, five years later he changed his mind and tried to get foreign partners to complete the construction of the reactors at Bushehr that had begun under the shah, and building new ones as well. The tense relationship between Iran and the West after the revolution meant that the necessary assistance was procured mainly from the Soviet Union and China.[372]

Back in 1968, Iran had signed the NPT. However, this did not keep Iran from launching a series of new projects from the 1990s – projects the Iranian government claimed had peaceful aims only, but which the USA suspected were intended to provide Iran with nuclear weapons. The most notable project was the construction of a facility at the city of Natanz; it was revealed shortly after 2000 that the facility housed a significant number of uranium enrichment ultracentrifuges, likely obtained through the A.Q. Khan network discussed in Chapter 6. Iran claimed that these centrifuges were only intended to enrich uranium up to 3.5 percent U-235, which was required for the country's light water reactors. But many were skeptical of this information.

The suspicions changed into something like certainty when the IAEA announced in 2006 that faint traces of uranium enriched to more than 3.5 percent U-235 had been found at a location where, according to Iran's own declarations, there was not supposed to be enriched uranium. A group of countries with detailed knowledge of nuclear energy and nuclear weapons, consisting of the five permanent members of the UN Security Council – the USA, the United Kingdom, France, Russia and China – supplemented by Germany, were tasked with keeping a close eye on the developments in Iran. The group, which went by the description P5+1, found no clear evidence of breaches of the NPT, but over the following years they found that the number of Iranian uranium centrifuges grew dramatically, having reached no fewer than 19,000 in 2015. This happened in spite of the fact that the Natanz facility in 2011 had been exposed to a cyber-attack via the so-called Stuxnet malware that was rumored to be developed in Israel and/or the USA. The attack incapacitated approximately a thousand centrifuges by making them spin so fast they broke down.[373]

The pressure on Iran steadily increased to the point that, in July 2015, the country entered an agreement with P5+1 and the EU called the Joint Comprehensive Plan of Action (JCPOA), entailing heavy limitations on Iran's nuclear ambitions in the following 25 years. The agreement required Iran to reduce its number of uranium centrifuges to 4,000 and to limit uranium enrichment to a maximum of 3.67 percent U-235. In return, the other parties would lift the sanctions introduced to pressure Iran. The vast majority of the sanctions were lifted on January 16, 2016.

Most observers viewed the agreement as a breakthrough that would contribute to stabilizing the situation in a part of the world marked by political, economic, social and religious unrest. But the cautious optimism was dashed after Donald Trump was inaugurated as president in January 2017. During his campaign, he had already called JCPOA a "disaster", mentioning it as "the worst deal ever negotiated", and predicting that it would lead to "nuclear holocaust" because it did not prevent Iran from recommencing its nuclear arms program as soon as the agreement terminated.[374] Trump also promised that soon after taking office, he would pull the USA out of JCPOA and reintroduce severe sanctions against Iran to punish the regime for supporting international terrorism.

Trump stuck to his word. In May 2018, he announced that the USA was pulling out of the agreement, that sanctions against Iran would be reintroduced and that companies – no matter where they were situated – would be subject to boycott if they traded with Iran. Even though the other members of JCPOA chose to follow the agreement, many non-American companies gave up their engagement in Iran, fearing they would be cut off from the US market and the US-dominated bank system. The Iranian leaders declared that Iran was no longer committed to the agreement, and the country's nuclear technicians began enriching uranium above the 3.67 percent U-235 limit stipulated in JCPOA.

In the period from 2019 to the beginning of 2020, tensions rose in the region around the Persian Gulf. There were almost daily reports of new attacks or provocations, including the Iranians' (or some of their proselytes') attacks on oil tankers in the Gulf of Oman in May/June 2019 and Saudi oil facilities a few months later; the American assassination of the high-ranking Iranian General Qassem Soleimani on January 3, 2020, and Iranian retaliation in the form of missile attacks on American bases in Iraq, as well as the introduction of new, advanced uranium enrichment centrifuges; and the murder of the leading Iranian nuclear specialist Mohsen Fakhrizadeh on November 27, 2020, which Iran accused Israel of having planned, and which Iran used as a reason to stop the IAEA's inspections of its nuclear facilities. Every time one of these events took place, the risk of the conflict getting out of hand increased and the risk of nuclear war in the Middle East increased. Behind it all loomed the constant threat that the USA and/or Israel would eventually deliver the final blow, as their leaders at the time, Trump and Netanyahu, had both vowed that Iran would never be allowed to possess nuclear weapons.

Joe Biden took the presidential oath in January 2021 and softened the aggressive policies of the first Trump administration towards Iran. Some of the sanctions were reduced, and he stated that on certain conditions the USA would be willing to re-enter JCPOA.[375] Negotiations for a renewal of the JCPOA treaty began in Vienna in early 2021, but on April 11 a new event struck in the form of a power outage at the uranium enrichment plant in Natanz. The Iranians were convinced it was sabotage and notified the IAEA that they would bring another 1,000 ultracentrifuges into use and begin to produce uranium enriched to a U-235 content of up to 60 percent.[376]

In the fall of 2021, the parties recommenced a renewal of the JCPOA treaty. The lengthy process was impeded further because in 2019 Iran had appointed a new president, the very conservative Ebrahim Raisi, who in contrast to his predecessor, Hassan Rouhani, was known as a hardliner in negotiations with the West. The negotiations also took place under heavy time pressure due to uncertainty and disagreements regarding how close the Iranian uranium enrichment program was to crossing the threshold that would make Iran a nuclear power.[377] If this threshold were crossed, the very basis for JCPOA would disappear.

On March 27, 2022 – i.e., about a month after the Russian army had invaded Ukraine – American Secretary of State Antony Blinken and Israeli Minister of Foreign Affairs Yair Lapid held a press conference in Jerusalem. This took place immediately before their extraordinary meeting in Israel's Negev Desert with the foreign ministers of four Arab states: the United Arab Emirates, Bahrain, Egypt and Morocco, all of which shared Israel's fear that Iran would become a nuclear power. At the press conference, Blinken was very outspoken when he promised Lapid that "We are both committed to, both determined, that Iran will never acquire a nuclear weapon".[378]

However, the question is whether the USA and Israel could prevent it from happening. Since 2015, Iran has produced significant amounts of enriched uranium, bringing the country very close to the lower limit for nuclear bomb uranium, which is approximately 90 percent. Also, Iran has distributed its nuclear facilities in many subterranean locations in the large, mountainous country, meaning that in practice it would be nigh on impossible to destroy them all with air raids. The fact that Iran openly supports Russia in the war against Ukraine further demonstrates that Iran's leadership does not refrain from challenging the Western powers.

On October 7, 2023, Hamas, a Palestinian militant group with ties to Iran, launched a devastating attack in southern Israel, resulting in the death of about 1200 Israelis, and more than 200 civilians and military personnel taken as hostages to Gaza. The awful events triggered the Gaza war, which reduced much of Gaza to a wasteland of destroyed buildings, with more than 55,000 Palestinian men, women and children killed, as of May 2025. At the same time, Israel clashed with the Iranian-backed Hezbollah in Lebanon, and through targeted surprise attacks, the Israelis killed a significant number of high-ranking military officials from Hamas, Hezbollah and the Iranian Revolutionary Guard. In April and October of 2024, Iran and Israel were on the brink of a full scale war when they launched against each other hundreds of missiles and drones, armed with conventional bombs.

One of the strikes by Israel was directed against an Iranian air base close to the Isfahan nuclear complex, which hosts nuclear reactors, a fuel production plant and other nuclear facilities. The complex was not hit on this occasion, but Iran's nuclear program is a tempting target for Israel, especially if its leaders sense that they have American support in carrying out a full scale attack. Iran, on the other hand, may feel tempted to speed up its efforts to obtain nuclear weapons.

In a 2024 report, the nuclear expert, Hui Zhang, who has studied the technical history of China's nuclear development program from 1955 onwards compared the program of the two countries. China, he notes, obtained the necessary amount of highly enriched uranium in 1964 and completed the final assembly and testing of its first atomic bomb within a few weeks. Zhang's conclusion is that if Iran has already made the necessary preparations, i.e. developed an initiator, a focusing system for imploding the U-235 target etc., then it would probably be able to pass the nuclear threshold only three weeks after the final decision has been taken by the Iranian leadership.[379]

What the USA and Israel intend to do if Iran were to become a nuclear state is uncertain, but undoubtably, the world would face a new, critical situation, with less room for diplomatic maneuver in this unstable nuclear hotspot. Indeed, it is highly likely that Iran's rivals, Saudi Arabia, Egypt and Morocco, would also attempt to acquire nuclear weapons. If that happened, the Middle East would end up in a nuclear armament spiral with immense consequences in the region and beyond (for most recent development see chapter 9).

USA–Russia

In a broader historical perspective, the years between 1985 and 1998 appear unusual in the long history of nuclear weapons: the Cold War enemies agreed to substantial mutual disarmament measures. The agreements behind the abbreviations ABM, SALT I, SALT II, INF, START I and START II were negotiated surprisingly quickly, offering, for the first time since 1945, real hope for a world (almost) free of nuclear weapons within a few years. But things turned out differently. The Indian and Pakistani nuclear tests in 1998, the inauguration of Vladimir Putin as Russian president whose top priority was to restore Russia as a superpower, and the terrorist attacks on the USA on September 11, 2001 caused both the USA and Russia to return to the trend during the Cold War: reinforcing the nation through armament, not least in regard to the quality of nuclear weapons.

During the Cold War, it had become increasingly clear to the leaders of the two superpowers that the thousands of nuclear weapons on both sides of the Iron Curtain only made sense as weapons of deterrence. Few responsible leaders truly believed that the smaller, so-called tactical nuclear weapons, designed for use on a limited battlefield, could be used without a great risk that the situation would escalate into an exchange of strategic nuclear weapons in the megaton range. Thus, all nuclear weapons were perceived as weapons of deterrence, produced to keep the enemy from attacking. If a nuclear attack occurred, both attacker and defender could expect total destruction in a devastating nuclear war. It was particularly this realization in both East and West that brought the parties to recognize the futility of producing more and more nuclear weapons and means of delivery, and they entered into the agreements discussed in Chapter 5 in the years 1985–98.

However, since the turn of the millennium, things have mostly gone downhill. It seems that the experiences from the Cold War have now been forgotten and that Russia, which as mentioned earlier inherited all the Soviet Union's nuclear weapons, and the USA have started acting again as if some nuclear weapons can be used for specific purposes in the same way as conventional weapons in a limited war. For instance, both the USA and Russia have developed hypersonic missiles that can be fired from aircraft. The missiles can carry relatively large although formally 'small' nuclear weapons with an explosive force less than that of the Hiroshima bomb, and can reportedly hit within 20 meters of a military target located two to three thousand kilometers away.[380] This is just one example of a development on a path to "new age of nuclear instability", as the then-CEO of the *Bulletin of the Atomic Scientists* Rachel Bronson wrote in an article in the *New York Times* in January 2019.[381] Stability is non-existent because it is tempting to use this type of weapon if the leaders reckon it will not result in total apocalypse. But what if they are wrong?

The lacking stability is obviously more than just a result of the development of hypersonic missiles. They are merely one example of a general drive to modernize and enhance the efficacy of the nuclear forces in all nine nuclear-armed states. Another example is that, in the mid-2010s, Russia developed a hypersonic variety of a well-known, short-range ground-to-ground cruise missile (Iskander-K), which the Russians claim is allowed under the INF Treaty signed by Reagan and Gorbachev in 1987. Western weapons experts, however, estimate its range to be far above the limit of 500 kilometers stipulated in the treaty.[382] In spring 2019, this brought President Trump to revoke the INF on the grounds that it was superfluous when Russia did not honor it anyway. This made Putin revoke the treaty as well. According to him, the USA was entirely to blame because they had begun installing anti-ballistic missiles near the Russian borders shortly after 2000. The rationale was that the missiles were intended to shoot down missiles from Middle Eastern rogue states and terrorist groups, but no one could deny that they could also be used against Russian missiles.

All this meant that the INF Treaty, which since 1987 had banned an entire class of nuclear-armed missiles in Europe, was now effectively neutralized, contributing to the return of uncertainty and instability. It is thus a discouraging fact that the USA and Russia are in these years conducting extensive, extremely expensive, once-in-a-generation modernizations of their nuclear arsenals. The current sizes and compositions of these arsenals are estimated in a number of articles by Hans M. Kristensen et al. in the *Bulletin of the Atomic Scientists*.[383] The term 'nuclear arsenal' here includes the warheads as well as the means of delivery – whether land-based, sea-based or air-based – the so-called Nuclear Triad.

Naturally, we know more about the American plans for modernization because every year Congress considers various requests from the three US forces for funding of specific arms systems. Recent plans include a new class of nuclear-powered submarine, called Columbus, to replace the current 40-year-old Ohio-class submarines, which seem menacing enough. When submerged, an Ohio-class submarine can fire up to 20 missiles with a range of 7,000 kilometers, the payload of each consisting of a number of individually controllable nuclear weapons. The price of this specific renewal of the nuclear-powered and nuclear-armed submarines, which is supposed to be finished in 20 years, is expected to be at least 128 billion dollars.[384] But this is only a fragment of the planned renewals within the sea-based leg of the nuclear triad. In addition to this, there will be upgrades of the land-based leg, including approximately 400 new, strategic ICBMs (called Sentinel) armed with nuclear weapons and installed in deep underground silos in the mid- and south-western US states. In 2020, the cost of the modernization program was estimated at $96 billion. However, as William J. Hennigan reported in an authoritative *New York Times* article from October 2024, "the price tag has skyrocketed to $141 billion".[385] For the air-based leg, there are plans for a new nuclear cruise missile called a Long Range Standoff Weapon, which can be fired from upgraded B-52 bombers and, in the future, the more advanced B-21 Raiders. The price tag for the entire modernization of the United States nuclear triad is estimated at 1,700 billion 2021 dollars over the next 30 years, i.e. $57 billion on average each year. This is nearly double the amount – when adjusted for inflation – that the US spent on the Manhattan Project during the Second World War. Many years' experience with large-scale military development projects causes many experts to be skeptical of this estimate and to expect large budget overruns.[386]

It probably irks American military staff and politicians when Russia's dictatorial President Putin claims that his country has already come a long way in modernizing its arsenals. In December 2020, Putin stated that modern weapons and equipment now made up 86 percent of Russia's nuclear triad, and that he expected that number to grow to 88.3 percent within a year.[387] He rubbed more salt into the wound by emphasizing how quickly the Russian defense could be modernized and made more efficient to ensure that the country remains on a par with its competitors: "It is absolutely unacceptable to stand idle. The pace of change in all areas that are critical for the Armed Forces is unusually fast today. It is not even Formula 1 fast – it is supersonic fast. You stop for a second and you start falling behind immediately."[388] However, in his speech Putin also expressed regret that the USA in the preceding years, "under contrived pretexts", had pulled out of several agreements such as the INF Treaty, which for many years had contributed to containing the nuclear arms race between the USA and Russia. And he added: "We have repeatedly stated our readiness to extend the New Start Treaty, but there has been no response."[389]

The background to this is that in 2011, the USA and Russia developed the so-called New START agreement which was set to remain in effect until 2021. The agreement aimed over a seven-year period to limit the number of deployed intercontinental strategic missiles to 700 and the number of deployed nuclear warheads to 1,550 for each country. These numbers could not be exceeded, regardless of whether they referred to land-based missiles (ICBMs), submarine-based missiles (SLBMs) or strategic bombers that could carry nuclear weapons. Through a significant number of mutual inspections, around 20 per year in each country, it was confirmed in 2018 that both nations had largely adhered to the agreement which, however, was set to expire three years later unless an extension was negotiated. During Trump's first presidency, this seemed unlikely because Trump and his administration believed

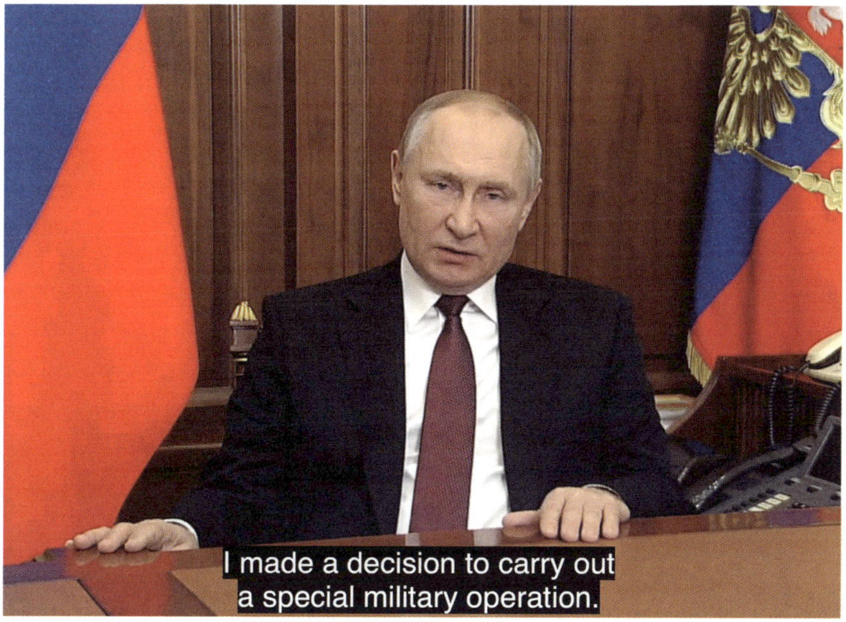

In a televised speech on February 24, 2022, President Putin warned the West that attempts to interfere with Russia's "special military operation" in Ukraine will lead to "consequences you have never seen before".

the Russians had not fully adhered to the agreement, and the Trump administration did not want any limitations on the ability of the US to further enhance its military armament. The agreement was salvaged at the last minute. Shortly after Joe Biden took office, the USA and Russia agreed to extend New START for five years – i.e., until 2026. However, this was the only bilateral armament limitation agreement from the later years of the Cold War and the immediate post-Cold War period to survive the turbulent years under the first Trump administration.[390]

During the first months of Biden's presidency, a series of promising discussions, known as the Strategic Stability Dialogue, was initiated between Washington and the Kremlin.[391] These discussions, addressed among other points a reinforced nuclear inspection system. However, the talks were discontinued in the beginning of 2022 as the growing Russian troop deployment along the Russian-Ukrainian border aggravated the tensions between the NATO countries and Russia. On February 24, 2022 Russian troops crossed the Ukrainian border and thus started a brutal full-scale war. The relationship between Russia and the Western powers worsened significantly with the outbreak of the war pushing the nuclear issue into a new, turbulent phase. Immediately after the invasion, Putin stated in a TV-transmitted speech that any foreign powers who would interfere would face "consequences greater than any of you have faced in history".[392] The veiled threat of using nuclear weapons became more explicit a few days later when Putin stated that Russian forces with access to nuclear weapons would be put on high alert. Such direct reference to nuclear weapons in connection with an ongoing conventional war had probably never been made at any point during the Cold War. The Russian attempt to quickly overthrow the government in Kiev failed, and Russian troops instead occupied the eastern regions of Ukraine along an unstable frontline. As the war stretched into its second and third years, Putin and his inner circle of military and political leaders issued both implicit and explicit warnings that the conflict might escalate to nuclear levels. NATO has not specified what its response would be in such a scenario. These statements issued from Moscow were particularly frequent during moments when Russia was struggling on the battlefield, and when Western powers provided more powerful conventional weapons to Ukraine, fueling ongoing speculations about Putin and his regime's nuclear red lines. The war continued unabated into 2025 (developments after january 2025 are discussed in chapter 9).

The war in Ukraine significantly worsened the relationship between the USA and Russia, with significant repercussions for arms control agreements. In March 2023, Russia suspended its participation in the New START agreement, with Putin declaring that the suspension would remain in effect until the USA halted its support for Ukraine.[393] In November 2023, Russia also officially withdrew its ratification of the Comprehensive Nuclear Test Ban Treaty (CTBT), placing Russia on the same footing as the USA, with both countries having signed but not ratified the treaty. This marked a significant setback, as the Biden administration had only a few years earlier indicated plans to pursue a ratification of the CTBT as part of efforts to play a more active role in international arms control. However, this did not materialize, and instead the two largest nuclear powers reached parity at a lower level, making the existing moratorium on nuclear testing less certain.[394]

The war in Ukraine thus dramatically increased nuclear tensions in a region in which the nuclear threat seemed, at least to observers outside the region, at one point to have been contained. The historical backdrop in this respect is the so-called Budapest Memorandum of 1994 in which Ukraine,

Belarus and Kazakhstan, following negotiations with the USA, the United Kingdom and Russia, gave up the nuclear weapons they inherited on their territories after the collapse of the Soviet Union.[395] Ukraine, Belarus and Kazakhstan also joined the NPT whose signatories, except for the five oldest nuclear powers, waive their right to ever acquire nuclear weapons. Ukraine's road to relinquishing the nuclear weapons was the most complicated. After the Soviet Union dissolved, Ukraine was left with the world's third-largest nuclear arsenal, behind only Russia and the USA. Although Ukraine did not have a complete nuclear weapons production cycle, it had greater nuclear expertise and a more profound fear of its eastern neighbor than did Belarus and Kazakhstan. However, post-Chernobyl there was little domestic political support for pursuing a "nuclear option" and, more importantly perhaps, the pressure from the major powers – Russia, the US and the UK – partly aided by the NPT framework left the Ukrainians with no real way of retaining or pursuing a status as a nuclear weapon state. As Ihor Pustovy, the general responsible for Ukraine's nuclear disarmament in the 1990s, put it, "Nuclear disarmament was the price of our independence".[396] After lengthy negotiations, in 1994 Ukraine relinquished its nuclear weapons systems and Russia agreed to respect the sovereignty and the existing borders of Ukraine. This assurance was broken in 2014 when Putin orchestrated a coup and annexed Crimea, and again in 2022 when Russian troops crossed into Ukraine.[397] The invasion fuels a deep sense of betrayal, as Ukraine gave up the world's third-largest nuclear arsenal in exchange for security assurances, only to be invaded by one of the countries – Russia, a nuclear weapon state – that had provided those assurances. Indeed, the invasion was not only an attack on Ukraine's sovereignty but also on the already fragile non-proliferation system. As we will discuss later in this chapter, the war in Ukraine highlights the weaknesses of the NPT and contributes to growing dissatisfaction among non-nuclear weapon states with the system's inequities and its lack of credibility in ensuring their security in a world in which nuclear weapons are part of the global order.

USA–China–Taiwan

Nuclear weapons play a central role in the geopolitical rivalry between the USA and China. China, like other nuclear-armed states, has been expanding its arsenal of nuclear weapons and delivery systems in recent years. This buildup is occurring at an accelerating pace, with China planning to double its stockpile of warheads within the next decade, or potentially sooner.[398] American military leaders refer in reports and news media to the Chinese armament as a reason for reinforcing the American nuclear triad and, particularly, its striking force in the Pacific region.[399] China ratified the NPT in 1992, and the country's official nuclear doctrine precludes 'first use' of nuclear weapons. But China has chosen to remain outside the New START Treaty arguing that it does not make sense to enter into negotiations on the reduction of nuclear arms as long as the American and Russian nuclear arsenals are much bigger than China's.[400]

In the first decade of the new millennium, the USA and China reached several technical agreements in the nuclear arms field. These included measures to prevent the spread of harmful radioactive material, for example, with American and IAEA assistance to convert small Chinese-developed neutron-source nuclear reactors from burning highly enriched uranium (HEU) to low-enriched uranium (LEU).[401] However, since 2010 there have been fewer examples of successful nuclear diplomacy between the two superpowers.

It is important to stress that there are many factors that weigh against a war between the USA and China – first and foremost the mutual economic dependency between the two countries, the mutual nuclear deterrence and the enormous expenses related to war, nuclear or otherwise. In the relationship between the USA and China, most experts point to Taiwan as the greatest risk factor in terms of nuclear weapons because there are special geopolitical and historical factors at play there.[402] Situated between the South and East China Seas, only 150 kilometers from the Chinese mainland, Taiwan has great strategic importance for China. Culturally and as a key aspect of Chinese national identity, Taiwan remains a central issue. The Chinese government has always maintained that the goal for the two republics is to eventually "reunite", as they frame the issue. In Beijing, Taiwan is considered an internal matter, and in 2005 China officially declared that any move by Taiwan to declare independence would be viewed as an act of war.[403] Some analysts assess that the long-term survival of the Chinese leadership depends on the promise of "reunion".[404] In any case, President Xi Jinping has stressed the importance of this objective and has invested much prestige in its realization.[405]

Conversely, the USA maintains that Taiwan's relationship to China cannot be changed by military means. As part of the normalization of the diplomatic ties to Beijing, the USA withdrew its troops (and nuclear arms) from the island in 1979. Instead, the USA and Taiwan entered into the so-called Taiwan Relations Act, which obliges the USA to equip Taiwan with the military means to defend its territory and maintain the capacity to resist Chinese initiatives to undermine Taiwan's security and freedom. Whether the USA is obliged to use this capacity in the event of Chinese aggression toward Taiwan is less clear and a sign of the deliberate strategic ambiguity intended to ensure American room for maneuver in the Taiwan issue.[406]

Taiwan raises difficult dilemmas in terms of the type of support the USA can give Taiwan and how much military assistance it could provide if China were to launch a blockade or a direct military attack on the heavily fortified island. For the USA, it is not just the obligation toward Taiwan that is at stake but the strategic position in the entire region – also in relation to nuclear arms. How would it impact the nuclear arms balance if Taiwan were not protected? It is easy to imagine a situation in which other countries in the region – most likely Japan, South Korea and Indonesia – would resort to developing nuclear weapons of their own if the USA's security guarantees to Taiwan were no longer regarded as trustworthy.

Moreover, Taiwan has the expertise and infrastructure to resume its military nuclear program – something that would undoubtedly prompt a very strong reaction from China. The historical context for this scenario is that American security assurances to Taiwan, as outlined in the Taiwan Relations Act, were a key factor in enabling the USA to use the IAEA system in 1988 to compel the shutdown of Taiwan's highly advanced military nuclear program.[407] By shutting down this secret program, which violated the NPT that Taiwan had joined in 1971, the USA prevented what they saw as a nightmare scenario: an open nuclear arms race between small Taiwan and large China, separated only by the narrow Taiwan Strait.[408] However, the consequence is that Taiwan's fate and the credibility of the non-proliferation system – possibly even its survival – are closely interconnected.

Both the USA and China thus have much at stake in the future status of Taiwan. The diplomatic and military balance is volatile. An example of this occurred in August 2022 when the Speaker of the House of Representatives, Nancy Pelosi, met with President Tsai Ing-wen in Taiwan in order to, as she wrote, send "an unequivocal statement that America stands with Taiwan, our democratic partner, as it defends itself and its freedom".[409] Pelosi was the highest-ranking US politician to visit Taiwan in 25 years, and in a conversation with President Biden before the planned visit, Xi condemned what he saw as unnecessary escalation of the tension and an interference in internal Chinese affairs.[410] During the tense period of Pelosi's visit, the Chinese military initiated its hitherto most comprehensive navy and air force exercise around Taiwan – according to international sources transgressing the recognized territorial demarcation lines in and around the Taiwan Strait.[411] Biden, who as part of a diplomatic balancing act did not support Pelosi's visit but defended her right to go through with it, subsequently deployed the aircraft carrier *USS Ronald Reagan* to the area in response.

This serves as an example of how the two superpowers flex their muscles and the situation concerning Taiwan is likely to intensify. The tensions entail a risk of confrontations that, in the worst-case scenario, could escalate to nuclear level if the situation got out of hand or as a result of misunderstandings or accidents. Security experts therefore point out that in light of the nuclear risk, there is a need to strengthen diplomacy between the United States and China to avoid accidents and misunderstandings regarding the handling of crises, and to secure communication channels at the highest political and military level.[412] So far, however, both countries appear to favor a strategic course based on massive, escalating nuclear armament in the attempt to maintain or change the balance of power regarding Taiwan and avoid the nuclear confrontation that no one desires.

In recent years, a troubling trend has emerged: increasing nuclear armament. This includes planned American billion-dollar investments in nuclear weapons while Russia is developing advanced weapon systems that include new 'doomsday' weapons like nuclear torpedoes designed to trigger massive tsunamis and spread devastating radioactive pollution.[413] Armament is not only limited to the USA and Russia. China is believed to have the fastest-growing nuclear arsenal among the nine nuclear-armed states, and it is now estimated to have more than 600 warheads for delivery by land- and sea-based ballistic missiles, and by bombers. The United Kingdom is currently building a new class of nuclear submarines and has decided to increase its nuclear stockpile to 260 warheads. Since 2018, France has substantially increased its budget to modernize its nuclear forces, with extensive plans that include new nuclear-armed submarines and upgrades to its SLBMs, which are already equipped with multiple independently targetable nuclear warheads.[414]

Unpredictability and Deterrence in the Second Nuclear Age

By the end of the Cold War, Fukuyama's and Huntington's stories of rupture resonated with many readers. But 'the end of the history' thesis did not hold up in a multipolar world with nuclear hotspots.[415] Instead, the nuclear arms issue of the 21st century is a condition we have to live with and try to handle during increasing levels of unpredictability, both in terms of the modernization of existing arsenals and the proliferation of nuclear weapons to new states and zones of conflict. Nuclear weapons and unpredictability are words that no one wants to hear in the same sentence, as security researcher C. Dale Walton writes, but unpredictability is indeed the central theme in the Second Nuclear Age.[416]

The guiding assumption in the First Nuclear Age (1945–91) was that the mere threat of using nuclear weapons would make both parties in a conflict more cautious and unwilling to engage in war. A central question is whether this logic of deterrence still applies to the more unpredictable geopolitical situation of the Second Nuclear Age. According to a noteworthy series of editorials published in 2007 by the four high-ranking American Cold War veterans George Shultz, William Perry, Henry Kissinger and Sam Nunn, the answer is no.[417] During their political careers, they supported American nuclear armament based on the deterrence rationale. But in 2007, they appealed to the American public with the message that nuclear weapons in the current geopolitical situation represent a security threat so immense that it is pivotal to focus on creating a world free of nuclear weapons. These weapons were crucial for geopolitical security during the Cold War, they wrote, but in the current situation when unstable states have nuclear weapons (or a realistic chance of procuring them), and with strong international terror movements, "reliance on nuclear weapons [...] is becoming increasingly hazardous and decreasingly effective". "Will new nuclear nations and the world be as fortunate in the next 50 years as we were during the Cold War?" the authors asked rhetorically, answering their own question with a 'no'.[418]

The issue is further complicated by the fact that it is very hard to tell if the deterrence logic did in fact work during the Cold War. While nuclear weapons have not been used since 1945, this is not necessarily a result of deterrence. In fact, there is no way we can know if nuclear war has been avoided because of this logic, and even less how the nuclear arms issue would have

Four Cold War veterans meeting the newly elected President Obama in the White House in 2009 to express their concern over the continued nuclear build-up. From left to right: William Perry, Sam Nunn, George Schultz, President Obama and Henry Kissinger.

developed if the path of openness regarding nuclear technology had been chosen, as suggested for example by Niels Bohr in his open letter to the UN. What we *do* know for sure is that the logic of deterrence in the current geopolitical configuration is much more complex, both technologically and politically.

For instance, can we rest assured that a country with nuclear weapons capability will refrain from using these weapons against an opponent that has a much larger arsenal of conventional weapons but no nuclear weapons? Or that a country that possesses nuclear weapons will refrain from using them against a neighbor that launches a limited, conventional attack in a border region between the two countries? Balance of threat and risk assessments look different now than in the Cold War MAD scenario, where it rested on the clear and unequivocal threat of mutual destruction. The technological aspect is further complicated by existing asymmetries in the ability of countries to defend themselves against nuclear weapons in a given conflict. If one part in a conflict, for example, assesses that they are capable of partly or entirely defending themselves against nuclear attacks from their opponent with ballistic missile defense weapons, the threat level calculation will change and become more complicated on both sides.

These considerations are not pure speculation; on the contrary, they directly affect the security doctrines of the superpowers. For instance, in the years surrounding the turn of the millennium, Russia developed a new security strategy that included a reconceptualization of the use of nuclear weapons in the event of a conventional military threat. The security doctrine developed by the Security Council of Russia and signed by President Putin in 2000 allows the use of nuclear weapons "in response to large-scale aggression utilizing conventional weapons in situations critical to the national security of the Russian Federation".[419] The doctrine on the use of nuclear weapons was elaborated in 2010 so that it applied to events in which the survival of the state of Russia is threatened. Both versions, however, establish that nuclear weapons can be used in certain instances even if Russia has not been attacked with this type of weapon.

In a well-researched analysis in 2014, security researcher Nikolai N. Sokov argued that the strategy is based on "nuclear de-escalation", i.e., that the use of smaller, tactical nuclear weapons can be seen as a de-escalation in situations in which the survival of the state of Russia is deemed to be under serious threat from another nuclear power, even though this power has not used nuclear weapons.[420] It may come across as highly paradoxical to perceive the involvement of nuclear weapons as de-escalation, but this should be considered in the light of concerns among Russian leaders and military strategists of being unable to match the USA's superior conventional military striking force. Based on this rationale the use of – or at lest the threat of using – small nuclear weapons can be seen as a legitimate defensive move to avoid another nuclear power (i.e., the USA) getting involved in vital conflicts compromising Russian security and survival. The doctrine of de-escalation presupposes as a minimum that Russia's threat of the limited use of nuclear weapons must be considered reliable. It also exemplifies how nuclear and conventional weapons are interconnected in the security assessments of the Second Nuclear Age. According to Sokov and several other experts, these factors seriously increase the risk that the threshold for the use of nuclear weapons will be crossed in the competition between the superpowers. In November 2024, Russia lowered the threshold for the use of nuclear weapons, specifying that it could launch nuclear strikes in response to an attack on its territory by a non-nuclear-armed state supported by a nuclear-armed one. This change was prompted by the war in Ukraine and was intended to send a message to Ukraine and its Western allies.[421]

We can and should not conclude from a state's official strategy on the use of nuclear weapons how that state will actually act in a conflict. Nevertheless, the strategies are significant signals internally within the states and externally between the nuclear powers. The USA's doctrine for the use of nuclear weapons is published in the *Nuclear Posture Reviews* (NPR). The most recent NPR from October 2022 states that the American nuclear arsenal is intended to deter other countries from attacking the USA and its allies with nuclear weapons, but it does not preclude the USA using nuclear weapons without having been attacked with them, e.g., if Russia, China or North Korea were to launch a large-scale attack with chemical or biological weapons.[422] In 2020, before he won the presidential election, Joe Biden publicly argued that the USA should adopt a so-called No First Use doctrine, but it is not part of the NPR from 2022 that was developed after war broke out in Ukraine.[423] Only two of the world's nuclear powers – India and China – have a no first use item in their official nuclear arms doctrines.

The logic of deterrence is thus intended to function in the current political situation with many hotspots and more unpredictable political players than during the Cold War. Typical examples include Iran and North Korea, which are both undemocratic and unstable countries. But Trump's first presidency and his reelection in November 2024 are a strong reminder that unpredictable governance can also take place in democratic countries and result in increased global instability.

Even if deterrence worked during the Cold War, we cannot just assume that it works now and will do so in the future. Failed deterrence is definitely a possibility. There is no sign of a quick fix that will fundamentally change the situation; we need continuous efforts toward disarmament, arms control and non-proliferation of nuclear weapons.

The Struggle for Future Disarmament Agreements

The dangerous nuclear hotspots and the extensive modernization and armament initiatives among the old nuclear powers have given rise to a reconceptualization of the nuclear arms opposition and new suggestions for disarmament. The current disarmament agreements, especially the NPT, have become central bones of contention in the new millennium. As described in Chapter 5, the NPT came definitively into effect in 1970 and still represents the cornerstone of the arms control regime under the UN's International Atomic Energy Agency (IAEA). As of January 2025, the treaty had been signed by 191 countries, including the old nuclear powers. In 1995, it was extended so that it no longer has an expiration date.[424]

In spite of the widespread backing for the NPT, there is a general consensus among experts that the treaty has inherent flaws and weaknesses. Firstly, as described in previous chapters, there have been several examples of countries successfully circumventing the NPT – or even using it actively, as did Libya – in their attempts to acquire nuclear weapons. Secondly, the NPT has the dual aims of preventing the proliferation of nuclear weapons at the same time as encouraging international collaboration on peaceful use of nuclear energy. As we have seen, it is extremely complicated to distinguish between civilian and military proliferation of nuclear technology. This fact gravely impairs the system and has caused problems in several hotspots. Thirdly, it causes imbalance in the NPT that the five old nuclear powers joined the NPT as de facto nuclear states, while the remaining NPT countries waived their possibility of becoming nuclear powers by joining. This historical asymmetry has had several consequences, one of which is that several countries with ambitions to develop nuclear weapons when the treaty was implemented chose not to join. Therefore, the nuclear weapon states Israel, India, Pakistan and North Korea are not members of the treaty, and in reality, they cannot become members now – even if they should wish to – without severely undermining it.[425]

The old nuclear powers that have signed the NPT are morally and legally obliged by the treaty's Article 6 to work for nuclear disarmament: "Each of the parties to the Treaty undertakes to pursue negotiations in good faith on effective measures to cessation of the nuclear arms race at an early date and to nuclear disarmament, and on a treaty on general and complete disarmament under strict and effective international control."[426] The nuclear weapon states' support for pursuing nuclear disarmament was obviously a decisive factor for many non-nuclear powers joining the asymmetrical treaty. However, the resolve among the nuclear weapon states to follow the course set in article 6 has been limited. Considering the planned investments in new nuclear arms technologies, the credibility of the nuclear-armed NPT countries is wearing very thin.

This situation has prompted efforts to develop a new treaty which, according to its proponents, will remedy the weaknesses of the NPT and provide a better framework for disarmament in the current geopolitical situation. The development of a new treaty gained momentum after the turn of the millennium when the NGO International Campaign to Abolish Nuclear Weapons (ICAN) took up the challenge of bringing it to a successful conclusion. A draft for a treaty was introduced under the auspices of the UN, leading in 2017 to the passing of the Treaty on the Prohibition of Nuclear Weapons (TPNW) or simply 'the Ban Treaty'. ICAN was awarded the Nobel Peace Prize in 2017 for its work on the Ban Treaty, which was ratified in the UN on January 22, 2021 when it had achieved the backing of 50 UN countries. As of January 2025, the TPNW has been signed by 94 member states, but 21 of these have not yet ratified it. The Ban Treaty differs from the NPT in shifting focus from the acquisition and use of nuclear weapons to a clear ban on possessing, developing and testing them.[427]

None of the nuclear powers or their close allies have ratified the TPNW. Critics of the treaty claim on those grounds that it is politically toothless and ill-suited to address the nuclear states' legitimate concerns regarding the security dilemma, i.e., how one nation that gives up its nuclear weapons can be sure that the other nuclear powers will follow suit. These weaknesses are generally acknowledged, but as security experts Rens van Munster and Casper Sylvest emphasize, the Ban Treaty is not a classical arms control agreement. Rather, it should be viewed as a sign of the non-nuclear powers' discontent with the current armament, and an attempt to pressure the nuclear powers and their allies to engage in serious disarmament.[428]

It is difficult to establish the effect of attempts like this, but they do not appear entirely futile in this respect. At least, the leaders of the five old nuclear powers issued a joint public statement on January 3, 2022 titled "On Preventing Nuclear War and Avoiding Arms Races". The statement stressed the need for increased efforts toward non-proliferation, disarmament and arms control and, more notably: "We remain committed to our Nuclear Non-Proliferation-Treaty (NPT) obligations, including our Article 6 obligation."[429] The joint statement should be viewed in the light of the heated debates around the world regarding the TPNW, including in Europe, where Austria and Ireland, among others, have joined.[430]

In a thought-provoking contribution to the discussion, political scientists and nuclear arms opponents Joelien Pretorius and Tom Sauer argue that the

The organization International Campaign to Abolish Nuclear Weapons (ICAN) received the Nobel Peace Prize in 2017 for its work on the Treaty on the Prohibition of Nuclear Weapons. In the photo, the Swedish lawyer and leader of the organization, Beatrice Fihn, gives the acceptance speech in Oslo, December 2017.

© Rune Hellestad/Lon20171210113_lg/Ritzau Scanpix

NPT should be dropped to ensure momentum for the TPNW.[431] The authors elaborate the weaknesses of the NPT, writing that today it is "the cornerstone of a severely hypocritical nuclear order in which a few states claim the right to wield their nuclear weapons while proscribing this right to other states".[432] They believe that the extension of the NPT in 1995, meaning that it has no expiration date, in reality allows the nuclear powers to postpone their disarmament to an indefinite point in the future at the same time as rearming at a staggering rate. Pretorius and Sauer conclude that an unequivocal Ban Treaty free from the NPT's flaws will have a better chance of clearing the path to nuclear disarmament.

Many – also within the disarmament movements – disagree on the controversial suggestion of dropping the NPT. They maintain that the TPNW can only function as a supplement to the NPT system.[433] They also believe that it will be too risky to discontinue the NPT, which is backed by the majority of the nuclear powers, and which includes an international control organ that to some extent has prevented the proliferation of nuclear weapons. Scrapping the NPT may open the floodgates for countries that want nuclear weapons, and it is not hard to imagine scenarios with several new, deeply disturbing nuclear hotspots, such as Iran and Saudi Arabia, armed with nuclear weapons. Hence, there are serious arguments against the controversial suggestion.

On the other hand, Pretorius, Sauer and other critics of the NPT make a strong case that Article 6 will probably not be realized in the foreseeable future, and, moreover, that the NPT system neither prevents further nuclear armament nor effectively curbs proliferation in the long term. Recent developments have indeed severely shaken the foundations of the NPT. In particular, the war in Ukraine is sending shockwaves through the international non-proliferation system, with unpredictable consequences. Since the onset of the war, leaders and populations of other vulnerable non-nuclear weapon states have been closely monitoring Ukraine's struggle. The stark fact is that Ukraine, a non-nuclear state and NPT signatory, was brutally assaulted by a nuclear-armed state, which used its nuclear capabilities to set the terms for a conventional war. Watching this scenario unfold strengthens the argument of those who contend that the safest – or perhaps only – way to avoid an attack by a nuclear-armed aggressor is to possess a nuclear deterrent. As mentioned, this discussion has for example taken place in South Korea during 2022–23, where prominent politicians and large segments of the population believe the country should possess its own nuclear deterrent, rather than relying solely on the US nuclear umbrella as it does now. The USA does not want South Korea to become a nuclear weapon state, which is why the two countries reached a new agreement in the spring of 2023, increasing the presence of American nuclear strike forces on the Korean Peninsula. However, the prospect of more American nuclear weapons in these strategically important waters fuels calls for nuclear armament in China. China's expanding arsenal, in turn, has led to demands for increased nuclear armament in the USA. Thus, we are witnessing overlapping and escalating arms race spirals within and across nuclear hotspots.

We are moving closer to a world where more countries keep each other in check – or engage in conventional wars – against the backdrop of nuclear weapons. In light of these troubling developments, there is a need to pressure nuclear powers to honor their stated goal of achieving a world free of nuclear weapons.

CHAPTER 8

Nuclear Weapons, Climate Crisis and the Doomsday Clock

Cold War Research and Climate Research

The past 50 years have brought increased attention to the accelerating and alarming human-made changes to the climate. In the new millennium, the climate crisis has even to some extent overshadowed the nuclear threat in many people's view of what constitutes the largest hazard to human existence. But rather than conceiving of nuclear weapons and climate change as separate (or even competing) crises, research today is coming to acknowledge that the nuclear threat and the climate crisis should be seen as interconnected global crises.

The advanced computer models that scientists develop today to predict the Earth's climate in the future originate largely from the results of large-scale studies on how radioactive isotopes from atmospheric nuclear tests in the period 1946–63 spread from the explosion site via prevailing winds in the atmosphere and stratosphere to a network of monitoring stations around the world.[434] One of the most interesting isotopes in this context is C-14, which has six protons and eight neutrons in each nucleus. This isotope is constantly created in small quantities when energetic particles from the sun and other sources in space hit nitrogen atoms in the Earth's atmosphere. During nuclear detonations, however, C-14 is created in large quantities. Regardless of how a C-14 isotope is created, it quickly combines with oxygen atoms in the atmosphere and forms a carbon dioxide molecule (CO_2), which then blends with the 'normal' carbon dioxide molecules in which the carbon isotope is the non-radioactive C-12 which only has six neutrons in its nucleus. But because C-14 is radioactive, it is easy to trace. A groundbreaking study on American nuclear tests, led by nuclear physicist Hans Suess and oceanographer Roger Revelle at the Scripps Institution of Oceanography in California, demonstrated in 1957 that the radioactive CO_2 quickly spread across the planet. The study also indicated that the oceans were not capable of absorbing all the carbon dioxide we humans emit into the atmosphere by burning fossil fuels – i.e., coal, oil and gas.[435] This was soon confirmed by climate scientist Charles Keeling, also financially supported by Scripps, which established observing stations in Antarctica and on Mount Mauna Loa in Hawaii. These stations have been constantly measuring the CO_2 content in the atmosphere ever since.[436]

Within a few years, it became evident that the CO_2 content of the atmosphere was increasing annually, a trend that has continued to this day. Today, the CO_2 concentration has surpassed 400 ppm (parts per million), compared to approximately 290 ppm before industrialization took off. This increase may not sound all that dramatic as carbon dioxide still only makes up less than 1/2,000 of the atmosphere, but it is in fact very serious because carbon dioxide is a greenhouse gas, like methane. Greenhouse gases allow most of the light from the sun to pass through the atmosphere and heat up the Earth, but absorb most of the heat emitted from the Earth toward space in the form of infrared light. The result is that Earth's temperature increases with the proportion of greenhouse gases in the atmosphere – analogously to what happens in a greenhouse.

Overall, the Cold War research in fields such as geophysics and climate modeling was instrumental to a dawning understanding of Earth and its atmosphere as a unified system. Military-based climate research, for example into the effect of atmospheric nuclear tests, was over the course of the 1970s supplemented with what science historians Matthias Heymann and Amy Dalmedico term "a new environmental paradigm which shifted the perspective from the Earth as a resource for human purposes to the Earth as a planet endangered by human activity".[437] Climate and nuclear weapons were interconnected in the research, meaning that nuclear researchers were among the first to establish connections between the two crises.

The Fate of the Planet Debate

The ties between research into nuclear weapons and climate were close during the Cold War. It was partly due to these research overlaps that a few scientists from the very beginning of the First Nuclear Age started pointing to the connection between the nuclear arms threat and growing climate and environmental problems. This connection, which is now obvious, was for example pointed out early on in the context of the UN by the British biologist, ecologist and diplomat Julian Huxley.[438]

In 1945, Huxley was appointed the first Director General of the UN Science Committee, UNESCO. Huxley conceived of the entire world in terms of evolutionary systems. He argued that the critical issue was that political evolution had not kept pace with the accelerating technological evolution that had now provided humankind with nuclear technology. Huxley highlighted that the technological capacity of humans – which was manifested in nuclear weapons, booming populations and negative impact on ecological systems – had consequences for all life on the planet, but that politics were stuck at a stage dominated by national units and interests. Via social organization, humankind throughout history had moved toward ever-larger social units, and now it was time to take the next step toward world citizenship or even world government to ensure peace and the survival of life in the Nuclear Age. In Huxley's view, humanity needed to perceive of itself as one whole biological species. This was the only hope for survival in the new circumstances that included nuclear weapons and increasing pressure on nature and its resources.[439]

In his invocation of the shared fate of humankind, Huxley's ideas were aligned with those of the anti-nuclear arms movement as expressed in the Einstein-Russell Manifesto, among other places, which also appealed to the human race as a biological species in its warning against the nuclear threat. However, Huxley further believed that humankind, due to its biological and technological evolutionary advantages, also had responsibility for other forms of life on the planet.

The connection between global environmental changes and the nuclear threat was also drawn immediately after the Second World War by other scientists and public debaters. Over the following decades, the connection became increasingly concrete, not least due to the recognition of problems caused by radioactive fallout. In a study on the Partial Nuclear Test Ban Treaty from 1963, which as described in Chapter 4 banned atmospheric but not underground nuclear tests, historian Toshihiro Higuchi demonstrates that much early opposition to nuclear arms revolved around environmental and health challenges. From early on, the nuclear powers had extensive knowledge of the atmospheric effects of the nuclear tests, and they also quickly began recording even low concentrations of fallout – not out of consideration for health or climate, but in order to monitor their opponents' nuclear activities. Higuchi describes how scientific studies of the effects on ecosystems, combined with the pressure from an increasingly concerned public through the 1950s, contributed to putting pressure on the nuclear powers. This became evident in different ways on both sides of the Iron Curtain. Moreover, Japanese researchers played a particularly important role with research indicating that the nutritionally and culturally central crop rice in many instances contained a higher concentration of radioactivity than, e.g., milk. Radioactive fallout became a UN matter, and Higuchi argues convincingly that the worldwide concern about the environmental consequences made it too contentious for the nuclear weapon states to recommence massive atmospheric nuclear test programs after 1963.[440]

Climate models, environmental issues and the nuclear arms race were also connected by influential critics of the arms race and its logic of deterrence.[441] One example of a noteworthy and influential voice towards the end of the Cold War is American author Jonathan Schell.[442] Schell became famous in particular for his bestseller *The Fate of the Earth* from 1982, which painted a bleak picture of the ecological consequences of a nuclear war. The book was based on new scientific results of climate modelling from Cold War research and argued that a nuclear war would cause a nuclear winter that in all likelihood would make the planet uninhabitable for humans and anything else except "grass and insects".[443] Schell described Earth as a complex and sensitive ecological system under significant stress due to the impact of humans. To Schell, it was not a great leap from the focus on worldwide atmospheric effects of nuclear tests and nuclear war to a warning that modern humankind could cause profoundly harmful and long-lasting changes to the environment on a global scale. Nuclear weapons and different global environmental crises were part of the same human-made, global threat. This point and approach became increasingly prominent in Schell's writings, which continued on into the new millennium.[444]

Huxley and Schell are here highlighted as examples of early voices arguing for the connection between nuclear weapons, environmental issues and climate change. They also shared the point of view that the nuclear arms threat and the environmental crisis were the products of accelerating scientific and technological development – something that, according to them, placed a heavy responsibility on scientists to analyze the nature of the threat and warn the public about its gravity.

These voices are important because they illustrate early reflections on the connections between the nuclear threat, the environment and the emerging climate crisis. However, it is important to stress that they remained relatively marginalized in the general threat assessment during the Cold War – in fact, all the way to its conclusion. It was difficult to put climate issues on the agenda, and the climate scientists were largely ignored. Both wealthy and poor countries gave higher priority to short-term economic growth than to the consideration for future generations. And climate skeptics, backed by financially strong multinational oil companies, succeeded for a long time in convincing leading politicians that rising global temperatures and more frequent extreme weather events were not linked to greenhouse gases, but just an example of the natural climate fluctuations that the planet had been exposed to for hundreds of millions of years. Science historians Naomi Oreskes and Eric Conway have described how these groups consciously acted as "merchants of doubt", cultivating strategies to sow doubt about the solid research that had established the reality and valid concern of human-made climate change.[445] These "merchants of doubt" were inspired by, among others, the strategies that the American tobacco industry had effectively employed to question the harmful effects of using its products. But the strategy is also closely related to the one that Teller and his supporters used to halt the opposition to nuclear weapons by questioning scientifically established commonplaces such as the harmful effect of exposure to significant levels of radiation.

It is a telling indication of how little attention the problem received that environmental and ecological crises as global threats were almost absent from Fukuyama's *End of History* from 1992, discussed in Chapter 7. In the book, Fukuyama did consider "some cataclysm, either a global war or an environmental collapse which, despite our best efforts, attacks the physical basis for contemporary human life".[446] But he believed that even in this extreme scenario, civilization and science could be rebuilt. As historian Paul Dukes has established, global climate issues and ecological challenges were also more or less absent in the widespread critical reception of Fukuyama's book.[447] And it is even more striking that Huntington's *Clash of Civilizations* from 1996 did not mention the issue at all.

Only toward the end of the 20th century did the climate crisis slowly begin to move up the international political agenda. This became evident in the UN's climate convention signed in 1992 at the World Conference on Environment and Development in Rio de Janeiro, and the adoption of the Kyoto Protocol – the first legally binding international agreement on (modest) reductions of greenhouse gases – which was signed in Kyoto in 1997, but did not enter into effect until 2005. The evidence of human impact on the climate through increasing CO_2 emissions into the atmosphere was becoming still more irrefutable. Year after year saw rising temperatures, in keeping with the predictions in the climate model. In 2007, the report *Climate Change* by the UN's Intergovernmental Panel on Climate Change established that 11 of the 12 warmest years since 1850 – when reliable records of the Earth's surface temperature began – occurred between 1995 and 2006.[448]

Around this time, the climate issue started make its way into mainstream Western media and culture. For instance, the documentary *An Inconvenient Truth* with former American Vice President and presidential candidate Al Gore premiered in 2006. The film became a surprise hit among audiences and increased awareness of the globally destabilizing consequences of growing CO_2 emissions. The same year, the Pugwash movement – the scientific anti-nuclear movement that originated in the Einstein-Russell initiative – launched a series of workshops under the title *The New Challenges to Human Security*, which established that conflicts, terrorism and environmental challenges had "put the 'classical' risks arising from armaments and especially weapons of mass destruction into a larger framework of human security and human development".[449] At this point, it was thus on the cards that the scientists behind the *Bulletin of the Atomic Scientists* would also take the global climate threat into consideration in future adjustments of the Doomsday Clock. As we will see in the next subchapter, this happened in 2007.

The following years showed that it was difficult for the global community to reach an agreement on a replacement for the Kyoto Protocol, and thus on setting substantial, binding targets for reducing global CO_2 emissions. However, at COP21 in Paris in 2015, 196 countries agreed to set goals and develop action plans to ensure CO_2 neutrality in 2050, and to keep the global temperature rise below 1.5 °C as compared to pre-industrial level. The Paris Agreement – which many critics view as insufficient considering the extent of the issue – has since come under political pressure, and substantial reductions in global CO_2 emissions have not yet occurred. The COP meetings between 2020 and 2024 were thus marked by rising desperation among many NGOs, scientists and politicians, as well as an increasing realization that it will be almost impossible to maintain Earth's mean temperature within the 1.5 °C goal of the Paris Agreement.

Countdown to 89 Seconds to Midnight (2000–2025)

Since the turn of the millennium, the alarming development regarding nuclear hotspots, the modernization of the nuclear states' nuclear arms systems and the escalating climate crisis have pushed the hands of the Doomsday Clock to indicate an increasingly gloomy state of the world.

As the new millennium began, it was undeniable that the existing nuclear powers were deploying new nuclear-armed ballistic missile systems, while several non-nuclear states were making strong efforts to acquire nuclear weapons. Obviously, this development was mirrored in the setting of the Doomsday Clock. In 1998, as mentioned, the clock was set forward to nine minutes to midnight, mainly due to the Indian and Pakistani nuclear tests. In 2007, the clock was set forward again, this time to five minutes to midnight, based on three tendencies that the editors of the *Bulletin* saw as serious blows to the future prospects for humankind: the USA and Russia had initiated wide-ranging modernizations of their nuclear arsenals; the poor and isolated country of North Korea had defied the world community's warnings by performing its first nuclear test; and, finally, ongoing climate change presented a threat to humanity that had long been underestimated. This was the first time that the *Bulletin* mentioned the climate crisis as an existential threat to the entire human race on a par with the nuclear arms crisis. The reason this happened in 2007 was that the Board of the journal, which had managed the Doomsday Clock since Eugene Rabinowitch's death in 1973, transferred the responsibility to a more diverse Science and Security Board. This new board included experts on nuclear, chemical and biological weapons, as well as specialists in climate, Earth systems theory and social media. After intense discussions, the board members – probably influenced by loud warnings from the high-profile environmentalists – agreed that in future, the journal needed to consider the ever more concerning changes in the global climate just as earnestly as the traditionally recognized dangers of nuclear armament and the proliferation of nuclear weapons to a growing number of countries.

According to the *Bulletin's* Science and Security Board, neither the nuclear threat nor the climate crisis has lessened since 2007 when the journal first mentioned the climate crisis as one of the main reasons for setting the

Doomsday Clock to five minutes to midnight. On the contrary. Both threats received roughly the same level of attention from the editors when in 2015 they moved the Doomsday Clock forward to three minutes to midnight. Due to the lack of political action to counter these existential threats, the clock was set forward another 30 seconds in 2017, and in 2018 again, now showing two minutes to midnight – the closest it had ever been to signaling the ultimate disaster since the first hydrogen bomb tests in 1952–53.[450]

Even though in January 2019 the *Bulletin* left the Doomsday Clock at two minutes to midnight, the Science and Security Board emphasized that what might look like some form of stability was in fact a sign of a "new abnormal".[451] For the first time, the editors also pointed to a new threat – likely a consequence of President Trump's actions – in the form of deliberate efforts to mislead the public with fake news. Powerful states and politicians exploited this by using social media to undermine global trust in science and democratic institutions. In terms of nuclear weapons, it was concerning that Trump had pulled the USA out of the Iran agreement (JCPOA) from 2015 and the agreement with the Soviet Union from 1988 on phasing out all medium-range missiles in Europe (INF Treaty). The only bilateral nuclear agreement between the USA and Russia that remained in force in 2019 was New START.[452] All this created a dangerous world in which the risk of open nuclear war had become all too realistic, concluded the *Bulletin*'s Science and Security Board.[453] In the conclusion of the 2019 article that argued for leaving the Doomsday Clock at two minutes to midnight, the *Bulletin*'s Science and Security Board made the following appeal:

> The 'new abnormal' that we describe, and that the world now inhabits, is unsustainable and extremely dangerous. The world security situation can be improved, if leaders seek change and citizens demand it. It is two minutes to midnight, but there is no reason that the Doomsday Clock cannot move away from catastrophe. It has done so in the past, because wise leaders acted – under pressure from informed and engaged citizens around the world.[454]

Another year went by without the leaders of the world doing much to address the pressing issues of nuclear armament and climate change. In fact, things were moving in the wrong direction, according to the *Bulletin*'s Science and Security Board, which on January 23, 2020 set the minute hand on the

On January 28, 2025, the Doomsday Clock was set by the *Bulletin of the Atomic Scientists'* Science and Security Board at the Washington Institute of Peace at 89 seconds to midnight – the closest it has ever been to midnight in its 78-year history. The people unveiling the clock are: Former president of Columbia Juan Manuel Santos (2nd L), chair of the Elders, and Robert Socolow (2nd R), professor emeritus at Princeton University, alongside Herb Lin (L), of the Center for International Security and Cooperation, and Suzet McKinney (R), of Life Sciences for Sterling Bay.

© Saul Loeb / AFP / Ritzau Scanpix

Doomsday Clock forward to 100 seconds to midnight and even closer to the apocalypse. To substantiate their decision, the Board mentioned a number of reasons, including that Iran had started producing enriched uranium again in new, improved centrifuges; that President Trump – despite his promises – had not been able to make North Korea give up its nuclear weapons; and that the USA had no intention of extending the New START. Finally, the climate conference in Madrid that year had demonstrated that almost all countries were miles away from meeting their emission reductions agreed at the Paris conference.

In January 2021, the *Bulletin*'s Science and Security Board left the Doomsday Clock at the time they had set the previous year – 100 seconds to midnight – in spite of several arguments for moving it even closer. The development of new nuclear arms systems continued at the same or faster pace, while it was also the second-warmest year on record globally. The board, however, refrained from adjusting the clock as there was also some positive news – most prominently Joe Biden's victory in the presidential election, in the light of the fact that two of his first initiatives were to extend the New START Treaty with Russia until 2026 and to rejoin the Paris Agreement.

The ratification of the TPNW in January 2021 was also part of the *Bulletin*'s appraisal. ICAN, the organization that had received the Nobel Peace Prize for initiating the treaty, argued in the *Bulletin* in early January that in light of the ratification, it was time to "Turn back the clock: The nuclear Ban Treaty is entering into force".[455] The editors of the *Bulletin* were not prepared to go that far, but did recognize the treaty's "intention of bringing pressure on the nuclear weapon states to move forcefully toward nuclear disarmament". The editors concluded their mention of the treaty by expressing tentative "hope that the treaty will lead to concrete actions by all states to address the challenges of disarmament and proliferation, including collective security and verification".[456] The *Bulletin*'s reservations regarding the treaty are precisely that it does not address the security dilemma mentioned in Chapter 7, and that it does not include a control or verification mechanism to discover and prevent non-compliance by the countries that have signed.

At the annual clock adjustment in January 2022, the Science and Security Board at the *Bulletin* stuck to the 100 seconds to midnight they had decided on two years before, but in 2023, the unsettling record was broken once again as the Doomsday Clock was set to only 90 seconds to midnight. 2022 had been weighed down by bad news: natural disasters, pandemics, increased geopolitical tensions in the nuclear hotspots and especially the war in Ukraine that began in February that year. The board explained that they had moved the hands of the Doomsday Clock, largely (though not exclusively) because of the mounting dangers of the war in Ukraine pointing out that

> Russia's war on Ukraine has raised profound questions about how states interact, eroding norms of international conduct that underpin successful responses to a variety of global risks. And worst of all, Russia's thinly veiled threats to use nuclear weapons remind the world that escalation of conflict – by accident, intention, or miscalculation – is a terrible risk.[457]

The editors mentioned the escalating modernization programs of the nuclear weapon states as well as Iran's ongoing efforts to become one. Moreover, in 2022 the world had witnessed huge natural disasters resulting partly from global warming. The Russian invasion of Ukraine was also concerning in this respect, as it triggered a new global arms race, diverting massive investments that could have addressed the climate crisis.

The Doomsday Clock setting changed again on January 28, 2025, when the minute hand was moved forward by just one second. The Science and Security Board explained that moving it "a single second should be taken as an indication of extreme danger and an unmistakable warning that every second of delay in reversing course increases the probability of global disaster".[458] Highlighting the growing dangers posed by nuclear weapons, climate change, biological threats and rapid advancements in artificial intelligence and other disruptive technologies, the Board concluded by identifying the three countries with the greatest responsibility:

> The United States, China and Russia have the collective power to destroy civilization. These three countries have the prime responsibility to pull the world back from the brink, and they can do so if their leaders seriously commence good-faith discussions about the global threats outlined here. Despite their profound disagreements, they should take the first step without delay. The world depends on immediate action. It is 89 seconds to midnight.

The Political Clock – Iconic and Alarmist

A phenomenon such as the Doomsday Clock, which within a few years of its introduction in June 1947 achieved iconic status in wide circles, has naturally prompted both praise and critique. Neither proponents nor critics doubt that the clock has had a substantial impact. It has been reproduced and mentioned time and again in various printed and electronic media over the years, securing the people behind the *Bulletin* more attention than they would have received without the iconic clock. But what is it that makes the clock such an effective means of communicating the threat of nuclear weapons? Finnish professor of international politics Juha Vuori has analyzed the Doomsday Clock from a "securitization perspective" and pointed out a number of significant factors.[459] Firstly, the Doomsday Clock has become a potent symbol for the anti-nuclear movement because it entails a strong plot structure. The icon illustrates that the threat is very urgent (acuteness), that the threat will bring about total doom (midnight expresses the existential aspect), and that the threat can be averted because the hands can be set back, away from midnight (there is a way out). Secondly, the plot structure is captured in an image that 'travels' more easily than text across language and cultural barriers. Regarding nuclear weapons, only the image of the mushroom cloud has a similar impact to the Doomsday Clock, but without its strong narrative structure. Thirdly, the clock speaks to both reason and emotions, which is connected to the sender's privileged status in relation to the threat. Physicists have been attributed great authority on nuclear issues – especially the physicists who contributed to the theoretical and experimental understanding of nuclear physics, and even more so the ones who took part in the Manhattan Project. Their knowledge of nuclear physics and expertise on the effects of nuclear war provided a solid basis for addressing the associated societal security issues. According to Vuori, regarding the Doomsday Clock, this allowed them to combine their scientific status with a prophetic role:

> Through the symbol of the Doomsday Clock, the scientists have been able to combine their social capital as voices of reason and objectivity with that of the soothsayer to influence society and behavior. While science deals with concepts, the symbol of the Clock relates to emotions.[460]

Effective plot structure, a strong visual message and the senders' authority all contribute to the Doomsday Clock's status as a powerful anti-nuclear icon. However, critics believe that this comes at a price. One of the major objections is that the Doomsday Clock leaves open or unclear who should act, and how, when the setting is minutes or seconds to midnight. The vast majority of people on Earth have limited opportunities to take direct and meaningful action to counter the nuclear threat. Because it is unclear who

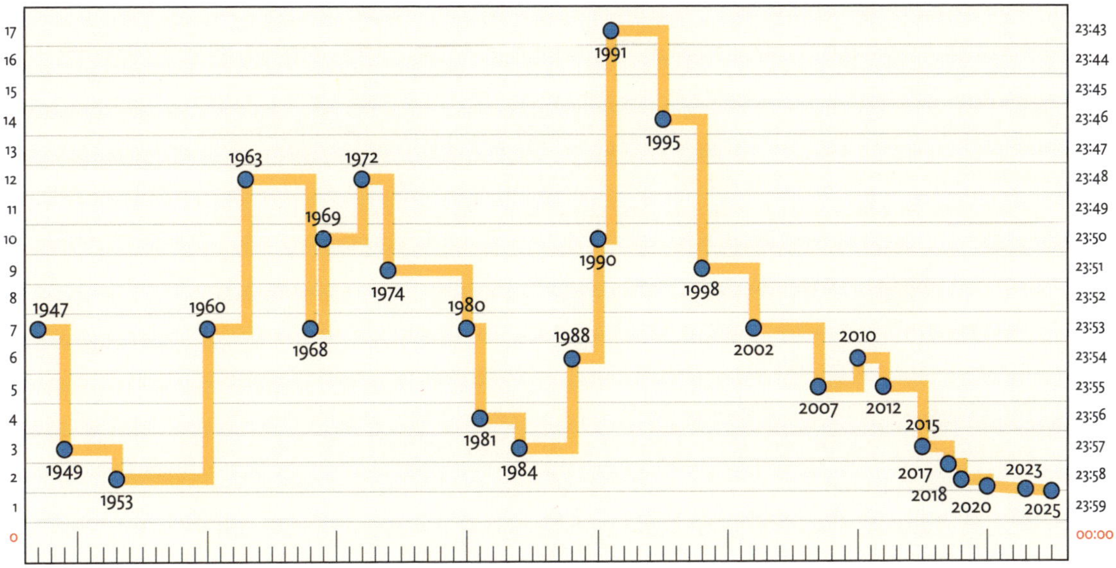

The changing settings of the Doomsday Clock from 1947 to 2025. In January 2020, the minute hand was moved forward to 100 seconds to midnight, in January 2023 to 90 seconds to midnight, and in January 2025 to 89 seconds to midnight.

is expected to do what, the risk is that the clock becomes merely alarmist ('doom is just around the corner') and fatalistic ('there is nothing we can do to avoid it'). As one critic states, the Doomsday Clock is a proclamation that screams PANIC all the way to the impending end.[461] Rather than encouraging action, the effect might be the opposite: the clock causes resignation and despair.

Apart from being alarmist and fatalistic, another major critique is that the clock as a symbol is one-dimensional in its risk assessment. Critics point to the obvious fact that the clock reduces a highly complex global threat to a single risk assessment expressed in the setting of time. This makes the Doomsday Clock a powerful cultural icon, but at the same time simplifies a complex technological and political landscape of costs and benefits that cannot so easily be condensed in the image the clock evokes in the viewer.[462]

It would be wrong to just dismiss this valid critique. However, the story of the Doomsday Clock, including the reasoning behind each new setting, shows that the messages communicated via the seemingly simple icon have often been nuanced. Warning, panic and fear have unquestionably been part of the clock's repertoire, and one concrete strategy to challenge the twisted logic (in the view of the *Bulletin*) of 'mutual assured destruction': "to preserve civilization by scaring men into rationality," as phrased by former editor Rabinowitch.[463] But as we have seen, another important aspect of the intention behind the clock has been to inspire hope, encourage action, and give legitimacy to initiatives that the editors of the *Bulletin* perceived as constructive and necessary: not least the disarmament and non-proliferation treaties, and international collaboration to reduce the level of threat.

The most powerful messages of hope have obviously been sent when the *Bulletin*'s editors and boards decided to set the clock back. The ultimate goal for the people behind the journal is a world without nuclear weapons, and only then will they be prepared to bury the clock. But the changing settings have made it possible to relate to the small yet positive steps. The instances when the clock has been set forward have entailed a tension within the icon itself between hope on the one hand and the acuteness of the threat on the other. The proximity of the minute hand to midnight has first and foremost signaled the urgent need to do something about the nuclear threat before it is too late. Conversely, when the time is set back, it inspires hope but this may also make it hard to stress as strongly that action is needed. In light of this, it probably was after careful consideration that Rabinowitch in 1960 moved the minute hand a few minutes back "with a hesitant hand". There is a core message in this phrasing. It expresses the constant balancing act between the need to insist on the gravity and reality of the nuclear threat at the same time as communicating hope that the efforts to reduce the threat are not in vain. In our view this awareness is perhaps the most convincing form of realism we can think of in relation to the nuclear threat.[464]

Another central point regarding the clock is that in the *Bulletin* it has been used to signal unity and universalism. The clock indicates a universal threat to the entirety of humankind, which transcends nation states, Cold War frontiers and other geopolitical rivalries past and present. It was crucial for the nuclear physicists west of the Iron Curtain that the threat be seen as universal, not just a result of Soviet aggression. During the Cold War, actions took place on both sides of the Iron Curtain that could affect the clock setting. This was also reflected in the iconography, with the clock sometimes depicted against a background of planet Earth. The *Bulletin* used the clock as a platform from which it insisted on the need for changes in the international system – not just changes on one side or the other of the Iron Curtain. Hence, the clock has become an element of a recurring theme in this book: scientists who insisted that it is 'one world or none'; figuratively speaking, scientists who were unwilling to accept President Truman's words to Oppenheimer, that the blood was solely on the hands of politicians. Accepting a position in which science renounces political responsibility in fact does seem completely untenable in a world where societal development is extremely influenced by scientific discoveries and technological choices. The Doomsday Clock is an example of how one group of scientists attempted to create a space in which science has a say in discussions about wider political and cultural orientations in society.

It is worth pointing out that both critics and proponents of the Doomsday Clock agree that the clock is not an objective representation of time; it is indeed political, aiming to highlight the nuclear threat and not least the fact that we need to act. In that respect, several observers have pointed to the broader implications of the clock in terms of how we perceive time in a situation where nuclear weapons have become a sword of Damocles. The Doomsday Clock is clearly not an ordinary clock that tracks time as we normally perceive it – i.e., chronologically, progressively and systematically split into units of seconds, minutes and hours. In its manner of showing time, according to historian and philosopher Michelle Bastian, the Doomsday Clock differs from 'clock time'.[465] Clock time is the time according to which we plan our life and activities: meetings on Tuesdays, summer holidays in a month's time, our retirement date, etc. Political life is also structured according to clock time: the new parliamentary year, electoral periods, 10-year economic plans and so on. Clock time is also vital in terms of the nuclear and climate crises. The entire historical course of events presented in this book plays out in clock time, starting with the fission of the uranium nucleus in the 1930s and so on all the way up to 2025. Clock time will also be vital in the near future: will the New START Treaty be extended beyond its present expiry date, 2026? Will the world's states succeed in bringing down CO_2 emissions to net zero by 2050 in accordance with the Paris Agreement?

Clock time is important, but it cannot be the sole measure of time in the world we live in. As described in Chapter 2, physicists realized in the 1930s that a chain reaction in uranium would release energy of unprecedented explosive force within millionths of a second. With thermonuclear weapons – the hydrogen bomb (or 'Super') – it became clear that the world could face a war in which the obliteration of the entire human race was a realistic scenario. Nuclear physicists realized this sooner than most others, and the

Doomsday Clock in the *Bulletin* was invented in 1947 because of this realization. It was a reminder that we had entered a new world – also in relation to time. If nuclear disaster comes – if the clock strikes midnight – clock time will cease to be relevant. No plans for Tuesday, no disarmament agreements, no electoral periods. Once, we could expect that wars come and go in human societies, but the Doomsday Clock has helped create awareness that in the Nuclear Age, a war fought with nuclear weapons could mean the end of all human societies.

It is fair to question how well the Doomsday Clock captures the existential threat that the climate crisis presents. The clock was designed to warn against the nuclear threat, and the physicists do not have the same authority when it comes to climate issues as they do in terms of nuclear weapons and their effects. Also, the climate crisis has a different plot structure from the nuclear apocalypse. The climate crisis is caused by a human-made gradual increase in the CO_2 content of the atmosphere. Climate researchers are of course working with tipping points to illustrate the escalating and cumulative effects on ecosystems, but even this type of scenario does not have the same character of instant, total disaster as nuclear war. Yet the similarities and connections between the two crises may also in this respect outweigh the differences. Security experts highlight that the climate crisis serves as a risk or threat multiplier in a world where nuclear weapons are spread across global hotspots. The climate crisis threatens political as well physical infrastructure – including nuclear weapon installations – in unprecedented ways, while nuclear modernization and proliferation continue. During the First Nuclear Age, the arms race unfolded against a relatively stable Earth system. This is not the case in the Second Nuclear Age if we choose to try our luck down this high-risk path again.[466]

The Doomsday Clock is a reminder of the new condition behind the assumption based on clock time that tomorrow will be more or less like today. It challenges our concepts of clock time and the stability it presumes. Reflecting on different concepts of time is an abstract exercise. The Doomsday Clock turns it into something concrete and existential.

CHAPTER 9

The Third Nuclear Age

In recent years and months, a growing number of scholars, security experts and think tanks have concluded that the world has entered a Third Nuclear Age.[467] While the starting point is debated, it is generally agreed that the shift has become evident in the past few years and especially after the outbreak of the war in Ukraine in February 2022. The Third Nuclear Age is defined by both technological and political changes. On the technological side, artificial intelligence (AI) and other emerging technologies are increasingly becoming intertwined with the development, command and control of nuclear weapons. A related concern is that cyberattacks could potentially disable or even highjack a state's nuclear capabilities.[468] Additionally, non-nuclear weapons that can be used strategically are adding to the technological complexity.[469] Underlying this new technological configuration is also the fact that ongoing modernization programs across all nuclear-armed states are now causing the number of nuclear weapons in the world to rise for the first time since the Cold War.

On the political side, the Third Nuclear Age is characterized by new complexities in the nuclear order among states. This means that nuclear-armed 'great powers' are increasingly locked in geopolitical competition with each other and with 'middle-range' powers, some of which are aspiring to become nuclear states. Some experts therefore argue that the Third Nuclear Age differs from the Second Nuclear Age because it marks a return to concerns over state and interstate relations, rather than the focus on 'rogue actors' like terrorists gaining access to nuclear weapons. However, in our view it is not so much that state actors were not central in the Second Nuclear Age, but rather that the current shift reflects a more pronounced willingness to employ the threat of using nuclear weapons to influence the outcome of conventional armed conflicts. This suggests that we have moved beyond the pretense that the only function of nuclear weapons is to serve as the ultimate deterrent or life safeguard for states. While history shows that nuclear weapons were never solely for deterrence, the active use of the threat of nuclear escalation – especially by Russia in the war in Ukraine – has highlighted how nuclear capabilities now openly impact conventional warfare and geopolitics in new ways. Other political characteristics of the Third Nuclear Age are the weakening of the political institutions and agreements concerning arms control, nuclear testing and non-proliferation that were developed around the end of the Cold War. Additionally, increased focus on civil nuclear technology to meet the energy needs of a warming world raises more concern about the entanglement of civil and military nuclear technology and the associated risks of proliferation.[470]

In this unstable technological and political situation, some think tanks argue that the best – or perhaps only – response is a strengthened deterrent, with expanded strategic and non-strategic nuclear weapons.[471] Others take the exact opposite view, contending that the only solution is the complete abolition of nuclear weapons – an agenda that is centered on the Ban Treaty driven by NGO efforts and supported by a significant number of non-nuclear states. The clash between those advocating for deterrence and those pushing for disarmament across traditional state alliances are also part of the complex situation characteristic of the Third Nuclear Age.[472]

It was in this volatile situation that Donald Trump's second presidency began in January 2025. As we write these lines in July 2025, much remains in flux, and it is uncertain how the change in Washington will influence the course of events in the Third Nuclear Age.

Trump and his inner circle are strong proponents of the so-called "Golden Dome" project — the establishment of a space-based missile defence system designed to protect the U.S. from any nuclear attack by any adversary.[473] According to the proposal which the Trump administration plans to present to Congress, the Golden Dome will be operational before the end of Trump's presidency. The proposal carries a price tag of $175 billion over those years, with the expectation that maintenance and further development could cost up to $800 billion over the next two decades.[474]

Solid information on technical (and contractual) details about the Golden Dome project are few and scattered. But clearly the project requires an unprecedented weaponization of space and technically it faces numerous challenges in all parts of the massive infrastructure. Indeed, the projected price tag and timeline of the project are, in the blunt word of one critical expert, 'insane'.[475] The political implications are no less forbidding. A Golden

Dome designed to prevent nuclear attacks may sound like a de-escalating defensive system. But in practice, the project shifts the balance of nuclear deterrence, because the United States' strategic rivals would, in theory, no longer be able to strike the USA with nuclear weapons, while the USA would still be able to strike them. A well-founded fear is that the dome project will further accelerate the ongoing nuclear arms race, as other powers will need to develop their offensive technologies to restore the balance of deterrence.

Inconsistency may be the appropriate word to describe the Trump administration's strategy on nuclear weapons. On the one hand, Trump has spoken about the need to 'denuclearize' so that funds could be directed to something more hopeful than nuclear weapons and on the other the Trump administration is putting the Golden Dome proposal before Congress. It is simply not possible to pursue 'denuclearization' and at the same time embark on a massive destabilizing project such as the Golden Dome.[476]

Inconsistencies aside one thing is clear: the Trump administration's shift in the policy of the USA regarding the war in Ukraine, to a position that appears largely supportive of Putin, is fundamentally changing the terms of the nuclear deterrence debate in Europe. French President Emmanuel Macron has reiterated his position that France's nuclear deterrence could be given a "European dimension", forming the backbone of a European deterrent less dependent on the USA. Macron's idea has moved to the center of the European security debate, but how it should be managed, both politically and technologically, remains unresolved, including how it should relate to the USA's nuclear umbrella (if such still exists in Europe). In other parts of the world, the uncertainty surrounding the USA's foreign policy – especially in Japan, South Korea and Taiwan – is fueling discussions about whether it is time to revive plans for extending civil nuclear programs with a military component to acquire nuclear weapons. If the international situation regarding nuclear weapons and their proliferation was already uncertain, that uncertainty has reached new levels in the first months of 2025.

The destabilizing effects of the USA under Trump are notable. However, recent events in the contested region of Kashmir are a stark reminder that other factors also play a role in the world's nuclear hotspots. On April 22 a terrorist attack near Pahalgam in the Indian administrated part of Kashmir left 25 Indians and one Nepali national dead. An Islamist terrorist group initially claimed responsibility for the attack. Claiming that he Pakistani government also played a role in the attack the Indian government launched airstrikes targeting alleged terrorist camps in Pakistan. Although the situation appears to be contained for now, many experts consider it the most severe skirmish in more than a decade between the two nuclear weapon states that do not have any formal bilateral crisis management mechanisms in place that could minimise the risk of further escalation.[477]

While tensions in Kashmir had somewhat eased, a new conflict erupted on June 14 in another nuclear hotspot when Israel launched an aerial attack on Iran, specifically targeting its nuclear program. Israel struck and killed several scientists involved in Iran's nuclear development and bombed multiple nuclear facilities, including the uranium enrichment plant at Natanz. The Israeli government's stated goal was to eliminate Iran's capability to develop a nuclear bomb – a threat that Prime Minister Netanyahu has repeatedly described as existential to Israel. In turn, the Iranian leadership, under Ayatollah Khamenei, views Israel's attack on its nuclear program as an existential threat and responded by launching missile and drone strikes on Israel. On June 22 the USA joined the Israeli airstrikes targeting Iran's nuclear facilities. In a brief but intense operation, B-2 Spirit stealth bombers dropped 14 GBU-57 "bunker buster" bombs, primarily on the heavily fortified Fordow nuclear site. The goal was to further destroy or at least significantly delay Iran's nuclear program. The technological and political impact of the Israel-USA bombings remain disputed and unclear. The attacks disrupted ongoing diplomatic negotiations between the USA and Iran over the Iranian nuclear program. When talks resume, they will undoubtedly occur under significantly altered terms and within a drastically changed security envionment. As Rafael Grossi, Director General of the IAEA, noted before the UN Security Council on June 20, at the height of the war: "The nuclear non-proliferation regime that has underpinned international security for more than half a century is on the line."[478]

Nuclear crises are not in short supply. However, it is important to recall that we have faced and addressed grave nuclear weapons crises before. In this respect history provides ample evidence that public protests, civil society actors and mass movements matter profoundly. Groups of concerned citizens, initially not expected to succeed, have historically managed to ignite mass movements and influence society and those in power to such an extent that policies have been radically changed. In the historical period that this book covers alone, it has happened several times, for example, when protests against nuclear armament and nuclear weapons testing erupted in many countries in the 1950s. A key factor in the coordination and widespread impact of the protests was the Russell-Einstein Manifesto and the closely associated conference at London's Caxton Hall in July 1955. In the wake of this event, protests spread to most Western European countries and the USA. The increasing pressure from numerous mass demonstrations influenced the governments of the USA and the Soviet Union to temporarily suspend their atmospheric nuclear tests between 1958 and 1961. After a short period of testing, which included a 50-megaton Soviet hydrogen bomb on the Arctic island of Novaya Zemlya, the two superpowers and the United Kingdom finally reached an agreement in August 1963 to ban all nuclear testing in the atmosphere, in outer space and underwater.

Another example, also discussed in this book, is the massive public protests in the early 1980s against the deployment of 572 medium-range nuclear-armed Pershing II missiles in Western Europe, along with an even larger number of similar SS-20 missiles in Eastern Europe. It was not one specific initiative, like the Russell-Einstein Manifesto, that sparked the resistance across countries in the 1980s. Instead, it was the creation of national and later international organizations within physics, chemistry, biology, medicine, psychology and law, which could provide the public with comprehensive and reliable information on the damage that nuclear warfare would cause to flora, fauna and human living conditions. Umbrella organizations also emerged, uniting the many diverse anti-nuclear groups, thereby enabling mass demonstrations across numerous countries. From a modest beginning in 1980, protests in the West grew from a few thousand people to massive crowds numbering in the hundreds of thousands. In the USA, the cross-political organization Nuclear Weapons Freeze Campaign succeeded in gathering over a million people in New York on June 12, 1982, likely the largest political rally in the history of the USA. The anti-nuclear-arms movements grew significantly between 1981 and 1985 and the protests continued to spread. By the second half of the decade they helped spark a mass movement in Eastern Europe with far broader political aims. The INF Treaty from December 1987 would probably never have come about without the massive popular pressure on Reagan and Gorbachev, and the collapse of the Eastern Bloc in 1989 would certainly not have occurred.

Nuclear weapons have now been part of our world for eighty years. This legacy provides us with valuable experiences that were not available to those who first developed nuclear weapons. Part of this legacy is a resounding warning "not to forget the apocalypse", as historian Daniel Immerwahr has reminded us.[479] The fact that nuclear weapons have not been used in warfare since 1945 means that we are entering an age with nuclear weapons but with only a fading collective memory of the terrible pain and suffering they can cause. Preserving this memory was part of the reason why the Nobel Peace Prize was awarded in 2024 to Nihon Hidankyo, the Japanese organization founded by survivors ('hibakusha') of Hiroshima and Nagasaki, "for its efforts to achieve a world free of nuclear weapons and for demonstrating through witness testimony that nuclear weapons must never be used again".[480]

The longstanding norm against the use of nuclear weapons is a valuable and hard-earned part of our shared nuclear heritage. In addition to the entrenched norm against using nuclear weapons, other key norms inherited from recent history include norms of non-proliferation and of the prohibition of nuclear testing. The norms – no use, no proliferation and no testing – are crucial for maintaining nuclear stability. Like a house of cards, the norms are interlinked and fragile (for instance, proliferation has historically been followed by testing). Yet, there is substantial international commitment to upholding the norms, which are grounded in the hard-earned lessons of living in a nuclear world.[481] They should continue to serve as important landmarks and guiding points as we pursue the more distant goal of a world without nuclear weapons.

We started this book with the Trinity Test in July 1945, the beginning of what was soon dubbed the Nuclear Age. Today, the event is perceived by many researchers as the beginning of something even bigger, namely 'the Anthropocene': an era in the history of the planet characterized by the activities of humankind, and their geological impact on the entire planetary system.[482] One aspect of the emerging Anthropocene condition was humans' new skill to exploit by way of science the immense forces hidden in the atomic nucleus, resulting within just a few years in the phenomenon we have called the nuclear crisis.

As integral parts of our Anthropocene condition, the nuclear crisis and the climate crisis represent the two greatest threats humankind has ever faced. Both threats are caused by humans. But our perceptions of these crises differ. The nuclear threat has been hanging over the population of the entire Earth as a sword of Damocles since around 1960. By this time there were already so many hydrogen bombs in the arsenals of the superpowers that detonating a large number of them would mean an abrupt end to human civilization. While nuclear weapons during the Cold War were regarded as the dominant global threat, the public awareness of the nuclear threat almost vanished in many parts of the world for a period after the end of the Cold War. Only very recently has it returned to the news stream and the top of global political agendas.

In recent decades the climate crises has received growing attention, especially among younger generations. The latest IPCC reports sound alarm bells, warning us that climate changes are fast, escalating, and in some cases irreversible. This is not a signal to give up but to realize that every decimal counts in the struggle against rising temperatures.[483] In many countries, it is now generally acknowledged as a very serious threat to the stability of the Earth system. But this recognition did not occur instantly unlike that of the nuclear threat. Rather, concerns about the climate slowly arose as systematic measurements of carbon dioxide in the atmosphere over the last 60–70 years showed an accelerating increase caused by the growing use of fossil fuels. The actual experience of increasingly extreme and violent weather phenomena undoubtedly also plays a role.[484] In recent years, popular concern has grown in many countries accompanied by a demand for international action. And international action is sorely needed because – like the nuclear crisis – the climate crisis is a global phenomenon that can only be effectively countered by massive global measures at an international level. Nevertheless, effective action is made difficult because the world is divided on the issue. The richest part of the world, where industrialization began, has contributed most to the climate crisis and at the same time, these societies also have more resources to mitigate its effects. In that sense, the climate crisis – again just like the nuclear threat – can be both a uniting and a dividing factor. The British chemist David King has used the image that the rich part of the world appears to be flying into the climate crisis in first class. The rich can, if they choose to, ignore the screaming of the many more people in economy class, but if the plane crashes, we are all in serious trouble.[485] In our Anthropocene era of climate and nuclear crises, humanity is tied together in a community of fate characterized by grave inequality.

This paradoxical, unequal community of fate provides a unique opportunity for people across ethnic, religious and social divides to acknowledge that the threats are so serious that we have to put our deeply entrenched conflicts and disagreements aside and join together in battling our common threats. As such the climate threat is directed at all of us. If people realize this – and there are many indications that at least a substantial part of the younger generation does so – there is hope that the nuclear threat will finally also be viewed through the same lens: it is a threat targeting all of humankind, and the continued development and proliferation of nuclear weapons does not provide the security that most of us long for.

Notes

Introduction

1. The Manhattan Project and Robert Oppenheimer's role in it have been treated in a vast number of books, e.g. in: Smyth (1945); Hewlett & Anderson (1962); Gowing (1964); Rhodes (2012; 1986); Badash (1995); Herken (2002); Hughes (2002); Bird & Sherwin (2005); DeGroot (2005); Wallace (2020).
2. Gutenberg (1946), 327–30.
3. Rabi comment after Trinity, quoted in Rhodes (2012; 1986), 672.
4. Masco (2004).
5. Rhodes (2012; 1986), 675.
6. Rhodes (2012; 1986). See also: https://www.wired.co.uk/article/manhattan-project-robert-oppenheimer.
7. Bensaude-Vincent, Boudia & Sato (2022).
8. Beard (2022) https://www.bbc.com/future/article/20220119-how-to-read-the-doomsday-clock.
9. A similar reading of the Doomsday Clock as an "utterance" has been performed by Juha A. Vuori from a perspective of *international relations* (Vuori 2010). By approaching the clock as an utterance, we can gain closer access to the possible intention of the sender and the changing settings of the hands. The Doomsday Clock has achieved an iconic status and become a well-known cultural symbol within many areas, from security policy to popular culture. This extended use is to a large extent beyond the sender's control. The present book is not an attempt to write an exhaustive cultural history on the Doomsday Clock, but the last part will include voices that have been critical of the Doomsday Clock as a symbol.

1 Discovering the Secrets of the Uranium Nucleus

10. Rutherford cited in the *New York Times*, September 12, 1933.
11. Noddack (1934).
12. Hahn to Meitner, quoted in Rhodes (2012; 1986), 253.
13. 1 electron volt (eV) is the energy an electron acquires when it is accelerated through a 1-volt potential difference.
14. Frisch about Bohr, as recollected in Frisch (1979), 116.
15. Bohr & Wheeler (1939).
16. Rhodes (2012; 1986), 27–28.
17. Lanouette (1992), 139–45, 172–73.
18. Wellerstein (2021), 21–26.
19. Einstein to Roosevelt, quoted in Cantelon et al. (1984), 9–11.
20. Title of the Frisch and Peierls memorandum, quoted in Cantelon et al. (1984), 11–15.
21. Karlsch & Walker (2005).
22. The committee's code, MAUD, was inspired by a telegram that Niels Bohr had sent to Otto Frisch in Birmingham after the German occupation of Denmark. The end of the telegram read: "Tell Cockcroft [well-known British physicist, ed.] and Maud Ray Kent", which by the English was perceived as code for an important message. Only after the war did it come to light that there was in fact a Maud Ray in the county of Kent, and that she had been the governess of some of Bohr's children!
23. The MAUD report and Frisch and Peierls' memorandum are reproduced in Gowing (1964), 389–436.

2
The World's First Nuclear Power

24. Wellerstein (2021).
25. In 1942, a nuclear reactor was referred to as a "pile".
26. Recent research indicates that uranium and other heavy elements found on Earth were created billions of years ago in a clash between neutron stars somewhere in our galaxy. See, e.g.: https://www.world-nuclear.org/information-library/nuclear-fuel-cycle/uranium-resources/the-cosmic-origins-of-uranium.aspx.
27. Groves (1962), 33–37.
28. Groves also included thorium (Th), which is element number 90 in the Periodic Table. Thorium was included in the search because it is radioactive like uranium, but mainly because its dominant isotope, Th-232, can be transformed via neutron radiation into the uranium isotope U-233 by absorbing a neutron and subsequent weak decay processes. This isotope undergoes fission in the same way as U-235 when hit by a neutron. In practice, thorium did not come to play any role in the American atomic bomb project.
29. Rhodes (1996), 130.
30. When the first nuclear reactor was referred to as a "pile", it was due to this layered construction.
31. Badash (1995), 36; Mania (2012), 236–39.
32. Szlard to Fermi, quoted in Lanouette (1992), 245.
33. In Groves (1962), 38–59. General Groves gives a detailed account of how he managed to get Du Pont to accept this task that involved so many unknown factors and dangers that it could have endangered the existence of the company if it had proven to be unsolvable.
34. https://www.atomicheritage.org/history/little-boy-and-fat-man
35. https://www.atomicheritage.org/history/little-boy-and-fat-man
36. Aaserud (2005), 23–27; Gowing (1964), 346–56; Christmas-Møller (1985), 64–66.
37. Churchill to Bohr and Cherwell, quoted in Rhodes (2012; 1986), 530; Gowing (1964), 355; Aaserud (2005), 26.
38. Rhodes (2012; 1986), 537–38; Aaserud (2005), 37–38; Pais (1994), 532–33.
39. Knudsen & Nielsen (2016), 39–50.
40. https://ahf.nuclearmuseum.org/ahf/history/interim-committee/. See also Rhodes (2012; 1986), 628–51.
41. Van Calmthout (2018), 77–128; Rhodes (2012; 1986), 605–14.
42. After the end of the war in Europe, ten leading German nuclear physicists were detained at an English estate (*Farm Hall*) that was rigged with microphones recording all conversations between them. It appears from these recordings that while the Germans were convinced in the beginning that they had been ahead of the physicists from the allied forces throughout the war, they kept trying to convince themselves and each other, after hearing and reading about the American nuclear attack on Hiroshima on August 6, 1945, that they had never wanted to develop an atomic bomb but only a nuclear reactor. See Walker (1995) and Bernstein (2001).
43. Rhodes (2012; 1986), 632.
44. Quotes from the Franck Report, in https://fas.org/sgp/eprint/franck.html.
45. Quotes from the Franck Report, in https://fas.org/sgp/eprint/franck.html.
46. Rabinowitch statement, quoted in Wittner (1993), 26.
47. General Lauris Norstad in a letter to General Curtis LeMay, see Coffey (1988), 474.
48. https://www.osti.gov/opennet/manhattan-project-history/Events/1945/debate.htm.
49. Rhodes (2012; 1986), 650–51.
50. Truman statement just before Trinity, quoted in Wittner (1974), 11.
51. Stalin to Truman, quoted in Rhodes (1996), 176.
52. Truman's diary for July 5, 1945, quoted in Boyer (1998), 23.

53. http://www.dannen.com/decision/index.html
54. Rhodes (2012; 1986), 640–41.
55. https://www.rerf.or.jp/library/scidata/scids/ds02/index.html
56. Truman statement after bombing of Hiroshima. Quoted in Rhodes (2012; 1986), 734.
57. Wellerstein (2024).
58. Wellerstein (2024), 734.
59. There are different reports on the number of victims of the nuclear attacks on Hiroshima and Nagasaki. Our numbers are taken from Badash (1995), 56.
60. Rhodes (2012; 1986), 740–42.
61. Truman in radio speech, August 10, 1945, quoted in Wellerstein (2020), 45.
62. Wellerstein (2020), 34–55.
63. Badash (1995), 64–65.
64. These numbers were presented to President Truman at his meeting with the Joint Chiefs of Staff and Service Secretaries, June 18, 1945; see Appendix K in Giangreco (2023), 163–76.
65. See Appendix B in Giangreco (2023), 118–20.
66. Alperovitz (1995).
67. Walker (1995); Craig & Radchenko (2008).
68. Walzer to Fussell, quoted in Fussell (1988), 23.
69. Fussell to Walzer, quoted in Fussell (1988), 28.
70. Oppenheimer on how to drop the atomic bomb, quoted in Bird & Sherwin (2005), 314.
71. Oppenheimer to Truman, and Truman to Dean Acheson, quoted in Bird & Sherwin (2005), 332.
72. Truman to Stimson, August 8, 1945, quoted in Craig & Radchenko (2008), 87.
73. Wallace diary for August 10, 1945, quoted in Boyer (1998), 23.
74. Teller on scientists and H-bombs, quoted in Shapin (2008), 71.
75. Oppenheimer to Stimson on August 17, 1945, quoted in Schweber (2003), 230.
76. Einstein and colleagues in *Bulletin of the Atomic Scientists*, June 1947, cover page 2.

3
All the Great Powers Become Nuclear Powers

77. Quoted in Weiss (2003), 37.
78. Badash (1995), 68–69.
79. Badash (1995), 69; Craig & Radchenko (2008), 122–24.
80. Halloway (1994), 161–63.
81. Craig & Radchenko (2008), 111–61, includes an analysis of the Baruch Plan and the surrounding circumstances in the years 1945–46.
82. Truman to Acheson, quoted in Weiss (2003), 37.
83. Extract from the McMahon Bill, quoted in Cantelon et al. (1984), 83–84.
84. Stalin to Milovan Djilas, cited in Rhodes (1996), 313.
85. Stalin to Kurchatov, quoted in Rhodes (1996), 177–78.
86. Kurchatov comment when first Soviet reactor became critical, quoted in Holloway (1994), 182.
87. Smyth (1945).
88. Solzhenitsyn (1975).
89. Holloway (1994), 172–77.
90. Hecht (2012); Pasternak (2011); Kuletz (1998).
91. Josephson (2005), 272–96.
92. McNiell (2001), 411–12.
93. Holloway (1994), 178–80.
94. Rhodes (1996), 273.
95. Holloway (1994), 182.
96. Holloway (1994), 184–89.
97. Holloway (1994), 187.
98. The third letter in the Russian alphabet corresponds to our V.
99. The first Soviet nuclear test is described in Holloway (1994), 213–20, and in Rhodes (1996), 364–68.
100. Gowin (2019).
101. Khariton comment after Joe-1, quoted in Holloway (1994), 216.
102. Groves and Bush to Senate Special Committee, Nov.–Dec. 1945 and Frank comment Oct. 1949. Quoted in *Bulletin of the Atomic Scientists*, October 1949, 264.
103. *Bulletin of the Atomic Scientists*, October 1947, 2.

104. Atlee in letter to Truman, quoted in Goldberg (1964), 410–11.
105. Bevin to cabinet colleagues, quoted in Baylis & Stoddart (2015), 32.
106. Dean (1954), 227; Baylis (1995), 451.
107. Baylis (1995), 60–63.
108. Gowing & Arnold (1974a), 179–85.
109. Baylis (1995), 52.
110. Gowing & Arnold (1974a), 41.
111. Gowing & Arnold (1974b), 194–96.
112. Gowing & Arnold (1974b), 498.
113. Chiefs of Staff Committee on H-bombs and Churchill to Cabinet, both quoted in Baylis (1995), 183.
114. Churchill to Plowden, quoted in Hennesy (2003), 52.
115. Arnold & Pyne (2001), 173–74.
116. Hecht (1998), 58.
117. President Auriol celebrating plutonium extraction, quoted in Hecht (1998), 2.
118. Hecht (1998), 59.
119. Hecht (1998), 60.
120. Hecht (1998), 64–78; 95.
121. https://nuclearweaponarchive.org/France/FranceOrigin.html
122. https://nuclearweaponarchive.org/France/FranceOrigin.html
123. General Galois' arguments for 'Force de frappe', quoted in Gunston (1973), 105.
124. *Gerboise* is the French word for *Gerboa*, which is a desert rodent living in the Sahara.
125. https://nuclearweaponarchive.org/France/FranceOrigin.html.
126. Regnault (2003), 1223–48.
127. https://en.wikipedia.org/wiki/canopus_(nuclear_test)
128. https://en.wikipedia.org/wiki/France_and_weapons_of_mass_destruction
129. Irène Curie to Yang Zhengzong, quoted in Lewis & Litai (1988), 36.
130. "New Look" and the associated term "massive retaliation" are discussed in more detail in chapters 4 and 5.
131. Chairman Mao on the need for Chinese nuclear weapons, quoted in Lewis & Litai (1988), 39.
132. Mao on possible effects of nuclear weapons, quoted in Lewis & Litai (1988), 69.
133. Lewis & Litai (1988), 62–65.
134. Lewis & Litai (1988), 72.
135. http://donwagner.dk/MS/StoreSpring.html.
136. Lewis & Litai (1988), 73–169.
137. Lewis & Litai (1988), 196–206.
138. https://media.nti.org/pdfs/china_nuclear.pdf
139. IPPNW (1991).

4
"Atoms for Peace" or "Atoms for War"

140. Archibald (2006), 36–40; Elzinga (1996), 89–132.
141. Wilkinson to UNESCO delegates, quoted in Beers (2016), 434–35. UNESCO had limited political power. Over the course of the 1950s, American mistrust in UNESCO increased, and the UN's function in relation to international monitoring of nuclear technology was transferred to other UN organs.
142. Rhodes (1986), 362–401; Compton (1956).
143. Davis (2009); Kevles (1971), 71–73.
144. Compton (1947c).
145. Compton in UNESCO 1947, quoted in Compton (1947a), 861.
146. Quoted in Compton (1947b), 303.
147. Masters & Way (1946).
148. Quoted in Sluga (2010), 56.
149. Aaserud (2005), 163–70; Christmas-Møller (1985), 117–31.
150. FRUS 1948, Vol. 1, Part 1, 388–99.
151. Quotes from Niels Bohr's open letter to the UN, Bohr (1950). The letter is reproduced in Aaserud (2005), 173–85.
152. Aaserud (2005), 185.
153. Villaume (2020), 82–84.
154. Gaddis (2008; 2005), 68.
155. Huntington (1961), 279–81.
156. Herken (1980), 193–256, 330–36.
157. Villaume (2020), 176–77, 222–24.
158. Rhodes (1996), 406–8; Villaume (2020), 154–55.

159. Bird & Sherwin (2005), 422–23.
160. Rhodes (1996), 407.
161. Rhodes (1996), 482–512.
162. Rhodes (1996), 523–29.
163. Strauss on USSR H-bomb test. Quoted in *Bulletin of the Atomic Scientists*, September 1953, 236.
164. Rhodes (1996), 541–42.
165. Mahaffey (2014), 74–82; Higuchi (2020), 23–35.
166. Strauss in press conference, March 1954. Quoted in DeGroot (2005), 185.
167. Churchill in British Parliament. The full speech is available at: https://winstonchurchill.org/resources/speeches/1946-1963-elder-statesman/never-despair/.
168. Bulletin statement after setting the Doomsday Clock in September 1953. Quoted in *Bulletin of the Atomic Scientists*, September 1953, back cover.
169. Osgood (2006), 153–86.
170. Eisenhower in UN, December 8, 1953 as quoted in Cantelon et al. (1991), 96–104; see also Hewlett & Holl (1989), 34–72.
171. In the years after the Second World War until Eisenhower's Atoms for Peace speech, many peace movements in Western Europe had been heavily influenced by Soviet peace initiatives. See e.g. Wittner (1993).
172. Osgood (2006), 156.
173. Strauss on nuclear generated electricity, quoted in Hecht (2012), 6.
174. Haber (1958), 14–21.
175. Haber (1958), 137–61.
176. van Munster & Sylvest (2016), 44–49.
177. Russell to Einstein, quoted in Wittner (1997), 6.
178. Wittner (1997), 7.
179. Russell at London Conference, July 9, 1955, quoted in https://pugwash.org/1955/07/09/statement-manifesto/.
180. Higuchi (2020).
181. https://pugwash.org/1955/07/09/statement-manifesto/
182. Wittner (1997), 35.
183. Wittner (1997), 35–37.
184. https://www.nobelprize.org/prizes/peace/1995/pugwash/facts/.
185. Rasmussen (2009), 49–63.
186. Lindell & Löfveberg (1972), 226.
187. https://www.rerf.or.jp/en/programs/roadmap_e/ (Accessed May 17, 2021).
188. Wittner (1997), 219–20.
189. Wittner (1997), 44–51.
190. Wittner (1997), 413–25.
191. Project Chariot is described in detail in O'Neill (1994). An essay on this case can be found in Boyer (1998), 87–94.
192. Teller joking with PNE, quoted in Boyer (1998), 89.
193. Fischer (1997), 29.
194. Nielsen et al. (1998), 113–23, 168–82.
195. Dulles reply to Molotov, quoted in Fischer (1997), 30. See also Hewlett & Holl (1989), 219–22.
196. The IAEA's objectives and functions, as quoted in Fischer (1997), 35–36.
197. Bunche on problems in IAEA's Board of Governors. Quoted in Fischer (1997), 74.
198. Fischer (1997), 84–85.
199. Scheinmann (1988), 37–38.
200. Dulles on USA's New Look Strategy, as quoted in Gaddis (2005), 145.
201. Huntington (1961), 282–83.
202. Dulles to British ambassador, July 21, 1958. Quoted in Villaume (2020), 369.
203. Gaddis (2005), 218.
204. Nielsen & Nielsen (2017); Nielsen & Nielsen (2021).
205. Dobbs (2009); Rhodes (2012; 1986), 570–76.
206. Rhodes (2007), 70–83.
207. Eden (2004).
208. Fermi and Rabi statements on H-bombs. Quoted in Rhodes (1995), 401.
209. Quoted in Rhodes (2007), 101.

5
The Role of Science During the Cold War

210. Agar (2012).
211. Knudsen & Nielsen (2012).
212. Pauling (1983).

213. Rubinson (2013).
214. Teller on H-bombs, quoted in DeGroot (2005), 185.
215. Teller (2002), 13–16.
216. Rubison (2011), 299–300.
217. Rubinson (2015), 93–106, 234–36.
218. Shapin on scientists endorsing military research, quoted in Shapin (2008), 74.
219. Sakharov on his contribution to the Soviet H-bomb, quoted in Sakharov (1990), 97.
220. Sakharov (1990).
221. https://www.osti.gov/opennet/hearing. The main points of the hearing are summarized and discussed in Bird & Sherwin (2005).
222. Bird & Sherwin (2005), 575–76.
223. Oppenheimer on Robert Kennedy proposal. Quoted in Bird & Sherwin (2005), 579.
224. Braun et al. (2007).
225. Norris & Kristensen (2010).
226. Fischer (1997), 86.
227. Fischer (1997), 93–95.
228. Beard (2022). https://www.bbc.com/future/article/20220119-how-to-read-the-doomsday-clock/
229. Rabinowitch on the new clock setting. Quoted in *Bulletin of the Atomic Scientists*, January 1960, 3.
230. *Bulletin of the Atomic Scientists*, October 1963, 2.
231. *Bulletin of the Atomic Scientists*, January 1968, 1–2.
232. Rabinowitch on the new clock setting. Quoted in *Bulletin of the Atomic Scientists*, April 1969, 48.
233. Norris & Kristensen (2010).
234. United States Treaties and Other International Agreements, Vol. 23, 846–55. See also Villaume (2023), 323–33.
235. Gaddis (2008; 2005), 252–58, 322–27, 348–49; Leffler (2007), 243–44.
236. https://www.nato.int/cps/en/natolive/official_texts_27040.htm.
237. Wittner (2003), 302.
238. Maar III (2022).
239. Gaddis (2005), 355–58.
240. Rhodes (2007), 187–211.
241. Jeremy Stone (1935–2017), mathematician and president of the Federation of American Scientists (FAS) from 1970 to 2000, where he was in charge of the organization's initiatives in arms control, human rights and foreign policy. Frank von Hippel (b. 1937), physicist, codirector of Princeton University's Program on Science and Global Security. Evgeny Velikhov (1935–2024), physicist, President of the Kurchatov Institute, and from 1986 scientific advisor to President Gorbachev. Andrei Sakharov (1921–1989), physicist, Nobel Peace Prize laureate 1975, and human rights activist in the USSR. In December 1986, President Gorbachev brought him back to Moscow after five years of forced exile in Gorky.
242. Evangelista (1999), 330. See also von Hippel & Kurokawa (2019), 7–8; Von Hippel (2025), 97-101.
243. Wittner (2003), 433–34; von Hippel & Kurokawa (2019), 6–9.
244. Evangelista (1999), 334.
245. von Hippel & Kurokawa (2019), 29–30; Neff (1991).
246. Yeltsin on START II, quoted in Wittner (2003), 442; see also https://fas.org/nuke/control/start2/index.html.
247. https://www.armscontrol.org/factsheets/start2chron.
248. Gorbachev in letter to Bernard lown, quoted in Wittner (2003), 404.
249. Evangelista (1999).
250. Rubinson (2015), 237–47.

6
Four New Nuclear Powers – and Several Candidates

251. Quote from Acheson-Lilienthal Report, see Weiss (2003), 17.
252. Fischer (1997), 30; Weiss (2003), 40.
253. https://world-nuclear.org/information-library/current-and-future-generation/thorium.aspx. See also: https://media.nature.com/original/magazine-assets/d41586-021-02459-w/d41586-021-02459-w.pdf.
254. This subchapter relies mainly on Cohen (1998). See also: https://www.nti.org/analysis/articles/israel-nuclear/.

255. Ben-Gurion on Israeli scientists, quoted in Cohen (1998), 10.
256. Bergmann on Israel's nuclear research program, quoted in Cohen (1998), 15–16.
257. The institute was set up in 1934 but did not get its present name until after the Israeli-Arab conflict in 1948, when the chemist Chaim Weizmann was appointed as the first president of the newly established state of Israel.
258. Cohen (1998), 81–82.
259. Cohen (1998), 54.
260. Cohen (1998), 52–54.
261. Bar-Zohar (2007), 216–17.
262. Cohen (1998), 73–75.
263. Cohen (1998), 60–62.
264. Cohen (1998), 84–87.
265. Ben-Gurion to Knesset, December 21, 1960. Quoted in Cohen (1998), 91.
266. Peres to Kennedy 1963. Quoted in Cohen (1998), 119.
267. *The Sunday Times*, October 5, 1986.
268. Cohen (1998), 297–98.
269. Hersh (1991).
270. Cohen (2010), 80–81.
271. https://thebulletin.org/premium/2022-01/nuclear-notebook-israeli-nuclear-weapons-2022/
272. The codeword for this policy in Israel is *amimut* – a Hebrew word that means something like "opaque" or "ambiguous". See Cohen (2010).
273. The present subchapter relies substantially on the authoritative work of Perkovich (1999).
274. Here cited from Perkovich (1999), 20.
275. Perkovich (1999), 26–27.
276. Apsara is a celestial nymph in Hindu mythology.
277. Abraham (1998), 105.
278. Perkovich (1999), 25–31.
279. Perkovich (1999), 69–74.
280. Perkovich (1999), 82.
281. Kaufman (2013).
282. Perkovich (1999), 170–78.
283. The Peaceful Explosion (atomicarchive.com) (Accessed February 10, 2022).
284. Perkovich (1999), 179.
285. Frey (2006), 169.
286. https://www.armscontrol.org/act/1998-05/news-briefs/india-conducts-nuclear-tests-pakistan-follows-suit (Accessed February 10, 2022).
287. Abraham (1998), 165–66.
288. https://world-nuclear.org/information-library/country-profiles/countries-g-n/india.
289. Weissman & Krosney (1981), 161. The present subchapter relies to a large degree on this book.
290. The meeting in Multan is described in detail in Weissman & Krosney (1981), 42–46.
291. Weissman & Krosney (1981), 45.
292. Weissman & Krosney (1981), 74–84.
293. Dr Abdul Qadeer Khan and his activities have been described in many books and articles. We base our description of the story mainly on Weissman & Krosney (1981); Corera (2006); the International Institute for Strategic Studies (2007); and MacCallan (2016).
294. Corera (2006), 7.
295. Corera (2006), 15; MacCalman (2016), 105.
296. Corera (2006), 41.
297. Corera (2006); The International Institute for Strategic Studies (2007); MacCalman (2016).
298. Weissman & Krosney (1981), 161–63.
299. Weissman & Krosney (1981), 194.
300. The International Institute for Strategic Studies (2007), 22.
301. The International Institute for Strategic Studies (2007), 31.
302. This subchapter relies to a large degree on an article published by the organization Nuclear Threat Initiative: https://www.nti.org/analysis/articles/north-korea-nuclear/.
303. Jae-Bong (2009); (Bermudez (1991); Bermudez (1999).
304. https://www.nti.org/analysis/articles/north-korea-nuclear/ (note 7). https://cisac.fsi.stanford.edu/content/cisac-north-korea.
305. https://www.nti.org/analysis/articles/north-korea-nuclear/ (note 9).
306. Hibbs (1993), 8–9; Oberdorfer (1997), 279.
307. Hecker et al. (2018).

308. Corera (2006); MacCalman (2016).
309. Corera (2006), ix–x.
310. Corera (2006), 196–216; The International Institute for Strategic Studies (2007), 93–106.
311. Musharraf press conference on February 6, 2004. Quoted in https://www.nytimes.com/2004/02/06/world/nuclear-expert-receives-pardon-from-musharraf.html.
312. North Korean News Agency on first nuclear bomb test, as quoted in https://www.nti.org/analysis/articles/north-korea-nuclear/ (note 38).
313. The bombing of the Osirak reactor is described in detail in Weissman & Krosney (1981), 3–10.
314. Eklund to IAEA's Board of Directors, quoted in Roehrlich (2022), 167.
315. UN Resolution 487, quoted in Roehrlich (2022), 173.
316. Roehrlich 2022, 170–72.
317. Weissman & Krosney (1981), 11–12.
318. Weissman & Krosney (1981), 11–21.
319. It should also be mentioned that Israel did something similar much later, namely on September 6, 2007, when Israeli fighters attacked and destroyed a secret nuclear reactor at Al-Kibar in northern Syria. It was not until 2018 that Israel admitted responsibility for the attack. https://www.armscontrol.org/act/2008-08/features/israel's-airstrike-syria's-reactor-implications-non-proliferation-regime.
320. https://nsarchive.gwu.edu/briefing-book/iraq-nuclear-vault/2021-06-07/osirak-israels-strike-iraqs-nuclear-reactor-40-years-later
321. https://www.nti.org/analysis/articles/iraq-nuclear/
322. https://www.isis-online.org/publications/iraq/iraqs_fm_history.html.
323. https://edition.cnn.com/2013/10/30/world/meast/iraq-weapons-inspections-fast-facts/index.html.
324. This subchapter relies mainly on https://www.nti.org/analysis/articles/libya-nuclear/ and https://www.armscontrol.org/factsheets/Libya-Chronology.
325. Most of these means are mentioned in the NTI research article mentioned in the above note.
326. https://isis-online.org/isis-reports/detail/libyas-gas-centrifuge-procurement-much-remains-undiscovered/11 (Accessed February 10, 2022).
327. The South African nuclear program has been described in, among others, the following articles: https://www.atomicheritage.org/history/south-african-nuclear-program and https://fas.org/nuke/guide/rsa/nuke/stumpf.htm.
328. Quoted in Hecht (2012), 29.
329. Beinart & Dubow (2021), 293–95
330. Beinart and Dubow (2021), 297–98.
331. Polakow-Suransky (2002).
332. Albright (1994).
333. Purkitt & Burgess (2005).
334. Beinart & Dubow (2021), 296–97.
335. Van Wyk (2010).
336. Hecht (2012).
337. https://www.atomicheritage.org/history/south-african-nuclear-program and https://fas.org/nuke/guide/rsa/nuke/stumpf.htm.
338. *Bulletin of the Atomic Scientists*, September 1974, 4–5.
339. Quoted in *Bulletin of the Atomic Scientists*, January 1980, 1–3.
340. *Bulletin of the Atomic Scientists*, January 1981, 1.
341. Quoted in *Bulletin of the Atomic Scientists*, January 1984, 2.
342. *Bulletin of the Atomic Scientists*, January 1988, 3; April 1990, 3; December 1991, 2.
343. *Bulletin of the Atomic Scientists*, January 1996, 2.
344. Quoted in *Bulletin of the Atomic Scientists*, September 1998, 4.

7
Nuclear Hotspots in the New Millennium

345. Fukuyama (1992); Huntington (1996).
346. Huntington (1996), 28.

347. Walton (2016), 202–6. *International relations* literature uses the term *Nuclear Age*.
348. Baylis (2016), 220–36.
349. https://www.bbc.com/news/10537286
350. https://edition.cnn.com/2013/11/08/world/kashmir-fast-facts/index.html
351. https://www.bbc.com/news/10537286.
352. Imre Khan statement, August 8, 2019, quoted in https://www.bbc.com/news/10537286.
353. https://pib.gov.in/Pressreleaseshare.aspx?PRID=1700682
354. https://pib.gov.in/Pressreleaseshare.aspx?PRID=1700682
355. Rehman (2024).
356. Toon et al. (2019). https://advances.sciencemag.org/content/5/10/eaay5478. In 2025 the countries had 350 nuclear warheads in total, and not 500 as the 2019 study projected. However, the calculations in the study were based on the firing of 250 nuclear warheads.
357. A brief overview of the North Korean nuclear program can be found here: https://www.nti.org/learn/countries/north-korea/.
358. https://www.armscontrol.org/factsheets/dprkchron
359. https://www.youtube.com/watch?v=8_rmhij41-U
360. https://www.armscontrol.org/factsheets/dprkchron
361. https://www.washingtonpost.com/national-security/biden-administration-forges-new-path-on-north-korea-crisis-in-wake-of-trump-and-obama-failures/2021/04/30/c8bef4f2-a9a9-11eb-b166-174b63ea6007_story.html
362. https://www.theguardian.com/world/2022/mar/31/testing-times-why-north-koreas-missile-launches-should-worry-the-west
363. Congressional Research Service (2024). https://crsreports.congress.gov/
364. Kristensen et al. (2024).
365. https://thebulletin.org/2023/01/the-us-has-a-new-nuclear-proliferation-problem-south-korea/
366. https://www.bbc.com/news/world-us-canada-65404805
367. Congressional Research Service (2024).
368. https://www.bbc.com/news/world-asia-62845958
369. Mackenzie & Comerford (2025).
370. An overview of the Iranian nuclear program until 2015 is provided in Juneau (2015), 169–202.
371. https://www.nti.org/learn/countries/iran/
372. https://www.nti.org/learn/countries/iran/
373. https://isis-online.org/isis-reports/detail/did-stuxnet-take-out-1000-centrifuges-at-the-natanz-enrichment-plant/
374. Quoted in https://www.reuters.com/article/us-usa-election-trump-iran-idUSKBN13427E.
375. https://www.bbc.com/news/world-middle-east-56643178
376. https://www.reuters.com/world/middle-east/iran-has-almost-completed-preparations-enrich-uranium-60-iaea-2021-04-14/
377. https://foreignpolicy.com/2021/12/28/iran-nuclear-deal-jcpoa-vienna-capabilities-biden/
378. Blinken to Lapid on Iran nuclear weapons, quoted in https://www.state.gov/secretary-antony-j-blinken-and-israeli-foreign-minister-and-alternate-prime-minister-yair-lapid-at-a-joint-press-availability/.
379. Zhang (2025).
380. *Politiken* July 29, 2019, 4.
381. https://www.nytimes.com/2019/02/01/opinion/inf-nuclear-weapons.html
382. https://www.armscontrol.org/act/2014-09/news/russia-breaches-inf-treaty-us-says
383. Kristensen & Korda (2021a) and (2021b). For the US nuclear modernization program, see the recent update in Kristensen et al. (2025).

384. https://armscontrolcenter.org/fact-sheet-u-s-nuclear-weapons-modernization-costs-constraints/
385. Hennigan (2024).
386. Hennigan (2024).
387. Kristensen & Korda (2021b).
388. Putin on Russia's nuclear arsenal, quoted in Kristensen & Korda (2021b).
389. Putin on New START, quoted in Kristensen & Korda (2021b).
390. https://www.state.gov/new-start/
391. https://www.armscontrol.org/blog/2021-12/us-russian-nuclear-arms-control-watch
392. Putin threatens to use nuclear weapons in the Ukraine conflict, quoted in https://theprint.in/world/full-text-of-vladimir-putins-speech-announcing-special-military-operation-in-ukraine/845714/.
393. https://www.armscontrol.org/act/2023-03/news/russia-suspends-new-start
394. https://www.armscontrol.org/factsheets/comprehensive-test-ban-treaty-glance; Podvig, (2024).
395. https://treaties.un.org/Pages/showDetails.aspx?objid=0800000280401fbb
396. Quoted in Budjeryn (2023), 230.
397. https://thebulletin.org/doomsday-clock/current-time/nuclear-risk/
398. For a detailed outline and evaluation, see Kristensen & Korda (2021c), 318–36. Sources in the US Department of Defense assess that we may be looking at a quadrupling of deliverable warheads by 2030 – a number that Kristensen & Korda are skeptical of.
399. US Department of Defense (2020). *Annual Report to Congress: Military and Security Developments Involving the People's Republic of China 2019*. Office of the Secretary of Defense, https://media.defense.gov/2023/Oct/19/2003323409/-1/-1/1/2023-MILITARY-AND-SECURITY-DEVELOPMENTS-INVOLVING-THE-PEOPLES-REPUBLIC-OF-CHINA.PDF.
400. There are differing assessments of China's *no-first-use* doctrine and its development: Sweeney (2021); Weidi, (2016); Kristensen & Korda (2021c), 326–27.
401. https://www.iaea.org/projects/crp/t12020
402. Bienen & Ostriker (2021); Riqiang (2013).
403. The Anti-Secession Law was passed at the 10th Party Congress in 2005 in Beijing and can be found in translation at http://us.china-embassy.gov.cn/eng/zt/twwt/200503/t20050315_4912997.htm (Accessed December 2, 2022).
404. See e.g. Sweeney (2021).
405. E.g., President Xi's speech in connection with the 100th anniversary of the Chinese Communist Party on July 1, 2021. The full speech in English translation can be found at http://www.xinhuanet.com/english/special/2021-07/01/c_1310038244.htm.
406. Chang-Liao & Fang (2021).
407. Albright & Stricker (2018) provide a solid and extensive analysis of Taiwan's nuclear program and its shutdown.
408. Albright & Stricker (2018), 195–202.
409. Pelosi statement when visiting Taiwan, July 2, 2022. https://www.washingtonpost.com/opinions/2022/08/02/nancy-pelosi-taiwan-visit-op-ed/.
410. https://www.ft.com/content/c8fc6efa-5429-4873-92c0-aae1134c7a14
411. https://www.cbsnews.com/news/china-missiles-waters-around-taiwan-regional-tensions-highest-levels-decades/(Accessed February 9, 2023).
412. Bienen & Ostriker (2021).
413. https://www.bbc.com/news/world-europe-34797252
414. https://thebulletin.org/premium/2025-03/chinese-nuclear-weapons-2025/; https://thebulletin.org/premium/2024-11/united-kingdom-nuclear-weapons-2024/; https://thebulletin.org/premium/2023-07/nuclear-notebook-french-nuclear-weapons-2023.

415. In fairness, it must be stressed that Fukuyama has revised his own thesis on the end of history several times.
416. Walton (2016), 217–18.
417. Dukes (2011), 121.
418. Schultz et al. on future nuclear dangers, quoted in Shultz, Perry, Kissinger & Nunn (2007), 2.
419. The security doctrine can be found in English translation at https://www.armscontrol.org/act/2000-05/russias-military-doctrine.
420. https://thebulletin.org/2014/03/why-russia-calls-a-limited-nuclear-strike-de-escalation/
421. https://www.icanw.org/new_russian_doctrine_increases_possible_nuclear_weapons_use_scenarios
422. Nuclear Posture Review 2022: https://crsreports.congress.gov/product/pdf/IF/IF12266.
423. Joe Biden, "Why America must lead again", *Foreign Affairs*, March/April, 2020. https://www.foreignaffairs.com/articles/united-states/2020-01-23/why-america-must-lead-again
424. Kierulf (2014), 230–50.
425. As mentioned earlier, North Korea withdrew from the NPT in 2003. The country had joined the treaty in 1985.
426. Article 6 in the NPT, as quoted in https://www.iaea.org/sites/default/files/publications/documents/infcircs/1970/infcirc140.pdf.
427. The Ban Treaty and the UN's summary of the course of events can be found at https://www.un.org/disarmament/wmd/nuclear/tpnw/.
428. https://www.un.org/disarmament/wmd/nuclear/tpnw/
429. https://www.whitehouse.gov/briefing-room/statements-releases/2022/01/03/p5-statement-on-preventing-nuclear-war-and-avoiding-arms-races/
430. For an updated list of countries that have acceded to and/or ratified the treaty, see https://treaties.unoda.org/t/tpnw.
431. Pretorius & Sauer (2021).
432. Pretorius and Sauer on problems with NPT, quoted in Pretorius & Sauer (2021), 402.
433. Harries (2021).

8
Nuclear Weapons, Climate Crisis and the Doomsday Clock

434. A brief but brilliant article on this topic: Edwards (2012). The topic is addressed in more detail in Weart (2007) and Edwards (2010).
435. Revelle & Suess (1957).
436. Keeling (1960); Keeling (1976).
437. Heymann and Dalmedico on a new environmental paradigm, quoted in Heymann & Dalmedico (2019); See also Caldwell (1996).
438. Waters & van Helden (1987).
439. Huxley (1946); Andersen (2019).
440. Higuchi (2020).
441. van Munster & Sylvest (2016), 88–89.
442. van Munster & Sylvest (2021a).
443. Schell (1982).
444. van Munster & Sylvest (2021a) argue convincingly that Schell in his writings foresaw the discourse on the Anthropocene, which became intense after the year 2000.
445. Oreskes & Conway (2010); Rich (2019).
446. Fukuyama (1992), 86.
447. Dukes (2011), 123–26.
448. IPCC (2007): AR4 Climate Change Synthesis Report. https://www.ipcc.ch/report/ar4/syr/.
449. Pugwash Community, New Challenges to Human Security. https://pugwash.org/2006/06/18/wageningen-meeting-on-new-challenges-to-human-security.
450. https://thebulletin.org/doomsday-clock/current-time/
451. https://thebulletin.org/doomsday-clock/current-time/
452. https://www.armscontrol.org/factsheets/NewSTART

453. https://thebulletin.org/doomsday-clock/2019-doomsday-clock-statement/
454. https://thebulletin.org/doomsday-clock/2019-doomsday-clock-statement/
455. https://thebulletin.org/doomsday-clock/2021-doomsday-clock-statement/
456. https://thebulletin.org/doomsday-clock/2021-doomsday-clock-statement/
457. https://thebulletin.org/doomsday-clock/2023-doomsday-clock-statement/
458. https://thebulletin.org/doomsday-clock/2025-doomsday-clock-statement/
459. Vuori on the doomsday clock, quoted in Vuori (2010). Studies of "securitization" address, among other things, who can convince others – and how – about what poses an existential, action-demanding threat to a given community. See also Wæver (1995); Buzan, Wæver & Wilde (1998).
460. Vuori (2010), 263.
461. https://slate.com/technology/2020/01/doomsday-clock-10000-year-long-now.html
462. This critique of the Doomsday Clock has, among other forums, been put forward in a publication by the American pro-nuclear power environmental movement *The Breakthrough Institute*. See e.g. https://thebreakthrough.org/journal/issue-5/fear-and-time.
463. Moore (1996). We often find in issues of *The Bulletin* reminders that the message behind the clock is *not* powerlessness and despair, which may be perceived as an acknowledgement that such an interpretation is rather tempting.
464. van Munster & Sylvest (2016), 132–39.
465. Bastian (2012).
466. Bulletin (2024): *Seminar: The climate-nuclear nexus: What climate change means for nuclear security*, https://www.youtube.com/watch?v=TzzJs3-vdFIXXX; Goodman (2024).

9
The Third Nuclear Age

467. Rhys (2023); Narang & Saga (2023).
468. https://www.kas.de/en/web/multilateraler-dialog-wien/to-the-third-nuclear-age-a-timeline?_CalendarPortlet_epoch=15723774&_CalendarPortlet_load-From=0
469. Futter et al. (2025), 2–3.
470. Futter et al. (2025), 4–5.
471. https://www.atlanticcouncil.org/in-depth-research-reports/issue-brief/strategic-stability-in-the-third-nuclear-age/
472. https://www.wagingpeace.org/thirdmeetingofstatesparties-3msp/; Futter et al. (2025), 3.
473. https://www.lockheedmartin.com/en-us/capabilities/missile-defense/golden-dome-missile-defense.html
474. https://www.bbc.com/news/articles/cwy33n484xoo
475. https://thebulletin.org/2025/05/the-15-minute-interview-joe-cirincione-on-golden-dome-and-the-long-running-us-missile-defense-debacle/
476. https://thebulletin.org/2025/04/trump-wants-denuclearization-and-a-golden-dome-he-cant-have-both/
477. https://thebulletin.org/2025/05/indias-missile-attack-shows-that-managing-an-india-pakistan-crisis-is-easier-said-than-done/
478. Rafael Mariano Grossi (IAEA) on Threats to International Peace and Security – Security Council, 9941st meeting. https://webtv.un.org/en/asset/k1h/k1h47d7kt5 (Accessed 15 July 2025).
479. Daniel Immerwahr (2022), "Forgetting the apocalypse", *The Guardian*, May 12, 2022, at https://www.theguardian.com/world/2022/may/12/forgetting-the-apocalypse-why-our-nuclear-fears-faded-and-why-thats-dangerous.
480. https://www.royalcourt.no/nyhet.html?tid=229383&sek=27262
481. Williams & Horschig (2024).
482. http://quaternary.stratigraphy.org/working-groups/anthropocene/; Waters et al. (2015).
483. https://www.ipcc.ch/ar6-syr/
484. Damsbo-Svendsen (2021).
485. King (2009), 10.

Bibliography

Aaserud, Finn, ed. (2005): *Niels Bohr Collected Works. Volume 11: The Political Arena 1934–1961* (Amsterdam: Elsevier).

Abraham, Itty (1998): *The Making of the Indian Atomic Bomb: Science, Secrecy and the Postcolonial State* (London & New York: Zed Books).

Agar, Jon (2012): *Science in the Twentieth Century and Beyond* (Cambridge: Polity Press).

Albright, David (1994): "South Africa's Secret Nuclear Weapons", *Institute for Science and Technology Policy*. ISIS Report, May 1994.

Albright, David & Andrea Stricker: "Taiwan's Former Nuclear Weapons Program", *Institute for Science and Technology Policy*, (2018), 1–222. https://isis-online.org/uploads/isis-reports/documents/TaiwansFormerNuclearWeaponsProgram_POD_color_withCover.pdf

Alperovitz, Gar (1995): *The Decision to Use the Atomic Bomb* (New York: Vintage Books).

Andersen, Casper (2019): "Julian Huxleys biokulturelle menneske og UNESCO". In Trine Kellberg Nielsen, Casper Andersen, Alexandra R. Kratschmer & Mathias Clasen (eds.), *Menneske, kultur, evolution: Et biokulturelt perspektiv* (Aarhus: Aarhus Universitetsforlag), 259–76.

Archibald, Gail (2006): "How the 'S' came to be in UNESCO". In Patrick Petitjean et al. (eds.), *Sixty Years of Science at UNESCO, 1945–2005* (Paris: UNESCO Publishing), 36–40.

Arnold, Lorna & Katherine Pyne (2001): *Britain and the H-bomb* (Basingstoke: Palgrave MacMillan).

Badash, Lawrence (1995): *Scientists and the Development of Nuclear Weapons: From Fission to the Limited Test Ban Treaty* (Atlantic Highlands, NJ: Humanities Press).

Barnaby, Frank et al. (1985): *Efter atomkrigen. Konsekvenser for mennesker og natur* (Aarhus: Forlaget Ask).

Bar-Zohar, Michael (2007): *Shimon Peres: The Biography* (New York: Random House).

Baylis, John (1995): *Ambiguity and Deterrence: British Nuclear Strategy 1945–1964* (Oxford: Clarendon Press).

Baylis, John & Kristian Stoddart (2015): *The British Nuclear Experience: The Role of Beliefs, Culture, and Identity* (Oxford: Oxford University Press).

Baylis, John (2016): "The Control of Weapons of Mass Destruction". In John Baylis, James Wirtz & Colin S. Gray (eds.), *Strategy in the Contemporary World. An Introduction to Strategic Studies* (Oxford: Oxford University Press), 220–36.

Beard, Simon (2022): "How to read the Doomsday Clock", BBC Future. https://www.bbc.com/future/article/20220119-how-to-read-the-doomsday-clock.

Beers, Laura (2016): *Red Ellen: The Life of Ellen Wilkinson, Socialist, Feminist, Internationalist* (Cambridge, MA: Harvard University Press).

Beinart, William & Saul Dubow (2021): *The Scientific Imagination in South Africa: 1700 to the Present* (Cambridge: Cambridge University Press).

Bensaude-Vincent, Bernadette, Soraya Boudia & Sato Kyoko (2022): *Living in a nuclear world. From Fukushima to Hiroshima* (Abingdon: Routledge).

Bermudez, Joseph S. (1991): "North Korea's Nuclear Programme", *Jane's Intelligence Review*, September 1991.

Bermudez, Joseph S. (1999): "Exposing North Korea's Secret Infrastructure – Part One", *Jane's Intelligence Review*, July 1999.
Bernstein, Jeremy (2001): *Hitler's Uranium Club. The Secret Recordings at Farm Hall* (2nd ed.) (New York: Springer Verlag).
Bienen, Henry & Jeremiah Ostriker (2021): "How the United States can chart a new path that avoids war with China", *Bulletin of the Atomic Scientists* 77(2), 1–12.
Bird, Kai & Martin J. Sherwin (2005): *American Prometheus: The Triumph and Tragedy of J. Robert Oppenheimer* (New York: Alfred A. Knopf).
Bohr, Niels (1950): "Åbent brev til De Forenede Nationer". In Stefan Rozental (ed.), *Niels Bohr. Hans liv og virke fortalt af en kreds af venner og medarbejdere* (Copenhagen: J.H. Schultz Forlag, 1964), 328–40.
Bohr, Niels & John A. Wheeler (1939): "The Mechanism of Nuclear Fission", *Physical Review* 56, 426–49.
Boyer, Paul (1994; 1985): *By the Bomb's Early Light: American Thought and Culture at the Dawn of the Atomic Age* (Chapel Hill and London: The University of North Carolina Press).
Boyer, Paul (1998): *Fallout. A Historian Reflects on America's Half Century Encounter with Nuclear Weapons* (Columbus: Ohio State University Press).
Braun, Reiner, Robert Hinde, David Krieger, Harold Kroto & Sally Milne (eds.) (2007): *Joseph Rotblat: Visionary for Peace* (Hoboken, NJ: John Wiley & Sons).
Budjeryn, Mariana (2022): *Inheriting the Bomb: The Collapse of the USSR and the Nuclear Disarmament of Ukraine* (Baltimore: JHU Press).
Buzan, Barry, Ole Wæver & Jaap de Wilde (1998): *Security: A New Framework for Analysis* (Boulder CO: Lynne Rienner Publishers).
Caldwell, Lynton C. (1996): *International environmental policy: From the twentieth to the twenty-first century* (Durham: Duke University Press).
Cantelon, Philip L., Richard G. Hewlett & Robert C. Williams (eds.) (1991): *The American Atom: A Documentary History of Nuclear Policies from the Discovery of Fission to the Present* (Pennsylvania, PA: University of Pennsylvania Press).
Cathcart, Brian (1995): *Test of Greatness: Britain's Struggle for the Atom Bomb* (London: John Murray).
Chang-Liao, Nien-chung & Chi Fang (2021): "The case for maintaining strategic ambiguity in the Taiwan strait", *The Washington Quarterly* 44(2), 45–60.
Christmas-Møller, Wilhelm (1985): *Niels Bohr og atomvåbnet* (Copenhagen: Vindrose).
Coffey, Thomas M. (1988): *Iron Eagle: The Turbulent Life of General Curtis LeMay* (New York: Avon Books).
Cohen, Avner (1998): *Israel and the Bomb* (New York: Columbia University Press).
Cohen, Avner (2010): *The Worst-Kept Secret: Israel's Bargain With the Bomb* (New York: Columbia University Press).
Compton, Arthur H. (1947a): "Atomic Power, Its Birth and Its Human Meaning", *Electrical Engineering* 66(9), 357–63.
Compton, Arthur H. (1947b): "The Place of Science in the Program of UNESCO", *Proceedings of the American Philosophical Society* 91(4), 303–6.
Compton, Arthur H. (1947c): "The World Educates for Peace". In Boyd Bode (ed.), *Modern Education & Human Values* (Pittsburgh, PA: Pittsburgh University Press), 48–53.
Compton, Arthur H. (1956): *Atomic Quest: A Personal Narrative* (Oxford: Oxford University Press).
Corera, Gordon (2006): *Shopping for Bombs: Nuclear Proliferation, Global Insecurity, and the Rise and Fall of the A.Q. Khan Network* (New York: Oxford University Press).
Craig, Campbell & Sergey Radchenko (2008): *The Atomic Bomb and the Origins of the Cold War* (New Haven & London: Yale University Press).

Crutzen, Paul J. (2006): "The Anthropocene". In Eckart Ehlers & Thomas Kraft (eds.), *Earth System Science in the Anthropocene* (New York: Springer).
Crutzen, Paul J. & John Birks (1982): "The Atmosphere After a Nuclear War: Twilight at Noon", *Ambio* 11, 114–25.
Damsbo-Svendsen, Søren (2021): "How weather experiences strengthen climate opinions in Europe", *West European Politics*, 1–15: https://doi.org/10.1080/01402382.2020.1792731.
Davis, Edward B. (2009): "Prophet of Science: Part I–III. Arthur Holly Compton on Science Freedom, Religion and Morality", *Perspectives on Science and Christian Faith* 61, 240–63.
Dean, Gordon (1954): *Report on the Atom. What You Should Know About Atomic Energy* (London: Eyre & Spottiswoode).
DeGroot, Gerard (2005): *The Bomb. A History of Hell on Earth* (London: Pimlico).
Dobbs, Michael (2009): *Cubakrisen – Kennedy, Khrusjtjov og Castro på randen af atomkrig* (Copenhagen: Informations Forlag).
Dukes, Paul (2011): *Minutes to Midnight. History and the Anthropocene Era from 1763* (London: Anthem Books).
Eden, Lynn (2004): *Whole world on fire: Organizations, knowledge, and nuclear weapons devastation* (Ithaca: Cornell University Press).
Edwards, Paul N. (2010): *A Vast Machine: Computer Models, Climate Data, and the Politics of Global Warming* (Cambridge, MA: MIT Press).
Edwards, Paul N. (2012): "Entangled Histories: Climate Science and Nuclear Weapons Research", *Bulletin of the Atomic Scientists* 68(4), 28–40.
Elzinga, Aant (1996): "UNESCO and the Politics of Scientific Internationalism". In Aant Elzinga & Catharina Landström (eds.), *Internationalism and Science* (London: Taylor Graham), 89–132.
Evangelista, Matthew (1999): *Unarmed Forces: The Transnational Movement to End the Cold War* (Ithaca, NY: Cornell University Press).
Fischer, David (1997): *History of the International Atomic Energy Agency. The First Forty Years* (Vienna: IAEA).
Frey, Karsten (2006): *India's Nuclear Bomb and National Security* (London: Routledge).
Frisch, Otto (1979): *What Little I Remember* (Cambridge: Cambridge University Press).
FRUS: *Foreign Relations of the United States* (https://history.state.gov/historical-documents).
Fukuyama, Francis (1992): *The End of History and the Last Man* (New York: Free Press).
Fussell, Paul (1988): *Thank God for the Atom Bomb and Other Essays* (New York: Ballantine Books).
Futter, Andrew, Ludovica Castelli, Cameron Hunter, Olamide Samuel, Francesca Silvestri & Benjamin Zala (2025): *The Global Third Nuclear Age: Clashing Visions for a New Era in International Politics* (London: Routledge).
Gaddis, John L. (2005): *Strategies of Containment: A Critical Appraisal of American National Security Policy During the Cold War* (Oxford: Oxford University Press).
Giangreco, Dennis M. (2023): *Truman and the Bomb: The Untold Story* (University of Nebraska Press, Potomac Books).
Goldberg, Alfred (1964): "The Atomic Origins of the British Nuclear Deterrent", *International Affairs* 40(3), 409–29.
Goodman, Sherri (2024): *Threat Multiplier: Climate, Military Leadership, and the Fight for Global Security* (New York: Island Press).
Gowin, Emmet (2019): *The Nevada Test Site* (Princeton, NJ: Princeton University Press).
Gowing, Margaret (1964): *Britain and Atomic Energy 1939–1945* (London: Macmillan & Co).

Gowing, Margaret & Lorna Arnold (1974a): *Independence and Deterrence: Britain and Atomic Energy, 1945–1952. Vol 1: Policy Making* (London: MacMillan).
Gowing, Margaret & Lorna Arnold (1974b): *Independence and Deterrence: Britain and Atomic Energy, 1945–1952. Vol 2: Policy and Execution* (London: MacMillan).
Groves, Leslie E. (1962): *Now it can be Told: The Story of the Manhattan Project* (New York: Harper & Brothers Publishers).
Gunston, Bill (1973): *Bombers of the West* (New York: Charles Scribner's & Sons).
Gutenberg, B. (1946): "Interpretation of Records Obtained in the New Mexico Atomic Bomb Test, July 16, 1945", *Bulletin of the Seismological Society of America* 36(4), 327–30.
Haber, Heinz (1956): *Our Friend the Atom* (Walt Disney Productions).
Harries, Matthew (2021): "Response: Keep the NPT", *Survival* 63(4), 125–30.
Hecht, Gabrielle (1998): *The Radiance of France: Nuclear Power and National Identity After World War II* (Cambridge, MA: MIT Press).
Hecht, Gabrielle (2012): *Being Nuclear: Africans and the Global Uranium Trade* (Cambridge, MA: MIT Press).
Hecker, Siegfried S., Robert L. Carlin & Elliot A. Serbin (2018): "A Comprehensive History of North Korea's Nuclear Program". https://cisac.fsi.stanford.edu/content/cisac-north-korea (download).
Hennessy, Peter (2003): *The Secret State: Whitehall and the Cold War* (London: Penguin Books).
Hennessy, Peter (2010): *The Secret State: Preparing for the Worst 1945–2010* (London: Penguin Books).
Hennigan, William J. (2024), "The Price". https://www.nytimes.com/interactive/2024/10/10/opinion/nuclear-weapons-us-price.html
Herken, Gregg (1980): *The Winning Weapon: The Atomic Bomb in the Cold War, 1945–1950* (New York: Alfred A. Knopf).
Herken, Gregg (2002): *Brotherhood of the Bomb: The Tangled Lives and Loyalties of Robert Oppenheimer, Ernest Lawrence and Edward Teller* (New York: Henry Holt & Company).
Hersh, Seymour (1991): *The Samson Option: Israel's Nuclear Arsenal and American Foreign Policy* (New York & London: Random House).
Hewlett, Richard G. & Oscar E. Anderson (1962): *The New World, 1939–1946* (University Park, PA: Pennsylvania State University Press).
Hewlett, Richard G. & Jack M. Holl (1989): *Atoms for Peace and War 1953–1961: Eisenhower and the Atomic Energy Commission* (Berkeley, CA: University of California Press).
Heymann, Matthias & Amy D. Dalmedico (2019): "Epistemology and Politics in Earth System Modeling: Historical Perspectives", *Journal of Advances in Modeling Earth Systems* 11(5), 1139–52.
Hibbs, Mark (1993): "Isotopics Show Three North Korean Reprocessing Campaigns Since 1975", *Nuclear Fuel*, March 1, 8–9.
Higuchi, Toshihiro (2020): *Political Fallout: Nuclear Weapons Testing and the Making of a Global Environmental Crisis* (Stanford, CA: Stanford University Press).
Holloway, David (1994): *Stalin and the Bomb* (New Haven & London: Yale University Press).
Hughes, Jeff (2002): *The Manhattan Project: Big Science and the Atom Bomb* (London: Icon Books).
Huntington, Samuel S. (1961): *The Common Defense: Strategic Programs in National Politics* (New York: Columbia University Press).
Huntington, Samuel S. (1996): *The Clash of Civilizations and the Remaking of World Order* (New York: Simon & Schuster).
Huxley, Julian (1946): *UNESCO, its Purpose and its Philosophy* (Paris: UNESCO Publishing).
International Institute for Strategic Studies (2007): *Nuclear Black Markets: Pakistan, A.Q. Khan and the rise of proliferation networks* (United Kingdom: Hastings Print).

IPPNW Report (1991): *Radioactive Heaven and Earth: The health and environmental effects of nuclear weapons testing in, on, and above the earth* (New York: The Apex Press).
Jae-Bong, Lee (2009): "US Deployment of Nuclear Weapons in 1950s South Korea & North Korea's Nuclear Development: Toward Denuclearization of the Korean Peninsula", *Asia-Pacific Journal*, Vol. 7, Issue 8, Number 3.
Josephson, Paul R. (2005): *Red Atom: Russia's Nuclear Power Program from Stalin to Today* (Pittsburgh, PA: University of Pittsburgh Press).
Juneau, Thomas (2015): *Squandered Opportunity: Neoclassical Realism and Iranian Foreign Policy* (Cambridge, CA: Harvard University Press).
Karlsch, Rainer & Mark Walker (2005): "New Light on Hitler's Bomb", *Physics World*, June 1. https://physicsworld.com/a/new-light-on-hitlers-bomb/.
Kaufman, Scott (2013): *Project Plowshare: The Peaceful Use of Nuclear Explosives in Cold War America* (New York: Cornell University Press).
Keeling, Charles D. (1960): "The Concentration and Isotopic Abundances of Carbon Dioxide in the Atmosphere", *Tellus* 7, 200–3.
Keeling, Charles D. (1976): "Atmospheric Carbon Dioxide Variations at the Mauna Loa Observatory", *Tellus* 28, 538–51.
Kevles, Daniel (1971): *The Physicists: The History of a Scientific Community in Modern America* (New York: Alfred A. Knopf).
King, David (2009): *The hot topic. How to tackle global warming* (London: Bloomsbury).
Knudsen, Henrik & Henry Nielsen (2016): *Uranbjerget – Om forsøgene på at finde og udnytte Grønlands uran fra 1944 til i dag* (Copenhagen: Forlaget Vandkunsten).
Knudsen, Henrik & Henry Nielsen (2012): "Pursuing common cultural ideals: Niels Bohr, neutrality, and international scientific collaboration during the inter-war period". In Rebecka Lettevall, Geert Somsen & Sven Widmalm (eds.), *Neutrality in Twentieth Century Europe: Intersections of Science, Culture and Politics after the First World War* (Abingdon: Routledge), 115–39.
Kristensen, Hans M. & Matt Korda (2020): "Status of World Nuclear Forces". https://fas.org/issues/nuclear-weapons/status-world-nuclear-forces/.
Kristensen, Hans M. & Matt Korda (2021a): "Nuclear Notebook: United States Nuclear Weapons, 2021", *Bulletin of the Atomic Scientists* 77(1), 43–63.
Kristensen, Hans M. & Matt Korda (2021b): "Nuclear Notebook: Russian Nuclear Weapons, 2021", *Bulletin of the Atomic Scientists* 77(2), 90–108.
Kristensen, Hans M. & Matt Korda (2021c): "Nuclear Notebook: Chinese Nuclear Weapons, 2021.", *Bulletin of the Atomic Scientists* 77(6), 318–36.
Kristensen, Hans M., Matt Korda, Eliana Johns & Mackenzie Knight (2025): "United States Nuclear Weapons, 2025", *Bulletin of the Atomic Scientists* 81(1), 53–79.
Kuletz, Valerie D. (1998): *The Tainted Desert: Environmental and Social Ruin in the American West* (New York: Routledge).
Lanouette, William (1992): *Genius in the Shadows: A Biography of Leo Szilard, the Man Behind the Bomb* (New York: Skyhorse).
Leffler, Melvyn P. (2007): *For the Soul of Mankind: The United States, the Soviet Union, and The Cold War* (New York: Hill and Wang).
Lewis, John Wilson & Xue Litai (1988): *China Builds the Bomb* (Redwood City, CA: Stanford University Press).
Lindell, Bo & Sven Löfveberg (1972): *Kärnkraften, människan och säkerheten* (Stockholm: Allmänna Förlaget).
Maar III, Henry Richard (2022): *Freeze! The Grassroots Movement to Halt the Arms Race and End the Cold War* (New York: Cornell University Press).
MacCalman, Molly (2016): "A.Q. Khan Smuggling Network", *Journal of Strategic Security* 9(1), 104–18.

Mackenzie, Jean & Ruth Comerford (2025): "Impeached S Korean president charged with insurrection", *BBC World News*, January 21.
Mahaffey, James (2014): *Atomic Accidents: A History of Nuclear Meltdowns and Disasters from the Ozark Mountains to Fukushima* (New York: Pegasus Books).
Masco, Joseph (2004): "Nuclear Technoaesthetics: Sensory Politics from Trinity to the Virtual Bomb in Los Alamos", *American Ethnologist* 31(3), 349–73.
Masters, Dexter & Katharine Way (eds.) (1946): *One World or None: A Report to the Public on the Full Meaning of the Atomic Bomb* (New York: McGraw Hill for the Federation of American Scientists).
McNiell, John R. (2001): *Something New Under the Sun. An Environmental History of the Twentieth-Century World* (New York: W.W. Norton & Company).
Narang, Vipin & Scott Saga (eds.) (2023): *The fragile balance of terror: Deterrence in the new nuclear age* (Ithaca: Cornell University).
Neff, T.L. (1991): "A Grand Uranium Bargain", *The New York Times*, November 4, 1991. https://www.nytimes.com/1991/10/24/opinion/a-grand-uranium-bargain.html
Nielsen, Henry, Keld Nielsen, Flemming Petersen & Hans Siggaard Jensen (1998): *Til samfundets tarv – Forskningscenter Risøs historie* (Roskilde: Forskningscenter Risø).
Nielsen, Kristian H. & Henry Nielsen (2021): *Camp Century: The UStory of America's Secret Arctic Military Base Under the Greenland Ice* (New York: Columbia University Press).
Noddack, Ida (1934): "About Element 93", *Angewandte Chemie* 47(1934), 653.
Norris, Robert & Hans M. Kristensen (2010): "Global Nuclear Weapons Inventories, 1945–2010", *Bulletin of the Atomic Scientists* 66(4), 77–83.
O'Neill, Daniel T. (1994): *The Firecracker Boys* (New York: St. Martin's Press).
Oberdorfer, Don (1997): *The Two Koreas: A Contemporary History* (Reading, MA: Addison-Wesley).
Oreskes, Naomi & Eric M. Conway (2010): *Merchants of Doubt: How a Handful of Scientists Obscured the Truth on Issues from Tobacco Smoke to Global Warming* (London & New York: Bloomsbury Press).
Osgood, Kenneth (2006): *Total Cold War: Eisenhower's Secret Propaganda Battle at Home and Abroad* (Kansas: Kansas University Press).
Pais, Abraham (1994): *Niels Bohr's Times: In Physics, Philosophy and Polity* (Clarendon Press).
Pasternak, Judy (2011): *Yellow Dirt: A Poisoned Land and the Betrayal of the Navajos* (New York: Free Press).
Pauling, Linus (1983): *No more war! 25th anniversary Edition* (New York: Dodd Mead).
Perkovich, George (1999): *India's Nuclear Bomb: The Impact on Global Proliferation* (Berkeley and Los Angeles, CA: University of California Press).
Podvig, P. (2024): "Preserving the nuclear test ban after Russia revoked its CTBT ratification", *Bulletin of the Atomic Scientists* 80(2), 75–80.
Polakow-Suransky, Sasha (2002): *The unspoken alliance: Israel's secret relationship with Apartheid South Africa* (Auckland: Jacana Media).
Pollack, Jonathan D. (2010): *No Exit: North Korea, Nuclear Weapons and International Security* (Abingdon: Routledge).
Pretorius, Joelien & Tom Sauer (2021): "Ditch the NPT", *Survival* 63(4), 103–24.
Purkitt, Helen E. & Stephen F. Burgess (2005): *South Africa's weapons of mass destruction* (Bloomington: Indiana University Press).
Rasmussen, Søren Hein (1997): *Sære allиancer. Politiske bevægelser i efterkrigstidens Danmark* (Odense: Odense Universitetsforlag).
Regnault, Jean-Mark (2003): "France's Search for Nuclear Test Sites, 1957–1963", *Journal of Military History* 67(4), 1223–48.

Rehman, Huma (2024): "What India's MIRV test adds to the 'strategic trilemma' in South Asia", *Bulletin of the Atomic Scientists, Newsletter*, May 3.

Revelle, Roger & Hans E. Suess (1957): "Carbon Dioxide Exchange Between the Atmosphere and Ocean and the Question of an Increase in Atmospheric CO_2 During the Past Decades", *Tellus* 9, 18–27.

Rhodes, Richard (2012; 1986): *The Making of the Atomic Bomb* (New York: Simon & Schuster).

Rhodes, Richard (1996): *Dark Sun: The Making of the Hydrogen Bomb* (New York: Simon & Schuster).

Rhodes, Richard (2007): *Arsenals of Folly: The Making of the Arms Race* (New York: Alfred A. Knopf).

Rhys, Crilley (2023): *Unparalleled catastrophe: Life and death in the Third Nuclear Age* (Manchester: Manchester University Press).

Rich, Nathaniel (2019): *Losing Earth. A Recent History* (London: MCD books).

Riqiang, W. (2013): "Certainty of uncertainty: Nuclear strategy with Chinese characteristics.", *Journal of Strategic Studies*, 36(4), 579–614.

Roehrlich, Elisabeth (2022): *Inspectors for Peace: A History of the International Atomic Energy Agency* (Baltimore: Johns Hopkins University Press).

Rubinson, Paul (2011): "Crucified on a Cross of Atoms: Scientists, Politics, and the Test Ban Treaty", *Diplomatic History* 35(2), 283–319.

Rubinson, Paul (2016): *Redefining Science: Scientists, the National Security State, and Nuclear Weapons in Cold War America* (Cambridge, MA: University of Massachusetts Press).

Sagan, Carl (1984): "Nuclear War and Climatic Catastrophe: Some Policy Implications", *Foreign Affairs* 62, 258–92.

Sakharov, Andrei (1990): *Memoirs* (New York: Alfred A. Knopf).

Scheinman, Lawrence (1988): *The International Atomic Energy Agency and World Nuclear Order* (Milton Park: Routledge).

Schell, Jonathan (1982): *The Fate of the Earth* (New York: Knopf).

Schweber, Silvan S. (2003): "J. Robert Oppenheimer: Prometheus Unbound", *Science in Context* 16(1/2), 219–42.

Shapin, Steven (2008): *The Scientific Life. A moral history of a late-modern vocation* (Chicago: Chicago University Press).

Shultz, George P., William J. Perry, Henry A. Kissinger & Sam Nunn (2007). "Toward a World without Nuclear Weapons", *The groundbreaking Wall Street Journal op-ed series* (Washington, DC: NTI).

Smyth, Henry D. (1945): *Atomic Energy for Military Purposes: A General Account of the Scientific Research and Technical Development that Went into the Making of Atomic Bombs* (Princeton: Princeton University Press).

Sluga, Glenda (2010): "Inaugural Lecture: Imagining Internationalism", *Arts: The Journal of Sydney University Arts Association* 32, 55–68.

Solzhenitsyn, Aleksandr (1973): *The Gulag Archipelago, 1918–56* (Vintage Publishing).

Sweeney, Mike (2021): "Why a Taiwan Conflict Could Go Nuclear". *Defense Priorities*. https://www.defense-priorities.org/explainers/why-a-taiwan-conflict-could-go-nuclear

Sylvest, Casper (2022): *Atomfrygt* (Aarhus: Aarhus Universitetsforlag).

Teller, Edward & Judith Shoolery (2012; 2002): *Memoirs: A twentieth-century journey in science and politics* (New York: Basic Books).

Toon, Owen B. et al. (2019): "Rapidly expanding nuclear arsenals in Pakistan and India portend regional and global catastrophe", *Science Advances* 5(10). https://doi.org/10.1126/sciadv.aay5478

van Calmthout, Martijn (2018): *Sam Goudsmit and the Hunt for Hitler's Atom Bomb* (New York: Prometheus Books).

van Munster, Rens & Casper Sylvest (2016): *Nuclear Realism. Global political thought during the thermonuclear revolution* (London: Routledge).

van Munster, Rens & Casper Sylvest (2021a): "Nuclear weapons, extinction, and the Anthropocene: Reappraising Jonathan Schell", *Review of International Studies* 47(3), 1–17.
van Munster, Rens & Casper Sylvest (2021b): "Atomtruslen er ikke forsvundet", *DIIS Policy Brief*, May 5, 2021. https://www.diis.dk/publikationer/atomtruslen-ikke-forsvundet
van Wyk, Anna-Mart (2010): "South Africa's nuclear programme and the Cold War", *History Compass* 8(7), 562–72.
Villaume, Poul (2020): *Frygtens logik. Den Kolde Krig – en ny global historie, 1917–1961* (Copenhagen: Gads Forlag).
Villaume, Poul (2023): *Mellem frygt og håb. Den Kolde Krig – en ny global historie, 1961–1977* (Copenhagen: Gads Forlag).
Villaume, Paul (2024): *Håbets gennembrud. Den Kolde Krig – en ny global historie, 1977–1991* (Copenhagen: Gads Forlag).
von Hippel, Frank & Tomoko Kurokawa (2019): "Citizen Scientist: Frank von Hippel's Adventures in Nuclear Arms Control. Part 3. Working with Gorbachev's Advisors to End the Nuclear Arms Race", *Journal of Peace and Nuclear Disarmament* 3(3), 1–32.
von Hippel, Frank (2025): *Ending the Nuclear Arms Race: A Physicist's Quest* (Boulder: Lynne Rienne Publishers, Inc.).
Vuori, Juha A. (2010): "A Timely Prophet? The Doomsday Clock as a Visualization of Securitization Moves with a Global Referent Object", *SAGE Publications* 41(3), 255–77. http://sdi.sagepub.com
Walker, Mark (1995): *Nazi Science. Myth, Truth, and the German Atomic Bomb* (New York: Plenum Press).
Wallace, Chris (2020): *Countdown 1945: The Extraordinary Story of the Atomic Bomb and the 116 Days that changed the World* (New York: Avid Reader Press).
Walton, C. Dale (2016): "The Second Nuclear Age: Nuclear Weapons in the Twenty-First Century". In John Baylis, James Wirtz & Colin S. Gray (eds.), *Strategy in the Contemporary World. An Introduction to Strategic Studies* (Oxford: Oxford University Press), 202–20.
Waters, C. Kenneth & Albert van Helden (1987): *Julian Huxley. Biologist and Statesman of Science* (Houston: Rice University Press).
Weart, Spencer (2007): *The Discovery of Global Warming: A Hypertext History of How Scientists Came to (Partly) Understand What Humans Are Doing to the Earth's Climate* (College Park, MD: Center for the History of Physics, American Institute of Physics).
Weidi, Xi (2016): "China's security environment and the role of nuclear weapons". In Li Bin & Tong Zhao (eds.), *Understanding Chinese Nuclear Thinking* (Washington, DC: Carnegie Endowment for International Peace), 48–87.
Weiss, Leonard (2003): "Atoms for Peace", *Bulletin of the Atomic Scientists* 59(6), 34–44.
Weissman, Steve & Herbert Krosney (1981): *The Islamic Bomb. The Nuclear Threat to Israel and the Middle East* (New York: Times Books).
Wellerstein, Alex (2020): "The Kyoto Misconception: What Truman Knew, and Didn't Know about Hiroshima". In Michael D. Gordin & G. John Ikenberry (eds.), *The Age of Hiroshima* (Princeton: Princeton University Press), 34–55.
Wellerstein, Alex (2021): *Restricted Data: The History of Nuclear Secrecy in the United States* (Chicago: Chicago University Press).
Wellerstein, Alex (2024): "Counting the dead at Hiroshima and Nagasaki", *Bulletin of the Atomic Scientists, Newsletter*, December 30.
Wilkinson, Ellen (1945). "Opening Address by the President of the Conference", *Conference for the establishment of the United Nations Educational, Scientific and Cultural Organization November 1945* (Paris: UNESCO Publishing).

Williams, Heather & Doreen Horschig (2024), "House of Cards. Nuclear norms in an era of strategic competition", Next Generation Nuclear Network: https://nuclearnetwork.csis.org/house-of-cards-nuclear-norms-in-an-era-of-strategic-competition/.

Wittner, Lawrence S. (1974): *Cold War America: From Hiroshima to Watergate* (New York: Praeger).

Wittner, Lawrence S. (1993): *One World or None: A History of the World Nuclear Disarmament Movement, 1945–1953* (Stanford, CA: Stanford University Press).

Wittner, Lawrence S. (1997): *Resisting the Bomb: A History of the World Nuclear Disarmament Movement, 1954–1970* (Stanford, CA: Stanford University Press).

Wittner, Lawrence S. (2003): *Toward Nuclear Abolition: A History of the World Nuclear Disarmament Movement, 1971 to the Present* (Stanford, CA: Stanford University Press).

Wæver, Ole (1995): "Securitization and Desecuritization". In Ronnie D. Lipschutz (ed.), *On Security* (New York: Columbia University Press), 46–86.

Zhang, Hui (2025): "How quickly could Iran build its first nuclear weapon? Look at China", *Bulletin of the Atomic Scientists, Newsletter*, January 22.

Index

See also Abbreviations page 9–10 regarding the different acronyms.

M

N

Author Biographies

Casper Andersen is Professor of the History of Ideas and Science at Aarhus University, Denmark. His research focuses on the history of ideas, science and technology in imperial and global contexts. He has written extensively on topics such as science and empire, the history of nuclear weapons, scientific internationalism, science diplomacy and the history of science in UNESCO. Andersen is the author/co-author of 11 books, and his work has appeared in leading international journals, including *Technology and Culture*, *Isis*, *International Journal of Heritage Studies*, *Global Perspectives* and the *Canadian Journal of African Studies*. He currently serves as Chair of the Danish Society for the History of Technology (since 2021) and is a member of the Learned Society at Aarhus University (since 2023). From 2015 to 2020, he was a member of The Young Academy of the Royal Danish Academy of Sciences and Letters. Andersen is also a frequently consulted expert in Danish media on the history and politics of the nuclear weapons crisis.

Henry Nielsen is Associate Professor emeritus at the Center for Science Studies, Aarhus University, Denmark. His research has mainly focused on the scientific and technological R&D in Denmark and Greenland after 1940, especially R&D related to nuclear power and nuclear weapons. Nielsen's work has been published in leading international journals, such as *Business History Review*, *Technology and Culture*, *Centaurus*, *History and Technology* and *Science as Culture*. He is the author/co-author of 15 books, including three which have been very relevant as background to the present book, namely *Exploring Greenland: Science and Technology on Ice* (Palgrave MacMillan, 2016), *The Uranium Mountain: On the Attempts to Find and Utilize Greenland's Uranium* (Vandkunsten, 2016, in Danish) and *Camp Century: The Untold Story of America's Secret Arctic Military Base Under the Greenland Ice* (Columbia University Press, 2021). Nielsen has also written numerous popular articles on the history of nuclear science and technology in Danish media.